Early Landowners
of
Maryland

Volume 1: Anne Arundel County
1650–1704

Robert W. Hall

HERITAGE BOOKS
2018

HERITAGE BOOKS
AN IMPRINT OF HERITAGE BOOKS, INC.

Books, CDs, and more—Worldwide

For our listing of thousands of titles see our website at
www.HeritageBooks.com

Published 2018 by
HERITAGE BOOKS, INC.
Publishing Division
5810 Ruatan Street
Berwyn Heights, Md. 20740

International Standard Book Number
Paperbound: 978-16-8034-977-1

CONTENTS

Preface

Mr. Hall has abstracted the earliest of the land records (the patents) and grouped this information by owners and by hundreds. The level of detail included clearly separates this work from mere abstracts of Rent Rolls and land records and makes it more useful for those without easy access to the Maryland State Archives.

He has greatly enhanced the value of *Early Land Owners of Maryland, Volume 1: Anne Arundel County,* by identifying patentees and other persons named in the patent document and by defining the relationships or involvement of such persons. This includes relatives, former tract owners, persons transported, persons completing service, surveyors, public officials, contributors of rights to acreage, trades and, occasionally, employers. The work is amply footnoted to include any unusual information found including personal relationships, disputes, and even an occasional reference to a burial site. Also included are tracts now located in adjoining counties that were granted as Anne Arundel tracts. Hall has identified virtually all the Anne Arundel patentees along with others who owned the land or warrant or acted as owner. In addition, he includes references to tract location by river, creek, or branch. In nearly all cases he identifies neighbors and their tracts and, using data gleaned from other records such as Probate, Judicial Proceedings, church and marriage records, he has identified and included many grants not included in the Rent Rolls.

F. Edward Wright
Lewes, Delaware
2003

Early Landowners of Maryland
Volume 1- Anne Arundel County

Introduction

The Conditions of Plantation, and amendments thereto, were codified and established by Lord Baltimore, the Lord Proprietor of Maryland, to provide Maryland settlers with the opportunity to become land holders, an opportunity that was often not available in their native land. The Conditions had many provisions and exclusions but they basically established a head-right system that provided that warrants for land would be awarded to persons who transported immigrants (including themselves) at their own expense to this Province here to inhabit. This included persons from other provinces of the New World. The Conditions also established and maintained land-management policy, procedures, and features such as annual rent for property owned and penalties (alienation fees) when rents were not paid on time. A rent amount and a payment schedule for each tract was shown in the survey/patent document. A detailed fee schedule of most of the Secretary's and Sheriff's fees can be found in the Acts of Assembly, 1650 (L7/33-35 SR7343).

Redemptioners or Indentured Servants were persons who entered agreements to work as servants for specific periods of time to redeem their passage costs. Indenture periods varied according to factors such as the age, sex, and skills of the persons involved. Land ownership in early Maryland featured most of the rights of present day ownership except that a fee (or rent) was required upon issuance of the patent and every year following. The "Conditions" were formally amended five times with some additional tinkering between amendments. The amendments usually augmented or supplemented the earlier versions except the "Fourth Conditions," which superseded and revoked all earlier versions. The following is a synopsis of the changes to the Conditions brought about by the amendments:

First Conditions (1633). Provided that a person transporting others to this Province here to inhabit received two hundred acres of land within this Province for each man transported, 100 acres for each woman, and 50 acres for each child.

Second Conditions (1636). Every "adventurer" who transported five men between the ages of 16 and 50 received 2,000 acres (i.e., 400 acres per man). Persons transporting less than five people received 100 acres per adult and 50 acres per child (under 16 years of age) and per maid servant (under 40 years of age) transported.

Third Conditions (promulgated in 1641, but did not take effect until 1642). Provided that anyone of English or Irish descent who transported 20 able-bodied men, between the age of 16 and 50, with arms and ammunition, or women between the age of 14 and 40, received 100 acres per person transported. If less than 20 persons were transported, the rate dropped to 50 acres per person, and the rate for children under 14 years of age was 25 acres per child transported.

Fourth Conditions (1648). This amendment replaced all earlier versions. Provision was made for land ownership by persons of French, Dutch, and Italian descent. A requirement was included that every prospective landowner take an Oath of Fidelity to the Lord Proprietor. The ground rules and ratio of land per person transported were not changed. Redemptioners of English or Irish descent, upon completion of an indenture period of not less than three years, were now entitled to "Freedom Rights" of 50 acres of land. Corporations, societies, fraternities, guilds, spiritual organizations and other groups were now prohibited from "new" or additional land ownership without permission from the Lord Proprietor.

Fifth Conditions (1649). Initially, the ground rules and acreage per person remained unchanged at 100 acres per person. This was reduced to fifty acres on 6/20/1652, except for several regions where settlement was to be encouraged (i.e., the Eastern Shore and areas of Prince George's County). Persons entitled to land were prohibited from assigning or selling rights to organizations, societies, etc. Head rights now had to be exercised within one year.

On October 2, 1680, Lord Baltimore issued an order to **John Lewellin,** Clerk of the Land Office, requiring him to issue warrants only upon due proof of rights thereunto made according to the oaths established in the order. This order applied to all phases of the patent process, i.e., certifications, surveys, and patents that had not been completed prior to the date of the order. (*LWC2/249 SR7340)*

Oath for Probate of Rights

You do sweare that the severall persons herein mentioned (*unless) their names are to be published in a list*) are to the best of your knowledge of British or Irish descent and, by your cost and charge are imported into this Province to inhabit in the year _ _ _ _ _, or otherwise at the proper cost and charge of your friends transported and consigned to you to be disposed of. And that neither you nor any other person or persons whatsoever for you or by your consent, priority, or knowledge has before proved or made over of the rights for same to any other person whatsoever, so help you God.

Oath Where a Person Proves His
Rights for Completion of
Service

You doe sweare that you are to the best of your knowledge of British or Irish descent and that at your friends proper cost and charges you were transported into this Province to inhabit in the year _ _ _ _ , and that you have truly performed your time of service within this Province and that you never before proved or made over of the right due you thereupon neither assigned the same over to any other person or persons whatsoever, so help you God.

Note 1: I found nothing in the land records that leads me to believe that any record of persons taking either of these oaths was ever made or maintained. Note 2: Although the Conditions of Plantation provided for land ownership by persons of Dutch, French, and Italian descent as early as 1648, these oaths (developed in 1680) require that land owners be of British or Irish descent.

Tracts that were deserted for four years (unless owned by orphans under 16 years of age), or if rents/alienation fees were unpaid for three years, and tracts belonging to deceased persons with no heirs reverted to the Lord Proprietor through a process called "escheat." Such tracts would usually be renamed, resurveyed (often with new shapes, metes and bounds), and granted to new owners. Unfortunately, there is no consolidated record of escheated tracts. Occasionally, however, a survey or patent document will provide a clue of prior ownership and some detail may be included.

Sales of tracts were extensive and immediate. Some sales were directly from one individual to another through a contract or indenture. Direct sales are recorded in the County Land Record Index (#73) held at the Maryland State Archives (MSA). Other "person to person" tract sales (e.g., Robinston, Deaver's Purchase, Duke's Cove Resurveyed, Greeniston, and Lydia's Rest) resulted in "regrants" by the Lord Proprietor who, "for a valuable consideration" provided by the buyer to the seller, regranted such tracts to a new owner. Such transactions, along with routine grants to private citizens, are recorded in MSA State Land Record Indices (#54 & #55), which were used for this project.

An exception to the above, concerning Anne Arundel County can be found in LCDi/109 SR7376, of the State Land Records. This is a contract, or Indenture, for the sale of three large tracts by **George White** of London, the heir of the former owner, to the Lord Proprietor, as follows:

> This Indenture dated 6/24/1693, between **George White** of England, brother and heir of the late **Jerome White, Esq.**, former Surveyor General of Maryland and the right honorable **Charles Lord Baltimore**. The s'd George for a summe of 125 lbs of lawful money of England paid by the

s'd Lord Baltimore hath bargained, sold, and confirmed to the s'd Lord Baltimore all of these three tracts and parcels of land lying in Ann Arundell County in the Province of Maryland. That is to say all of those tracts or parcels of land in Portland Manor near RidgeManor containing by estimate 1,700 acres and all of that land in White Planes near Taylor's land containing by estimate 1,200 acres and all of that land in White's Ford on South River containing by estimate 1,800 acres.

> **John Tashburg** of St. James Parish
> & **Alex Standish** of St. Elyse in the
> Fields make oath that the s'd George
> White aforementioned signed, sealed
> and delivered this deed to the afores'd.
> Examined
> **Andreas Young**

Note: The size of the tract Whites Plaines is 200 (not 1,200) acres.

The patent process involved three steps beginning with the certification of the rights of an individual to a given number of unidentified acres. It included a brief explanation of how and when those rights were earned. Like survey and patent documents, the certification was usually recorded in one of the land record libers and a copy may have been provided to the owner. The next step was a survey of a specific parcel of land in the amount of acreage certified. My experience has been that certification and surveys were often combined into one step. The third and final step is the "Letters Pattent" granting the tract to the individual named in the Survey. At some point in the late 1880s, the survey and patent steps were merged. Ownership rights began upon certification. A certificate of rights or a surveyed tract could be divided, sold, traded, or willed to an heir. Tracts could be inhabited on the basis of a survey with or without a patent. Many settlers built homes and lived on surveyed tracts for years before patenting and, perhaps due to the added expense, some tracts were settled but never patented.

Another reason for the failure of some to obtain a patent is that many within the large Puritan population of Anne Arundel County found oath taking and any other act requiring formal acknowledgement of governmental authority to be repugnant. On October 8, 1649, a court in Jamestown expelled three hundred Puritan families for failure to conform to the rituals and traditions of the Church of England. This came as no surprise to Puritan community leaders who had already explored the possibility of relocating their group to Maryland. At the invitation of **Thomas Stone**, then Governor of Maryland, many of these people did resettle in Maryland at a settlement they called Providence, which became Anne Arundel County in 1650.

A 1648 amendment to the Conditions of Plantation required that persons receiving Letters Pattent take an Oath of Fidelity to the Lord Proprietor. Oath taking was a prerequisite to the acceptance of public employment or service as a Burgess or Clerk in the General Assembly, and in the probation of wills and other situations including obtaining patents (but not surveys) for a tract of land. As mentioned above, after October1680, the requirement for oaths was confirmed as a part of the probate process and to claim Freedom Rights to fifty acres of land upon completion of service indenture periods. It is impossible to know how many tracts were surveyed and inhabited, but not patented for these and other reasons. We can never know with certainty whether a tract was actually not patented or the patent record was lost or burned during the move of the Capitol to Annapolis or the courthouse fire in 1704.

The early development of a class of "head-right brokers" was, I believe, a natural spin-off of the head-right system as established in Maryland. Rights brokerage offered a needed career ladder for surveyors and others involved in the affairs of the land office. To other enterprising settlers it presented a unique opportunity to obtain wealth. Unlike modern real estate brokers these early businessmen sold rights to random vacant acreage rather than specific properties. Grant documents indicate that some individuals such as surveyors, land office personnel, and wealthy citizens held warrants for thousands of acres. These were usually obtained from individuals such as sea captains, former indentured servants, widows and orphans with inherited rights, wealthy citizens who "transported" settlers to this province, or anyone with accumulated rights to land but not interested in obtaining land.

Remarks recorded in 1676 (L19/459) show that **Charles Calvert** believed that the headright system was too expensive for settlers and that land titles were dubious and incomplete due to poor performance by his land office personnel. He also believed that he was losing a great deal of money and it was his intention to discontinue the system within two years. The head-right system dragged on, however, until 1683, when it was abolished. From then on, the Lord Proprietor sold land to anyone willing to pay the required fee. The mechanics of the grant process continued generally as before and it appears that "unused" rights continued to be honored. The average number of grants per year dropped from 22.7 (1650-1684) to 10.4 (1685 to 1704). During the same period average tract size rose from 217 to 457 acres. Sometime in the mid 1690s the "Letters Pattent" format changed from a separate document to a statement added to the bottom of the survey document to indicate that a patent was "thereby" issued.

Initially, I restricted the scope of the project to actual patents. My purpose was to identify land that was owned and inhabited by individuals in Anne Arundel County during the period targeted. As indicated above, surveyed tracts might be inhabited without ever being patented. Also, tracts were added to the rent roles when surveyed. In order to produce a more complete record of who lived here, when they were here, and what property they owned I have included tracts surveyed but not known to have been patented, and tracts surveyed by one person and patented by another. Also included are "resurveys" and "regranted tracts" whether or not a change in acreage or ownership was involved. For convenience, I refer to all of these as "grants." In addition, a small number of patents occurring after the period addressed (up to 1710) have been included because either the grant process was begun prior to 1704, or the tract location is a key to the geographical placement of other tracts granted within the specified period.

Lord Baltimore adopted the "hundred system" shortly after the establishment of St. Maries. Hundreds in Maryland are usually described as geographical subdivisions that served as voting districts until about 1671. Like the hundreds in England, there was a military aspect to the hundred. The Assembly of February/March 1638/9 established that each hundred be under the management of a commander empowered to appoint a high constable and a sergeant to train all able men to bear arms. I was unable to find anything that established individual hundreds or actual boundaries in Anne Arundel County. However, the rent rolls for the period targeted do list tracts by hundreds and I have included hundred designations in each tract description as follows:

> B&TNH - Broad and Town Neck Hundred
> HCH - Herring Creek Hundred
> MNH - Middle Neck Hundred
> SRH - South River Hundred
> WRH - West River Hundred

The first step was to identify individual tracts, by hundred if possible, within the scope of the project. I found three slightly varying sources of Rent Roll information, as follows:

> Anne Arundel County Rent Rolls 1651-1774, MSA Microfilm Reel SR4376
> Anne Arundel County Rent Rolls 1702-1790, MSA Microfilm Reel SR4382
> Maryland Rent Rolls, Anne Arundel & Baltimore Counties 1700-1707, 1705 -1724, by Clearfield, Baltimore, MD, 1996

These lists were transcribed from the records, loaded into a database, merged, sorted, and culled of duplicate entries and tracts granted after the period targeted. The result was a consolidated list of 917 tracts comprising a mix of surveys, patents, and resurveys. Patent records for 885 (96.5%) of these were found in the Maryland State Archives (MSA) State Land Records, Indices (#54 & #55). These records contain no mention of the 32 unfound tracts under the owners or tract names as shown in the rent rolls. An additional 234 tracts not included in the rent rolls, although geographically located in the area covered, were found by a variety of means. These include looking up adjoining tracts and searching the land records for persons mentioned in other MSA records of Wills, Probate, Judicial Proceedings, marriage records, etc.

A total of 1,119 grants to 569 individuals were found. The boundaries of each tract found were drawn according to the metes and bounds specified and the actual acreage was measured. One hundred fifty nine tracts, involving 38,305 acres of land, could not be drawn or measured due to incomplete or inaccurate course (boundary) data (ICD) in the grant document. Individual tract drawings according the original metes and bounds with a brief synopsis of the grant document and individual tract drawings including adjoining tracts are available. Please contact the publisher for details.

The targeted period covers 54 years. There were no certifications, patents, or surveys during periods of Puritan control of Maryland (1653, 1656, 1657, 1660) or during the Lord Proprietor's rule in 1691. Following the English Civil War and takeover in England by the **Cromwell** Government, Puritan Settlers in Maryland rebelled successfully and wrested control of Maryland from Lord Baltimore and his Governor on two occasions extending from December 1652 to July 1654, and again between March 1655 and March 1658. There were 12 patents in 1652 before that point in December when Puritan Control was established. Three more grants occurred during the portions of 1654/1655 in which the Lord Proprietor was in control. Strangely, the only grant in 1655 was to Puritans **Thomas** and **Edward Selby**, in September, during a period when the Puritans had temporarily lost control. Cromwell was persuaded to restore control of Maryland to the Lord Proprietor on March 3, 1658. There were 35 patents or grants that year. The following graphs depict the distribution of grants and acreage over the years studied:

Certified Acreage (292,809) By Decade

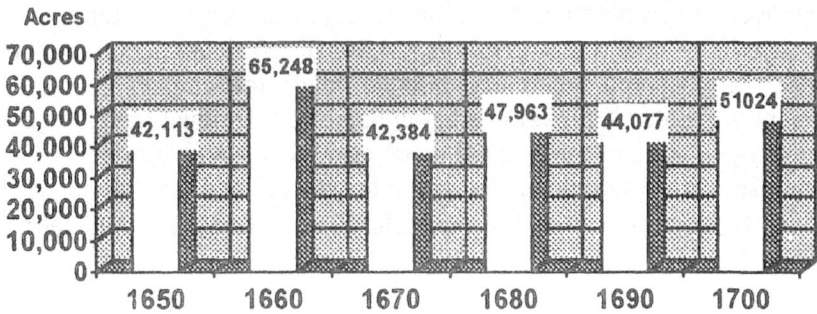

Acres

	1650	1660	1670	1680	1690	1700
	42,113	65,248	42,384	47,963	44,077	51024

Grants (1,119) By Decade

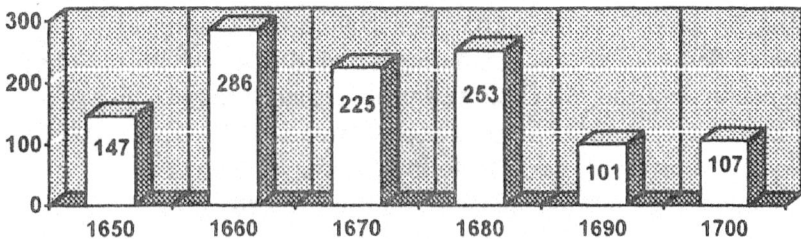

	1650	1660	1670	1680	1690	1700
	147	286	225	253	101	107

Although surveying methodology and equipment was on the cutting edge of 17th century technology, it was primitive by today's standards. As a result, there are errors in acreage and some tracts overlap others and/or do not "close." Numerous complaints by landowners over acreage significantly less than the amount certified have been found. It was a fairly common for owners to seek a Special Warrant of Resurvey to verify shortages or to locate "surplus" land within their boundaries or "vacant" land contiguous to their boundaries. When found, such land was usually granted to the owner or petitioner subject to his making rights and paying retroactive land rent for any land gained back to the date of the original survey. There are instances of tracts being reduced in size because a boundary was found to encroach on that of a "more ancient tract." I found one tract (Slatbourne) that was surveyed, patented, and later found to be entirely within the bounds of another tract (Abingdon).

Differences in certified and actual acres exist for 72% of the tracts found. This includes the 159 tracts that could not be drawn or measured due to incomplete boundary course data. A total of 292,809 acres were certified but only 254,809 acres were actually conveyed. Discounting the 159 "unmeasurable" tracts, however, an overall acreage discrepancy of only - 415 acres existed for the entire period. Although the overall acreage discrepancies did nearly balance over the years it should be noted that 72% of the tracts surveyed had either some acreage discrepancy or the metes and bounds were so poorly documented that the tract could not be measured.

At first I attributed this to the relatively basic state of the art of surveying at the time. I found a number of tracts with simple geometric shapes (squares, rectangles, and triangles) such as Porter's Hill and Pierpoint's Rocks with significant acreage discrepancies. I also found some complex tracts (both large and small) with unconventional shapes such as Ben's Discovery, Davistone, and Ridgely's Chance with little, if any, acreage discrepancy. Obviously, methods for determining the area of odd shaped tracts were known, but not always (or even often) correctly applied. Mistakes were so frequent that I began to look for explanations such as random error, survey error/bribery, or any other explanation including a mix of the above. I considered surveying errors by grant year, by tract size, by general location, and by possible favoritism to prominent persons or families without finding any sustained pattern or ongoing irregularities. It is a fact that the six largest tracts collectively experienced an overwhelmingly favorable acreage discrepancy of +6,293 acres. Five of these tracts were owned by the Lord

Proprietor, the Surveyor General of Maryland, and a prominent citizen (**Charles Carroll**) favored by the Lord Proprietor and used to oversee those Land Office functions that personally involved then Surveyor Generall **Henry Darnall** (see LDD5i/58). In contrast, the next six largest tracts have a collective acreage shortfall of -299 acres. Favoritism does not seem to be a driving factor in overall acreage discrepancies. Wealthier landowners may have had some slight advantage with their larger tracts but their smaller tracts were "shorted" at about the same rate as those of everyone else.

Toward the end of the period a trend toward consolidating smaller tracts into larger holdings was developing. The certified acreage per tract rose from 287 in 1650s to 436 in the 1690s. By the end of the period, ten families owned over 17% of Anne Arundel County acreage, as follows:

	No. Of Tracts	Certified Acres
Carroll	6	8,505
White (Jerome)	6	6,800
Howard	43	6,719
Duvall	12	5,605
Dorsey	11	5,230
Warfield	10	4,823
Beard	10	4,295
Chew	5	3,447
Snowden	3	2,607
Lynthicum/Linthicum/ Linnescomb	4	2,278
Total	110	50,309

The acres certified for each tract included is shown as the first number before the slanted line in the heading of each tract description. The number following the slanted line is the actual acreage conveyed. There is no slanted line for tracts that could not be measured and the only number shown is the certified acreage.

Toward the end of the 1680s, later generations of Anne Arundel families began a suburban movement northward toward Laurel, Huntington (Savage), and Elk Ridge, areas now wholly or partially in present day Howard County. Some of the more prominent names involved are Brown, Carroll, Chew, Gather, Owing, Ridgely, Carroll, and Worthington. "Upper Arundell," as the area was sometimes called, was less densely populated and large areas of contiguous acreage were still available. The air was said to be fresher. The Ridge of Elks was to become a kind of summer resort extending from Elk Ridge Landing to Ellicott City to Clarksville, to Laurel, and back. Elk Ridge Landing became a port of entry at least 25 years before the founding of Baltimore Town in 1729 (Old Homes and Families of Howard County, Maryland, written and published by Cecilia Holland, 1987). This area, located about 25 miles from the port of Annapolis, was primarily residential and agricultural. Prior to the establishment of Elk Ridge Landing as a port in about 1703, the delivery of commodities to Annapolis shipping points proved to be a problem. Initially it was the responsibility of the shipper (not the farmer) to collect and deliver goods to the ship. An Act of Assemby (1696) required that four roads be cleared and marked to accommodate the rolling of tobacco hogsheads from Northern or Upper Anne Arundel County to the ports. As a result of complaints by London merchants, an act requiring farmers to deliver their goods to ports was enacted in 1727.

Anne Arundel County, called Providence by many of the residents before 1650, included all that part of the Maryland north of St. Mary's on the west side of the Chesapeake Bay westward from the Isle of Kent. Later, with the establishment of Prince George's and Baltimore Counties, the western and southern bounds of Anne Arundel evolved to extend to the Patuxent River with Prince George's on the western side and Calvert to the south. To the north and east, the Patapsco River separated Anne Arundel and Baltimore Counties. Apparently there was some confusion over this and a proclamation in 1674, further declared that the north side of the Patapsco was Baltimore County and the south side was Anne Arundel.

Changes in the boundaries of Anne Arundel, Baltimore and, much later, Howard Counties have presented a problem identifying tracts to be included. For example, a portion of what is now Howard County (formerly called Upper Arundel) was officially in Anne Arundel until 1659, when it was transferred to the newly established Baltimore County. This was without protest by the Anne Arundel citizens. The area transferred, roughly to the north and west of Elk Ridge, was considered at that time to be frontier or surplus land. In 1698, the entire area now known as Howard County became a part of Baltimore County. This was reversed in 1727, when approximately the same area was returned to Anne Arundel to eventually become Howard County. As a result, tracts in and near this region (roughly from Elk Ridge to Ellicott City to Clarkesville to Laurel and back) are a confusing mix of Anne Arundel and Baltimore Manor patents depending on the date of the patent/survey. I have included all of these tracts found and I have also included all tracts located on the south side of the Patapsco River (regardless of date).

Land records of this era sometimes directly or indirectly reveal unexpected information involving personal and family relationships, burial sites, employer's names, trades, disputes, and religious and political involvement. Special instructions from the Lord Proprietor regarding a number of matters such as suspended surveyors, gifts to his relatives and special friends, the location of special springs reserved for his use, and much more were found. The entire Acts of Assembly, 1650, were found in Liber 3 (folios 29-61) of the land records. These are well worth a read in themselves. Among the topics addressed are corporal punishment (i.e., the removal of ears or hands) for swearing, the collection of ransom to rescue hostages from the Indians, retaliation against the Indians, requirements that Indians provide 24-hour notification before visiting a settlement (and then, only in limited numbers), and the refurbishment of the fort at St. Inegoes to control the behavior of the crews of foreign trading vessels while in port. All persons named in the land records are shown in boldface type and are included in the People Index.

I have tried to retain the special flavor of the records by including many of the consistently misspelled words and some of the less wordy quaint phrasing found. Apparently words were often spelled according to the way they sounded. This created some interesting variations. For example, a tract called Broughton Ashley became known as Broad Nashley. The Magothy River became the Maggity or Maggoty River. The Rhode River was the Rode or Road River and Anne Arundel was Ann Arundall, Ann Arundall, or Anarrundell.

Appendices A-F are included to assist in determining the relatively correct historical location of individual tracts. Appendix A is an exploded view of the entire county showing the placement and size of the hundreds in relation to each other. Appendices B-F are individual hundreds showing many of the water landmarks with the old names used in the patent documents.

Although nothing I could say would be adequate, I would like to express my appreciation and gratitude to my wife Sandy for all that she did to help and for her unlimited patience with me while we worked on this project.

Tracts on the west side of Broad Creek at the South River

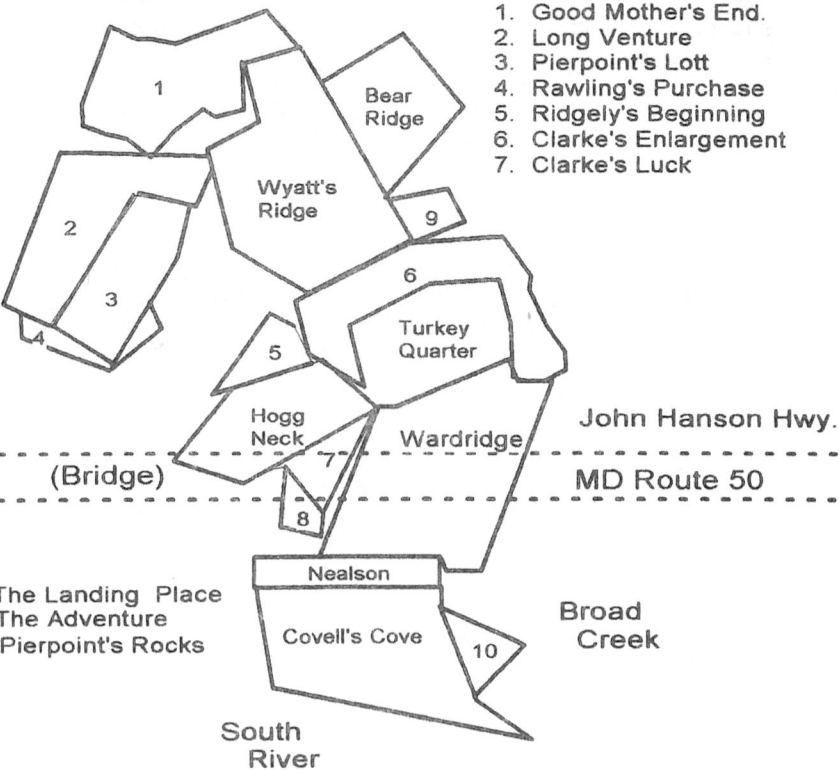

1. Good Mother's End.
2. Long Venture
3. Pierpoint's Lott
4. Rawling's Purchase
5. Ridgely's Beginning
6. Clarke's Enlargement
7. Clarke's Luck

Bear Ridge

Wyatt's Ridge

Turkey Quarter

Hogg Neck

Wardridge

John Hanson Hwy.

(Bridge)

MD Route 50

Nealson

8. The Landing Place
9. The Adventure
10. Pierpoint's Rocks

Covell's Cove

Broad Creek

South River

Tracts located in the Herring Creek Hundred near Lyon's Creek

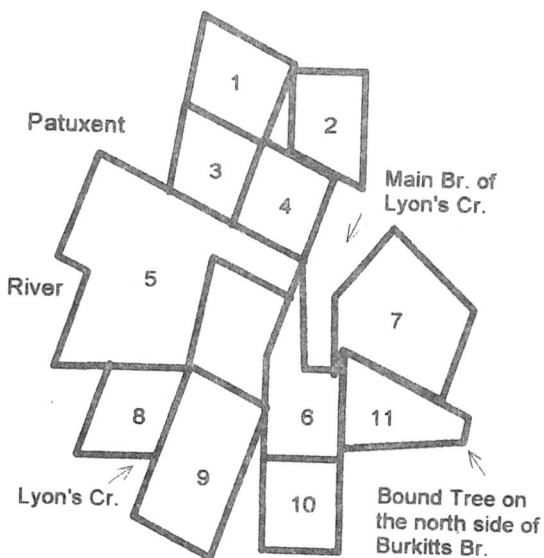

1. James' Fancy
2. Talbott's Search
3, Vale of Pleasure
4. Birkhead's Chance
5. The Rainge
6. Birkhead's Right
7. Birkhead's Mill
8. Abraham
9. Bersheba
10. The Hamm
11. Bedworth'a Addition

Abbreviations:

B&TNH - Broad & Town Neck Hundred

HCH - Herring Creek Hundred

MNH - Middle Neck Hundred

SRH - South River Hundred

WRH - West River Hundred

Format

Following the name of the patentee is the name of the tract/date of the patent/**certified acreage**/actual acreage/liber (book)/folio (page). When there is only one number, it is the certified acreage (as with "undrawable" tracts).

Early Landowners of Maryland
Volume 1
Anne Arundel County

Acton, Richard (*Carpenter*)

> **Acton 8/11/1658 – 100/107 acres.** LQ/117 SR7345
> <u>Location</u>: MNH near Severn River at Todd's Branch.
> <u>Persons mentioned</u>: None.

Alcott, Samuel

> **Alcott's Triangle 10/1/1672 – 70 acres.** L16/551 SR7357
> <u>Location</u>: B&TNH on the east side of the Severn River adjoining Long Neck Branch.
> <u>Persons mentioned</u>: **Robert Ridgely, William Thurgood, & George Yate** (assignors of land rights). **William Davis, William Blaies, & William Slade** (neighbors). *Note: William Thurgood assigned the 50 acres he received for completing his time of service in this Province.*

Alderidge, Nicholas

> **Alderidge His Beginning 7/11/1681 – 300/285 acres.** LCB2i/257 SR7366
> <u>Location</u>: B&TNH on the south side of the Maggity River opposite a small island.
> <u>Persons mentioned</u>: **Henry Hanslap** (assignor of land rights).

Arbuckle, Archibald/Archer

> **Elk Thickett 1/28/1659 – (two tracts) 150/142 acres.** L4/438 SR7376
> <u>Location</u>: SRH on the west side of the South River adjoining Arbuckle's Branch and South River.
> <u>Persons mentioned</u>: Rights based on Arbuckle and his wife **Dyna** completing their time of service in this Province. *Note:*

Tract one (50/50 acres was unnamed). Tract Two (10 /92 acres was named Elk Thickett).

Arnold, Richard *(Planter)* **& Gray, John**
Arnold Gray 8/3/1688 – 300 acres. L12/121 SR7354
Location: MNH on the north side of the South River.
Persons mentioned: None. *Note: Arnold's share of the land rights included fifty acres due him for completing his time of service in this Province.*

Ashman, George
George's Fancy 6/1/1687 – 100/94 acres. LIB&ILC/207 SR7368
Location: B&TNH on the south side of the Patapsco River and on the west side of Curtis Creek adjoining Cabbin Branch.
Persons mentioned: **George Hope** (neighbor). *Note: The patent/survey document places this tract in Baltimore County. MSA Land Index #55 places it in Anne Arundel County. I have included it here based on its location.*

Ashman's Hope 11/10/1695 – 512/558 acres. LCC4i/113 SR7375
Location: BNTNH on the north side of the Patapsco River on Hunting Ridge.
Persons mentioned: **Thomas Preston & Michael Judd** (assignors of land rights). *Note: The patent document places this tract in Baltimore County and the location tends to support this. However, it is included in the Anne Arundel County Rent Rolls (1753-1777- SR4382). I have included it here because it might have been in Anne Arundel County.*

Askew, John
Asketon 2/15/1659 – 230/240 acres. L4/459 SR7376
Location: B&TNH on the east side of the Severn River.
Persons mentioned: **William Crouch** (neighbor).

Netlam 4/4/1664 – 50/50 acres. L7/221 SR7349
Location: B&TNH on the north side of Severn River
adjoining the Maggity River.
Persons mentioned: Joyce Williams (transported by Askew to
this Province here to inhabit).

Little Netlam 8/20/1665 – 50/50 acres. L8/143 SR7350
Location: B&TNH on the north side of the Severn River
adjoining a tract called Netlam.
Persons mentioned: Edward Bates & Thurman Salley
(assignors of land rights).

Baker, Morris
The Range 6/10/1671 – 50/50 acres. L16/181 SR7357
Location: B&TNH on the north side of the Severn River.
Persons mentioned: John Homewood (assignor of land
rights). John Green (neighbor).

Baker's Chance 6/1/1687 – 330/330 acres. LIB&ILC/317
SR7368-2
Location: B&TNH near the head of Deep Creek.
Persons mentioned: John Harwood (assignor of land rights).

Charles His Forrest 2/11/1688 – 295/302 acres.
LNSBi/625 SR7370
Location: B&TNH on the north side of Deep Creek next
adjoining a tract called Locust Thickett.
Persons mentioned: Thomas Richardson (assignor of land
rights).

Baker's Addition 2/18/1688 – 263/265 acres. LNSBi/627
SR7370
Location: B&TNH on the north side of Deep Creek adjoining
his own land.
Persons mentioned: Thomas Richardson (assignor of land
rights). Thomas Tench & Amos Pierpoint (neighbors).

Baker's Increase 6/20/1688 – 80/87 acres. L12/21 SR7354
Location: B&TNH on the north side of the Severn River.
Persons mentioned: **George Yate** & **Phillip Thomas**
(assignors of land rights). **John Green, John Askew,** &
Elizabeth Hill (neighbors).

Baker, Ralph

Gray's Adventure 6/1/1667 – 184/185 acres.
LIB&ILC/433 SR7368-2
Location: B&TNH on the north side of the Maggity River
and on the southwest side of Bodkins Creek.
Persons mentioned: **Robert Proctor** (assignor of land rights
and neighbor). **John Gray** (original owner).

Baldwin, John

Baldwin's Neck 1/7/1651 – 260 acres. LAB&H/267
SR7344
Location: MNH on the north side of the South River at
Beard's Branch next adjoining a tract called Baldwin's
Addition.
Persons mentioned: None.

Baldwin's Addicion 8/11/1664 70/63 acres. L7/368
SR7349 (Two tracts)
Location: WRH in the swamp between Herring Creek and
The Three Islands at the head of Deep Creek.
Persons mentioned: None.

Baldwin's Addicon 8/11/1664 – 120/102 acres. L7/356
SR7379
Location: MNH on the north side of the South River
adjoining his own land.
Persons mentioned: None. *Note: On the same day,* **Baldwin**
and his wife **Ruth** *patented another tract called Baldwin's
Addicon (70 acres) in the West River Hundred of Anne
Arundel County. This variation in the spelling of the word
"addition" was not uncommon.*

Brushy Neck 8/24/1665 – 150/151 acres. L8/148 SR7350
Location: MNH on the north side of the South River
adjoining Acton's Creek.
Persons mentioned: None.

Lydia's Rest Res. 7/8/1681 – 210/134 acres. LCBi/148
SR7366
Location: MNH on the north side of the South River at
Oatley's Point on Oatley's Creek.
Persons mentioned: **Christopher Oatley** (former owner).
Elizabeth Caplyn (daughter of **Henry Caplyn**, deceased,
widow of **Thomas Watkins**, deceased, who was the former
husband of **Lydia**, now the wife of **Edmund Beetenson**).
*Note: The tract was initially patented by Christopher Oatley
as Oatley. Ownership somehow passed to the Caplyns who
died without an heir and the tract escheated to the Lord
Proprietor. Apparently it was then regranted to Lydia, who
was also, at some point, married to Thomas Watkins.
Through Lydia, ownership passed to a later husband,
Edward Beetenson (See LWC2/344 SR7340). The
Beetensons sold the tract (and the LOP regranted it) to
John Baldwin.*

Baldwin's Chance 11/10/1695 – 451/493 acres. L23/265.
SR7364
Location: MNH on the north side of the South River at
Baldwin's Point.
Persons mentioned: **Richard Beard & Daniel Ellet**
(assignors of land rights). *Note: Following the death of John
Baldwin in 1729, this tract was divided among his children
John, Thomas, & Catherine, the wife of Charles Griffen.*

Ball, William
Bare Neck 10/10/1671 – 140/123 acres. L14/359 SR7356
Location: B&TNH on the south side of Patapsco River at
Curtis Creek.
Persons mentioned: **George Yate** (assignor of land rights).

Ball's Enlargement 7/15/1674 – 100/100 acres. L15/272
SR4327
Location: B&TNH on the south side of the Patapsco River
next adjoining his own tract called Bare Neck.
Persons mentioned: **Robert Wilson & William Wheatly**
(assignors of land rights).

Baltimore, Lord

**Mannors of Ann Arundell & Portland Resurveyed 1698 –
15,356/17,255 acres.** LCDi/54 SR7346
Location: HCH adjoining the Patuxent River.
Persons mentioned: **Coll. Henry Darnall** (Surveyor
Generall). **Coll. Thomas Taylor & John Burrage**
(neighbors).

Barwell, John

Barwell's Choice 2/1/1671 – 100/100 acres. L14/390
SR7356
Location: WRH in Herring Creek Swamp adjoining The
South Creek.
Persons mentioned: George Yate (assignor of land rights),
Thomas Hooker, Thomas Pratt & Matthew Selby
(neighbors). *Note: A later patent was issued on 7/2/1681
(CB2i/151). Except for the dates and references, both
patents are the same except that George Yate is described in
the latter as the assignee of Richard Hill.*

Barwell's Purchase 7/10/1671 – 115/115 acres. L20/259
SR7361
Location: WRH in Herring Creek Swamp adjoining Barwell's
Enlargement.
Persons mentioned: **George Yate & Richard Hill** (assignors
of land rights). **Thomas Hooker, Thomas Pratt & Matthew
Selby** (neighbors).

Barwell's Enlargement 4/4/1682 – 50/47 acres.
LCB3i/139 SR7367
Location: WRH in Herring Creek Swamp adjoining a tract
named Barwell's Purchase.
Persons mentioned: None. *Note: Barwell's rights were
based on completion of his time of service in this Province.*

Bates, Edward

Brushy Neck 7/13/1665 – 150/150 acres. L8/503 SR7350
Location: B&TNH on the south side of the Maggity River at
the mouth of Bate's Branch.
Persons mentioned: Hermann Rollen (assignor of land
rights).

Bate's Chance 5/1/1672 – 80/76 acres. L14/548 SR7356
Location: B&TNH on the north side of the Ann Arundell
(Severn) River.
Persons mentioned: George Yate (assignor of land rights).
John Askew, George Norman, & Christopher Rowles
(neighbors).

Batten, Ferdinand & Skinner, Andrew

Hopewell 5/7/1666 – 300/288 acres. L9/306 SR7351
Location: HCH in the woods near the beaver dams on
Herring Creek.
Persons mentioned: John Burrage (neighbor). Capt.
Thomas Besson & John Gray (assignors of land rights).

Batten, Fernando/Ferdinand

Essex 8/5/1664 – 300/337 acres. L7/299 SR7349
Location: WRH on the north side of the West River.
Persons mentioned: Himself, Millicient (his wife), **Seaborn**
(his son), and daughters **Dina, Mary, & Ruth** (all transported
by Fernando Batten into this Province here to inhabit).
Richard Talbott & Richard Ewen (neighbors).

Kent 7/20/1673 – 48/45 acres (two tracts). L15/7 SR4327
Location: WRH.
Persons mentioned: George Yate (assignor of land rights).
Thomas Mills, Richard Ewan, & Richard Talbott,
(neighbors).

Batten's Due 9/20/1677 – 100/111 acres. L19/507 SR7360
Location: WRH next adjoining his own tract (Essex).
Persons mentioned: Richard Talbott (deceased neighbor).

Suffolk 6/18/1683 – 52/52 acres. LSDA/412 SR7369
Location: WRH adjoining Essex.
Persons Mentioned: William Richardson (assignor of land
rights).

Bayly/Bayley/Bailey, Richard

Baker's Folly 7/10/1671 - 100/112 acres. L16/240 SR7357
Location: B&TNH on the north side of the Maggity River.
Persons mentioned: Robert Wilson & Thomas Wellborne
(assignors of land rights).

Ferfatt 5/1/1672 – 30/34 acres. L14/519 SR7356
Location: B&TNH between the Severn & Maggity Rivers on
the east side of Maggity Br.
Persons mentioned: George Yate (assignor of land rights).
John Ray (neighbor).

Piny Plaine 5/10/1685 – 70/71 acres. LNS2i/215 SR7371
Location: B&TNH on the north side of Maggity River on the
west side of Bayly's Creek.
Persons mentioned: None.

Betty's Poynt 5/10/1685 – 90/93 acres. LNSBi/217
SR7370
Location: B&TNH on the south side, at the mouth, of the
Maggity River and on the west side of Maggity Creek.
Persons mentioned: Henry Woolchurch (neighbor).

Bayly's Content 6/1/1687 – 24/36 acres. LNS2i/345
SR7356
Location: B&TNH on the south side of the Maggity River.
Persons mentioned: George Burges (assignor of land rights).
Richard Moore (neighbor).

Beard, Hester

Hester's Habitation 6/24/1679 – 118/124 acres. L20/187
SR7361
Location: SRH on the south side of the South River at
Burges' Branch.
Persons mentioned: George Yate (assignor of land rights).

Beard, Richard

Brampton 2/15/1659 – 100/91 acres. L4/442 SR7346
Location: MNH on the north side of the South River and on
the east side of Broad Creek.
Persons mentioned: John McCubbin (neighbor).

Broome 2/15/1659 – 220/202 acres. L4/41 SR7346
Location: MNH on the north side of South River and on the
east side of Broad Creek.`
Persons mentioned: None.

Beard's Dock 9/20/1663 – 250/254 acres. L5/585 SR7347
Location: MNH on the north side of the South River at
Beard's Branch.
Persons mentioned: Richard & Rachel (children of Richard
Beard) & Thomas Gearfe (all transported by Beard into this
Province here to inhabit). *Note: On the same day Richard
Beard made over (sold) the tract to John Taylor.*

Beard's Habitation 9/22/1663 – 1,260/1,247 acres. L5/590
SR7347
Location: SRH on the south side of the South River next
adjoining a tract called West Puddington.

Persons mentioned: Richard Preston, Gent. (assignor of land rights and transporter of the following persons into this Province to inhabit: Richard Orchard (1650), William Jones & Richard Foster (1667). George Puddington (neighbor).

Poplar Neck 9/20/1663 – 200 acres. L5/588 SR7347
Location: SRH near the South River.
Persons mentioned: Rachell Beard (wife of Richard. Transported by him in 1650).

John's Cabbin Ridge 9/18/1666 – 30/30 acres. L10/748 SR7352
Location: SRH on the north side of the Flatt Creek.
Persons mentioned: None.

Bare Neck 9/1/1671 – 290/265 acres. LNS2i/388 SR7371
Location: B&TNH between the branches of Curtis Creek.
Persons mentioned: George Burges (assignor of land rights).

The Pound 10/14/1687 – 68/68 acres. LNS2i/573 SR7371
Location: B&TNH on the south side of Maggity River west of Beard's Creek.
Persons mentioned: Thomas Richardson (assignor of land rights). Francis Mondo (neighbor).

Huckleberry Forrest 10/1/1687 – 1,611/1,620 acres. LNS2i/564 SR7371
Location: B&TNH on the south side of the Maggity River by the side of Wolf Pitt Br.
Persons mentioned: Thomas Richardson (assignor of land rights). John Gray, Abraham Child, Walter Phelps, Henry Hanslap, Matthew Howard, George Saughier, Thomas Sutton, William Gibbs, & Francis Modre (neighbors).

Fortaine 2/10/1698 – 148/108 acres. LCC4i/134 SR7375
Location: B&TNH on the north side of Plott's Creek.

Persons mentioned: Charles Carroll (assignor of land rights). James Jackson (neighbor).

Bedworth, Richard & Thornbury, Samuel
The Hamm 4/15/1668 – 100/102 acres. L11/406 SR7353
Location: HCH on the Main Branch of Lyon's Creek.
Persons mentioned: John Wilson & Robert Paca (neighbors).

Bedworth, Richard
Bedworth His Addition 5/1/1672 - 52/54 acres. L16/571 SR7357
Location: HCH on the north side of Lyon's Creek.
Person's mentioned: George Yate (assignor of land rights). Abraham Birkhead (neighbor). *Note: The patent document identifies this tract as Bedworth His Addition and as Bedworth's Addition.*

Beetenson, John
Beetenson's Adventure 9/23/1680 – 82 acres. LCBi/47 SR7366
Location: MNH on the north side of the South River.
Persons mentioned: George Yate (assignor of land rights). Thomas Bell (neighbor).

Bell, Thomas
Bell's Haven 2/17/1665 100/122 acres. L9/184 SR7351
Location: MNH on Besson's Creek.
Persons mentioned. Elizabeth Bell (wife of Thomas who was transported by him to this Province here to inhabit).

Bennet, John
Bennet's Chance 5/25/1684 – 124/108 acres. L22/106 SR7363
Location: B&TNH on the north side of Homewood's Creek by Blay's Creek.

Persons mentioned: **Robert Jones & George Yate** (assignors of land rights). *Note: George Yate was also the surveyor for this tract.*

Bennet's Park 6/12/1688 – 81/68 acres. LNS2i/694
SR7371
Location: B&TNH on the south side of Homewood's Creek at Dawson's Long Point.
Persons mentioned: **Madame Ursala Burges & Coll William Burges,** deceased (assignors of land rights).

Benson, Daniel
Benson's Park 3/26/1696 – 250/250 acres. LC3i/262
SR7377
Location: B&TNH at Elk Ridge adjoining tracts named Chew's Vinyard & Chew's Resolution Mannor.
Persons mentioned: None. *Note: This tract lies in present day Howard County.*

Benson, Steven
Kequeston Choice 9/4/1663 – 300/282 acres. L4/458
SR7347
Location: HCH in the woods among the branches of Herring Creek.
Persons mentioned: **Thomas Turner & Walter Carr** (assignors of land rights). **Elizabeth Benson, Mary Smith, David Rosse, & Mary Clark** (persons transported into this Province here to inhabit.). **William Ayres, Samuel Chew, John Burrage, & William Selby** (neighbors).

Besson, Thomas, Capt
Besson's Den 2/11/1650 – 450/430 acres. L4/405 SR7375
Location: SRH on the south side of the South River and on the south side of Besson's Br.
Persons mentioned: **Ann** (his wife), **Thomas & Ann** (his children), & **Edward Cox** (persons transported by Besson into this province here to inhabit).

Bessonton 2/10/1650 – 350/350 acres. L4/504 SR7346
Location: SRH on the west side of the Rode River at Muddy Branch.
Persons mentioned: Thomas Sparrow & George Nettlefold (neighbors).

Besson, Thomas (the younger)

Younger Besson 2/6/1659 – 50/49 acres. L4/7 SR7346
Location: SRH on the south side of the South River next adjoining a tract called Bessonton.
Persons mentioned: Thomas Besson (the elder) & George Nettlefold (neighbors).

Bewsey, William

The Heart 8/31/1681 – 60/49 acres. L12/350 SR7362
Location: B&TNH on the south side of the Maggity River at Back Creek.
Persons mentioned: Thomas Taylor & Henry Hanslap (assignors of land rights). George Yate (Deputy Surveyor). John Smith (neighbor).

Biggs, Seth

Bigg's Purchase 3/18/1701 – 334/334 acres. LWD/372 SR7372-2
Location: HCH next adjoining a tract named Samuel's Purchase.
Persons mentioned: Samuel Turner (neighbor). Note: MSA Land Records (Index #54) places this tract in Calvert County. However, the patent document states that it is in Ann Arundel Mannor.

Billingsly, Francis

Selby Clifts 11/26/1650 – 200/200 acres. LQ/233 SR7345
Location: SRH
Persons mentioned: Edward Selby (former owner) Thomas Forby & Mary Slade (persons transported into this Province

by Selby). **Thomas Meers** (neighbor). *Note: The patent document places this tract in St. Mary's County. MSA Land Index #54 places it in AA County. There is no definitive location information in the patent document. I have included it here because it may have been in Anne Arundel County.*

Birkhead, Abraham

Abraham 11/14/1665 –50//52 acres. L9/97 SR7351
Location: HCH in the woods.
Persons mentioned: **John Wilson** (neighbor). *Note: A marginal note on the survey document states that the tract was patented and that the patent is on Folio 97. It was not found on Folio 97 of this Liber, however, it is assumed that it was patented at some point.*

Birkhead's Chance 9/10/1666 – 50/50 acres. L10/142 SR7352
Location: HCH.
Persons mentioned: **George Yate** (assignor of land rights). **John Wilson** (neighbor).

Birkhead's Choice 1/10/1667 - 750/747 acres. L11/206 SR7353
Location. HCH at a Great Branch of the Patuxent River.
Persons mentioned: **George Yate** (assignor of land rights.) **Thomas Turner & John Grammar** (neighbors).

Birkhead's Adventure 5/10/1679 – 420/421 acres. L20/246 SR7361
Location: HCH on the north side of the main branch of Lyon's Creek.
Persons mentioned: **George Yate** (assignor or land rights). **John Grammar & William Mears** (neighbors).

Birkhead's Mill 5/1683 – 100/104 acres. LCB3i/308 SR7367

Location: HCH on the Main Branch of Lyon's Creek.
Persons mentioned: Henry Hanslap (assignor of land rights).

Birkhead's Right 5/10/1685 – 55/65 acres. LNS2/99
SR7371
Location: HCH beginning at bound tree of Birkhead's Chance.
Persons mentioned: Robert James (assignor of land rights).
Nathan Smith, Samuel Thornbury, & Richard Bonwart neighbors).

Birkhead, Christopher
Birkhead's Parcell 1/5/1663 – 600/524 acres. L6/91
SR7348
Location: HCH on the west side of a great swamp near a pond.
Persons mentioned: Samuel Chew (assignor of land rights).
John Burrage (owner at the time of survey).

Birkheads Meadow 8/25/1664 – 50/49 acres. L7/376
SR7349
Location: HCH next adjoining a tract called Birkhead's Parcell.
Persons mentioned: David Frye (assignor of land rights).
John Burrage (neighbor).

Birkhead's Lott 8/24/1665 - 434/438 acres. L8/95 SR7350
Location: HCH in the woods on the west side of the plantations of Herring Creek.
Persons mentioned: David Frye (assignor of land rights who also transported himself to this Province here to inhabit).
Abraham Pritchard, Anne Anderson, Henry Anderson, Richard Breadwart, William Harris, John Prosser, Elizabeth Jones, & John Williams (Persons transported by Birkhead to this Province here to inhabit in 1662). Samuel Chew &Thomas Truman (neighbors).

Birmingham, Jacob

West Quarter 6/24/1663 – 100/100 acres. L5/352 SR7347
Location: MNH on the south side of the Severn River and on the south side of Howell's Creek.
Persons mentioned: Mary Combs, servant (transported to this Province in 1659, by Birmingham, here to inhabit). *Note: From MSA Tract Index# 73: West Quarter is within the bounds of Read's Lott and the Widow's Addition.*

Birmingham, Michael

All Cussack's Land 5/28/1692– LBB3B/451 SR7374
Location: MNH
Persons mentioned: Michael Cussack (former owner). *Note 1: A note found in the Rent Rolls states the following, "Cussack dead and can find no heirs." The following was extracted from a grant to Michael Birmingham (LBB3/451 SR7374- 5/29/1692): "Whereupon it has been made manifestly clear to me that Michael Cussack, deceased, was in his lifetime legally possessed of about two hundred acres of land in the County of Ann Arundell between the South and Severn Rivers and two or more parcels as by patents for same as is sett forth. And, Whereas the s'd Michael Cussack made no disposition of the land and dyed without heirs, all of the lands ought to revert to and devolve again to the honorable Charles, Land Barron of Baltimore. Know yee that for and in consideration of the singular love and affection I have for Michael Birmingham of London, Gent, and likewise to prevent further charges concerning the s'd lands in the office of escheat, or otherwise, do hereby grant unto him the s'd Michael Birmingham all of the lands belonging to the s'd Michael Cussack." According to the Rent Rolls this would have included Garrett's Town, Welfare, Cussack's Forrest, and Come By Chance. About two months later, Birmingham sold these tracts to **Richard Hill** of Ann Arundell County. Note 2: No specific acreage, location, or boundary courses are provided.*

Bishop, Roger

Talbott's Land 10/1/1687 – 44 acres. LNS2i/506 SR7271
Location: HCH among the branches of Lyon's Creek adjoining tracts called Portland Landing & Portland Mannor.
Persons mentioned: Richard Beard (assignor of land rights). Abraham Birkhead (neighbor).

Talbott's Search 10/1/1687 – 50/51 acres. LNS2i/537 SR7171
Location: HCH among the branches of Lyon's Creek next adjoining a tract called Portland Landing.
Persons mentioned: Richard Beard (assignor of land rights).

Blackwell, Thomas

Blackwell's Search 10/10/1694 – 439/449 acres. LB23i/330 SR7365
Location: B&TNH at Elk Ridge on the Middle Runn of the Patapsco River.
Persons mentioned: None. *Note: The tract lies in present day Howard County.*

The Desert 6/12/1696 – 148/138 acres. LWDi/124 SR 7372-2
Location: B&TNH on the west side of the North Branch of the Patuxent River next adjoining a tract called The Diamond.
Persons mentioned: Thomas Browne (neighbor).

Bladen, William

Hawkins Habitation Res. 12/30/1703 - 100 acres. LDD5i/123 SR7378
Location: BNTNH on the north side of the Severn River in a neck of land called the Broad Neck at the head and on the north side of Hawkin's Branch.
Persons mentioned: James Kile (former owner of one moiety). *Note 1: The tract was initially patented by Ralph Hawkins on 8/12/1665. Subsequently, one moiety escheated unto his LOPS for want of heirs of James Kile, to whom the moiety was conveyed by one of the Devisees. The other*

moiety was purchased by Bladen. Note 2: The patent document does not include boundary courses. Actual acreage could not be determined.

Bland, Thomas

Bland's Quarter 9/21/1681 – 200/150 acres. LCB2I 329 SR7366
<u>Location:</u> B&TNH on the north side of the Severn River adjoining a tract called Martin's Nest.
<u>Persons mentioned:</u> **Martin Faulkner, John Gray, & Edward Phillips** (neighbors).

Blay, Edward

Blay's Neck 11/20/1678 – 200/243 acres. L20/109 SR7261
<u>Location:</u> B&TNH on the south side of Blay's Branch.
<u>Persons mentioned:</u> **William Blay** (father of Edward Blay).
Note: Apparently there was some confusion on the part of the clerk who transcribed the patent over the identity of Edward, son and heir of William Blay. The name William is used as the grantee throughout the document but the grant is actually to Edward.

Blay, William

Unnamed Cert 11/19/1652 – 600/520 acres. LAB&H/285 SR7344
<u>Location:</u> B&TNH on the west side of the Patapsco River at Duck Cove.
<u>Persons mentioned:</u> **Richard Ewen** (neighbor).

Boarman, Edward

Phantascoe 2/17/1704 – 100/100 acres. LCDi/267 SR7376
<u>Location:</u> B&TNH on the south side of the Patapsco River descending into Curtis Creek and the north side of Long Branch.
<u>Persons mentioned:</u> None. *Note: The patent/survey document places this tract in Baltimore County. MSA Land Index #55 places it in Anne Arundel County. I have included it here based on its location.*

Bodware, Richard

Thornbury's Addition 10/5/1684 – 16/19 acres.
LSDA/421 SR7369
Location: HCH adjoining land he now liveth upon.
Persons mentioned: **Henry Hanslap** (assignor of land rights).

Body, John, Capt. *(Marriner)*

Body's Adventure 4/20/1676 – 700/710 acres. L19/488
SR7360
Location: B&TNH on the south side of the Patapsco River
and on the north side of Curtis   Creek next adjoining a tract
called Morley's Choice.
Persons mentioned: **James Pauley, George Garrish,
Thomas Fisher, Dorothy Chapman, Thorus Packogells,
Ann Eleson, Richard Chandler, Sarah Clarey, Ann
Glover, Robert Owens, George Clarge, Henry Oswald,
Robert Hubbard,** & **Francis Beatson** (persons transported
by Body into this Province here to inhabit). **Joseph Morley**
(neighbor).

Bond, Benjamin

The Favor 4/2/1696 – 123/121 acres. LC3i/420 SR7377
Location: MNH on the north side of the South River at the
mouth of Oatley Creek.
Persons mentioned: **George Puddington, William
Pennington, Ester Gossum,** & **Adam De Lapp** (former
owners). **George Yate** (Deputy Surveyor).

Bond, Peter

Bond's Forrest 2/18/1678 – 381/298 acres. LNSBi/628
SR7370
Location: B&TNH near the head of Deep Creek, a branch of
the Patapsco River.
Persons mentioned: **Thomas Richardson** (assignor of land
rights). **Morris Baker** (neighbor). *Note: The discrepancy
between certified and actual acreage is extreme, even for
this period. However, the boundary courses have been*

verified and the acreage is correct as shown above.

Bond, Thomas

Lucky Hole 9/1/1702 – 100/106 acres. LDD5i/63 SR7378
<u>Location:</u> BNTNH next adjoining a tract called Point Thickett.
<u>Persons mentioned:</u> **James Carroll** (assignor of land rights). *Note: The patent/survey document places this tract in Baltimore County. MSA Land Index #55 places it in Anne Arundel County. I have included it here based on its location.*

Bonner, James

Bonnerston 2/16/1659 – 100 acres. L4/510 SR7346
<u>Location:</u> WRH on the north side of the West River on the west side of Cedar Creek and on the north side of Bonner's Branch.
<u>Persons mentioned:</u> None. *Note: The tract could not be drawn and actual acreage could not be determined due to incomplete boundary course information in the patent document.*

Great Bonnerston 2/16/1659 – 150/147 acres. L4/512 SR7346
<u>Location:</u> WRH on the north side of the West River at Cedar Creek.
<u>Persons mentioned:</u> **Hugh & Emmanuel Drew & Jacob Duhatton** *(probably Duhaddaway) neighbors.*

Boon, Humphrey

Brown's Adventure 9/10/1672 – 160/150 acres. L17/294 SR7358
<u>Location:</u> B&TNH on the south side of the Patapsco River on the north side of Rock Cr.
<u>Persons mentioned:</u> **George Yate, ThomasTaylor, Jerome White, Esq.** (assignors of land rights). **Paul Kinsey** (neighbor).

Boyde, John

Boyde's Chance 5/4/1685 – 60/80 acres. LNS2i/108 SR7371

Location: MNH on the north side of the South River at the Head of Indian Branch.

Persons mentioned: Matthew Howard (neighbor).

Brewer, John

Brewerston 2/16/1659 – 400/396 acres. L4/505 SR7346

Location: SRH on the west side of the Rode River adjoining a tract called Bessonton.

Persons mentioned: Thomas Besson (neighbor).

Larkington 9/2/1663 – 300 acres. L5/462 SR7347

Location: SRH on the south side of the South River by Pyther's Creek.

Persons mentioned: Ellis Brown (assignor of land rights and transporter of Edward Stone & John Macubbin into this Province here to inhabit in 1649). John Larkin (former owner).

The Security 9/10/1664 – 66/49 acres. L7/267 SR7349

Location: SRH on the south side of the South River.

Persons mentioned: William Burges (neighbor).

Brewer's Chance 9/1/1667 – 152/154 acres. LNS3i/402 SR7371

Location: SRH on the south side of the South River on the north side of Pyther's Creek.

Persons mentioned: Richard Beard (assignor of land rights).

Brewer, John, Jr.

Collierby 4/13/1678 – 150 acres. L10/68 SR7361

Location: SRH adjoining the riverside.

Persons mentioned: John Collier (former owner). Ellis Brown & Edward Selby (neighbors).

Brewer, Joseph

>Brewerston Res. 11/4/1710 – 400/360 acres. LDD5i/669 SR7378
>
>Location: WRH on the west side of the Rode River.
>
>Persons mentioned: Thomas Odall (arranged for resurvey on behalf of Brewer). *Note: This patent is included because the Cert and/or Survey were within the targeted period.*

Brice, John

>Escheat Land called Barron Neck 5/20/1704 – 124/123 acres. Two Tracts. LDD5i/733 SR7378
>
>Location: B&TNH adjoining Ferry Creek, Coxes Cove, and Strong's Cove.
>
>Persons mentioned: William Taylord (former owner). *Note: The following is written on the same Folio immediately following the patent which, at this point, shows William Taylord as the patentee: "Then issued pattent for the s'd two parcells of escheat land to Mr. John Brice of Ann Arundell County (Wm. Taylord dyed without paying the purchase money agreed upon) for the summe of 15 lbs sterling paid in hand."*

Brooksby, John

>Brooksby's Point 7/11/1681 – 350/396 acres. LCBi/257 SR7366
>
>Location: MNH on the south side of the Ann Arundell *(Severn)* River adjoining Indian Branch.
>
>Persons mentioned: George Yate (assignor of land rights). John Sutton (neighbor). *Note: The tract was sold to John Moyatt in 1686, for 12,000 lbs of tobacco. Three years later Moyatt sold a 60-acre portion to Thomas Alderich for 3,500 lbs of tobacco.*

Brown, Ellis

>Unnamed Cert 10/21/1652 – 300 acres. LAB&H/277 SR7344
>
>Location: SRH on the south side of the South River at

Pyther's Creek.
Persons mentioned: Edward Selby (neighbor). *Note: The tract cannot be drawn and the actual acreage cannot be determined due to incomplete boundary course information in the patent document.*

Brown, James *(of New England, Merchant)*
Brown's Quarter 10/16/1677 – 20/20 acres. L15/413 SR4327
Location: BNTNH on the north side of the Severn River in a neck of land called theTown Neck on the east side of Durand's Creek at Broad Creek.
Persons mentioned: George Yate (Deputy Surveyor). Ralph Williams (neighbor).

Brown, John & Clark, John
Brownton 1/2/1650 – 650/599 acres. LQ/2778 SR7345
Location: WRH on the west side of the West River at the mouth of Deep Creek.
Persons mentioned: John, Patient & Mary Brown (transported by Brown in 1649), John Clark, Elizabeth, wife, and children John & Ann (all transported by Clark to this Province here to inhabit).

Brown & Clark 10/2/1666 – 50/83 acres. L10/189 SR7352
Location: B&TNH on the north side of the Severn River by a marsh.
Persons mentioned: William Hopkins & Peter Porter (assignors of land rights). Phillip Howard (neighbor).

Brown, Thomas & Hopkins, William
The Friendship 5/26/1682 – 100/80 acres. LSDA/94 SR7369
Location: MNH in the woods about 2 miles from the head of the Ann Arundell *(Severn)* River.
Persons mentioned: Francis Marlow & John Yates (persons transported by Hopkins to this Province here to inhabit).

Brown(e), Thomas

> **Brownley 2/15/1659 – 150/147 acres.** L4/452 SR7346
> Location: MNH on the west side of the Severn River near
> unto the head adjoining tracts called Brown's Increase and
> Brown's Peace.
> Persons mentioned: None.

> **Brownston 2/16/1659 –100/102 acres.** L4/500 SR7346
> Location: B&TNH on the north side of Severn River.
> Persons mentioned: Henry Cattline & William Hopkins
> (neighbors).

> **Brown's Peace 2/20/1677 – 52/51 acres.** L20/75 SR7361
> Location: MNH on the west side of the Ann Arundell
> *(Severn)* River next adjoining a tract called Henry's Increase.
> Persons mentioned: George Holland & David Frye
> (assignors of land rights). Henry Sewell (neighbor).

> **Brown's Folly 7/1/1680 270/257 acres.** LCB2i/13 SR7366
> Location: MNH on the south side of the Ann Arundell
> *(Severn)* River on the north side of Plum Creek.
> Persons mentioned: George Holland (assignor of land
> rights). William Hopkins (neighbor).

> **The Diamond 8/10/1684 – 200/207 acres.** LSDA/414
> SR7369
> Location: B&TNH about four miles from the head of Severn
> River in a marsh.
> Persons mentioned: Coll. William Burges & Henry Hanslap
> (assignors of land rights).

> **Brown's Chance 10/1/1687 – 98/98 acres.** LNSBi/489
> SR7370
> Location: MNH on the south side of the Ann Arundell
> *(Severn)* River next adjoining a tract called Warfield's Plaine.

Persons mentioned: **Richard Beard** (assignor of land rights). *Note: Brown sold the tract to Daniel Macomas for 4,000 lbs of tobacco in 1692.*

Brown's Forrest 3/10/1695 – 387/519 acres. LWD/129 SR7372-2
Location: MNH on the west side of the North Branch of the Patuxent River.
Persons mentioned: None. *Note 1: Another patent is found on LC3i/379 SR7377. Note 2: The discrepancy between certified and actual acreage is extreme, even for this period. However, the boundary courses have been verified and the acreage is correct as shown above.*

Brown's Chance & Capt Dorsey's Friendship 7/3/1702 – 574/435 acres. LDD5i/61 SR7378
Location: B&TNH on the north side of Bacon's Branch (the northmost of two branches of Carrol's Great Branch) on the west side of a tract called Doughoregan.
Persons mentioned: **Charles Carroll** (neighbor). *Note 1: This tract was located in Baltimore County at the time of the patent/survey. I have included it because the land had been, and would again be, designated as Anne Arundel County before being absorbed into present day Howard County. Note 2: The discrepancy between certified and actual acreage is extreme, even for this period. However, the boundary courses have been verified and the acreage is correct as shown above.*

Rantor's Ridge 5/30/1705 – 415/434 acres. LDD5i/175 SR7378
Location: B&TNH on the south side of the Patapsco River at the head of a branch.
Persons mentioned: None. *Note 1:This tract was surveyed during the targeted period on 75/7/1703. Note 2: This tract was located in Baltimore County at the time of the patent/survey. I have included it because the land had been, and would again be, designated as Anne Arundel County*

before being absorbed into present day Howard County.

Brown, William

Brown's Fancy 10/11/1692 – 200/142 acres. LB23i/306
SR7376
Location: B&TNH between Elk Ridge and the head of the
Ann Arundell *(Severn)* River.
Persons mentioned: None. *Note: This tract lies in present day
Howard County.*

Bruer, John

Bruerton 9/7/1659 – 250 acres. L4/93 SR7346
Location: SRH on the west side of the South River next
adjoining Pyther's Creek.
Persons mentioned: **William Pyther** transported himself,
Ann, his wife and son **William** to this Province here to
inhabit. Pyther assigned these rights to **William Taylor**, who
assigned them to **Ellis Brown**, who further assigned them to
**John Milliken, Archer Arbuckle, Robert Maharty, & John
Maccubbin**, executors of the elder **John Milliken**, deceased.
Patrick Gossum (neighbor). *Note: The tract cannot be
drawn and the actual acreage cannot be determined due to
incomplete boundary course information in the patent
document.*

Bruton, John & Grimes, William

Bruton Grimes 1665 – 150/139 acres. L9/114 SR/7351
Location: MNH on the south side of the Severn River at Plum
Creek.
Persons mentioned: **Henry Sewell** (former owner). *Note:
Surveyor's note from the Rent Rolls (pg. 205): "Upon
reading the Cert of this land to **Coll. Hammond** he informed
me that William Grimes possesses this land but Grimes
denyes it nor can I find anyone who claimes it."*

Bruton/Burton, John

Bruton 6/1664 – 50/58 acres. L9/114 SR7351
Location: MNH on the south side of the Severn River in the woods.
Persons mentioned: John Sisson (neighbor). *Note: MSA Land Index #73 shows the name as* **John Burton.**

Bruton's Hope 4/10/1671 – 40/55 acres. L14/207 SR7356
Location: MNH South side of the Severn River next adjoining a tract called Salmon Hill.
Persons mentioned: Matthew Howard (assignor of land rights). Ralph Salmon (neighbor). *Note: Bruton's Hope along with a 40-acre portion of Huckleberry Forrest was made over to* **Thomas Rolls** *(Cooper) and by him sold in 1704 to* **Edward Hall** *(MSA Tract Index #73).*

Budd, William
Timber Neck 11/10/1695 – 132/115 acres. L23 252 SR7364
Location: B&TNH in Elk Ridge standing by the Middle Runn of the Patuxent River.
Persons mentioned: John Dorsey (assignor of land rights). *Note: This tract is located in present day Howard County.*

Burges, Edward
The Rainge 7/2/1684 - 211/208 acres. L22/101 SR7363
Location: HCH by the Patuxent River adjoining a tract called Birkhead's Choice
Persons mentioned: George Yate (assignor of land rights). Abraham Birkhead (neighbor).

Burges His Right 12/18/1688 – 153/153 acres. LNSBi/627 SR7370
Location: SRH on the south side of the South River at the mouth of Jacob's Creek.
Persons mentioned: Thomas Richardson (assignor of land rights).

Burges, William (Capt/Coll)

The Burgh 2/9/1650 – 300/249 acres. LQ/403 SR7345
Location: SRH on the south side of the South River adjoining a tract called Scornton.
Persons mentioned: **Anthony Holland & Thomas Hilliard** (persons transported to this Province by William Burges).
George Westhill & Thomas Besson (neighbors).

Burges 12/9/1651- 200 acres. LAB&H/263 SR7344
Location: SRH on the south side of the South River.
Persons mentioned: None. *Note: Surveyor's note from the Rent Rolls (SR4376): "I did not find that **Coll Burges** ever pattented this land nor do I find he ever pay rent for it nor left it for any person in his will nor has anyone claimed it.*

Burges'Choice 12/9/1666 – 400/436 acres. L10/421 SR7352
Location: SRH on the South side of the South River next adjoining a tract called Covell's Folly.
Persons mentioned: **Robert Franklin & George Puddington** (assignors of land rights).
Ann Covell, Richard Cheney, Marin Duvall (neighbors).
*Note: The tract was initially patented by **John Covill, Sr.,** in 1664. However, the same four hundred acres was surveyed for **John Shaw** in 1665 (reason unknown). Shaw assigned the tract to Robert Franklin the same day. Franklin subsequently assigned the tract to **William Burges**. Ownership was contested and The Provincial Court decided the matter in favor of Burgess after Ann Covill, widow, and guardian of **John Covill, Jr.,** son and heir of John Covill, Sr. failed to show up for court on several court dates specified.*

Burle, Robert

Burle Bank 6/15/1650 450 acres. LAB&H/43 SR7344
Location: B&TNH bounding on The Chesapeake Bay.
Persons mentioned: None. *Note: The tract cannot be drawn and the actual acreage cannot be determined due to*

incomplete boundary course information in the patent document.

Burle's Hill 2/11/1658 – 200/197 acres. LQ/206 SSR7345
<u>Location:</u> B&TNH at Burle's Pond.
<u>Persons mentioned:</u> **Neale Clark & Rebecca Ketteridge** (persons transported by Burle into this Province here to inhabit).

Burle's Town Land 12/18/1665 – 100/96 acres. L6/68 SR7348
<u>Location:</u> B&TNH on the east side of Ferry Creek in a neck of land called The Broad Neck at the mouth of Burle's Br.
<u>Persons mentioned:</u> None.

Burle, Stephen

Locust Thickett 8/10/1684 - 200/199 acres. LSDA/441 SR7369
<u>Location:</u> B&TNH on a branch of Deep Creek.
<u>Persons mentioned:</u> **Henry Hanslap** (assignor of land rights).

Burle's Park 8/10/1684 – 200/205 acres. LSDA/451 SR7369
<u>Location:</u> B&TNH on a forke of Rock Creek of the Patapsco River.
<u>Persons mentioned:</u> **Henry Hanslap** (assignor of land rights).

Burnett, Richard & Elizabeth

Bell's Haven Res. 6/30/1684 – 55/55 acres. L22/94 SR7363
<u>Location:</u> MNH in a swamp.
<u>Persons mentioned:</u> None. *Note: From a surveyor's note found in the margin of the patent document, " Formerly laid out for one hundred acres but now for fifty five by reason that the lines of the first survey runs into the land of a more ancient tract."*

Burradge/Burrage, John:

Burradge 2/22/1659 – 500/462 acres. L4/524 ST7346

Location: HCH on the south side of Herring Creek.
Persons mentioned: None. *Note: The tract following this one (Burrage, also patented by John Burrage) is the same size as this one in terms of both certified and actual acreage. The shapes of the two are remarkably similar although slightly different. However, they were patented at different times and the later patent makes no mention of it being either a resurvey or a patent of confirmation of an earlier tract of the same (or a similar) name. Burradge is located on the south side of Herring Creek Bay and Burrage on the northwest side of the branches of Herring Creek. I have included both tracts because there is no way of knowing with certainty if these are the same tract (patented twice with a spelling error in the earlier patent), or if they are two distinct tracts.*

Burrage 9/3/1663 – 500/462 acres. L5/451 SR7347
Location: HCH on the northwest side of Herring Creek.
Persons mentioned: **Maj. John Billingsly** (assignor of land rights). *Note: See footnote for preceding tract (Burradge).*

Burrage Blossom 9/4/1663 – 200/196 acres. L5/452 SR7347
Location: HCH adjoining the land he now liveth upon.
Persons mentioned: **Robert Clarkson** and **Thomas Lawrence** (persons transported to this province here to inhabit in 1649, and assignors of land rights to **John Burrage**). *Note: MSA Land Index# 54, places this tract in Calvert County. However, the patent document and the Anne Arundel County Rent Rolls place it in the Herring Creek Hundred of Anne Arundel County.*

Quick Sale 8/26/1664 – 300/206 acres. L7/393 SR7349
Location: HCH on the east side of the Patuxent River in the woods among the branches of Lyon's Creek.
Persons mentioned: **Christopher Burkitt** *(possibly Birkhead)* neighbor.

Burrage's End 3/20/1665 – 150/151 acres. L9/287 SR7351
Location: HCH adjoining the land he now liveth upon.
Persons mentioned: William _____, Matthew Erkson, &
Bridgett Larrey (persons transported by Burrage into this
Province here to inhabit). John Hall (neighbor).

Herring Creek Road 3/22/1665 – 100/106 acres. L9/291
SR7358
Location: HCH near Herring Creek Bay.
Persons mentioned: George Yate & Thomas Taylor
(assignors of land rights). Richard Wells & Anthony
Salloway (neighbors).

Unnamed Certification 11/1665 – 150/138 acres. L19/153
SR7351
Location: HCH adjoining his own land
Persons mentioned: John Hall (neighbor).

Unnamed Certification 11/1665 – 100/100 acres. L19/153
SR7351
Location: HCH.
Persons mentioned: Richard Wells & Anthony Salloway
(neighbors).

Burroughs, William & Ann
   Surplus Land Within Cheney Neck 6/1/1696 – 80/82 acres.
   LC3i/390 SR7377
   Location: SRH on the south side of the South River.
   Persons mentioned: Ann Barnett (daughter of Ann
   Burroughs). Richard Cheney (owner of Cheney's Neck).
   John Horring (husband of Ann Barnett).

Butler, Francis & Custins, Robert
   Francis & Robert 5/19/1679 – 300/297 acres. L15/903
   SR4327
   Location: WRH in Herring Creek Swamp.
   Persons mentioned: George Yate, William Jones, &

Nicholas Gassaway (assignors of land rights). **Matthew Selby & John Burwell** (neighbors).

Butler, Tobias
The Coombe 1/22/1659 – 150/149 acres. L6/432 SR7346
Location: MNH on the west side of the South River near the head.
Persons mentioned: Edward Lloyd Esq., **Richard Deaver, & Marin Duvall** (assignors of land rights). **John Freeman** (neighbor).

Calvert, William
Maryes Delight 7/18/1669 – 500/500 acres. L12/395 SR7354
Location: WRH on the northern border of a tract called Ann Arundall Mannor
Persons mentioned: **Charles Calvert** (son of William). **Jerome White** (Surveyor Generall). **Thomas Taylor** (neighbor). *Note: Memorandum from the LOP to Jerome White dated 5/10/1669 (same reference): "You are impowered to lay out 500 acres between Thomas Taylor and my Quarter at the Ridge for my Godson Charles Calvert. The certificate should be returned in the name of William Calvert, father of the above named Charles."*

Carr, Nicholas
Carr's Forrest 2/17/1661 – 400/400 acres. L5/53 SR7347
Location: HCH.
Person's mentioned: **John Scotcher & Robert Rockhold** (assignors of land rights). **William Parker** (neighbor).

Carroll, Charles
Doughoregan 4/30/1700 – 7,000/7,824 acres. LDD5i/710 SR7378
Location: B&TNH on the Middle Runn of the Patuxent River beginning at an Indian Path leading to Indian cabbins near the river.

Persons mentioned: None. *Note 1: Doughoregan was surveyed on 4/30/1700 although not patented until 2/28/1709 (LDD5i/712), when it was merged with The Addition to form a single tract of 10,000 "certified" acres. The actual acreage was 10,564. Note 2: This tract was located in Baltimore County at the time of the patent/survey. I have included it because the land had been, and would again be, designated as Anne Arundel County before being absorbed into present day Howard County.*

Port of Annapolis 10/10/1701 – 2.5 acres. LWD/371 SR7346
Location: MNH "...in a place now commonly known as the Port of Annapolis."
Persons mentioned: **John Perry** (former owner). **Sarah Perry Evans** (widow and heir of John Perry). *Note: The patent document did not include a specific location or any boundary course information. The tract cannot be drawn and actual acreage cannot be determined.*

The Addition 11/20/1701 – 3,000/2977 acres. LDD5i/711 SR7378
Location: B&TNH between the North & Middle Runns of the Patuxent River next adjoining his own tract called Doughoregan.
Persons mentioned: None. *Note 1: The Addition was "surveyed into" Doughoregan on 2/28/1709 (LDD5i/712), to form a single 10,000-acre tract. Note 2: This tract was located in Baltimore County at the time of the patent/survey. I have included it because the land had been, and would again be, designated as Anne Arundel County before being absorbed into present day Howard County.*

Chance 2/30/1705 – 203/222 acres. LDD5i/442 SR7378
Location: MNH above the head of the South River adjoining a tract called Herford.
Persons mentioned: **John Marriott** (neighbor).

33

New Year's Guift 2/20/1706 – 1,300/1,352 acres.
LDD5i/718 SR7378
Location: B&TNH in Elk Ridge next adjoining a tract called
Major's Choice.
Persons mentioned: **John Cross, Walter Phelps, & John
Dorsey** (neighbors*). Note 1: This tract was located in
Baltimore County at the time of the patent/survey. I have
included it because the land had been, and would again be,
designated as Anne Arundel County before being absorbed
into present day Howard County. Note 2: This tract was
surveyed during the targeted period (1/3/1700).*

Dourghegan 2/15/1709 – 10,000/10.654 acres. LDD5i/712
SR7378
Location: B&TNH beginning at a blind path leading from a
tract called Brown's Chance & Capt. Dorsey's Friendship to
some Indian cabbins near the Middle Runn of the Patuxent
River.
Persons mentioned: **Thomas Browne** (neighbor). *Note 1: This
tract was formed via the merger of The Addition (Carroll)
and this tract. It was certified during the targeted period
(4/30/1700) and it is a key tract in determining the relative
geographical placement of other tracts within the area.
Note: This tract was located in Baltimore County at the time
of the patent/survey. I have also included it because the land
had been, and would again be, designated as Anne Arundel
County before being absorbed into present day Howard
County.*

Carroll, James *(Deputy Surveyor)*
  Fingaul 10/10/1704 – 402/366 acres. LDD5i/519 SR7378
  Location: SRH between the lands called The South Addition
  and the land of the Stocketts next adjoining tracts called The
  Obligation, Bridge Hill, and Beard's Habitiation.
  Persons mentioned: **Nicholas Sporne** (assignor of land
  rights). *Note: Carroll assigned 402 acres to Sporne on
  6/18/1703. Sporne had the tract surveyed on 6/19/1703.*

Sporne then assigned rights back to Carroll on 4/25/1704, and Carroll patented the tract on the date shown above.

Carter, Edward (Capt)

Bennett's Island - 920/1658 - 275 acres. LQ/190 SR7345
Location: HCH on the east side of the Patuxent River on the west side of Lyon's Creek.
Person's mentioned: **Richard Bennett, Esq.**, hath transported **John Scaper, Mary & Edward,** two mulatto children born of English women in Virginia into this Province for land rights. **John Warfield** (former owner).

Unnamed Patent 9/20/1651 – (two tracts) 900/585 acres. LQ/152 SR7345
Location: HCH near Herring Creek Bay and Carter's Creek adjoining his own land.
Persons mentioned: **Ann Bennett** transported **Robert Grammar, Henry Taylor, & John Nottingham** into this Province and assigned the corresponding land rights to **Richard Bennett, Esq.** Bennett then assigned these rights to **Capt. Edward Carter.** Carter also transported **James Allen, Andrew Hay, James Dike, Quintan Conen, John Pert, & Henry Piny** into this Province, for additional land rights. *Note: The certification is for 600 acres. However, two tracts totaling approximately 900 acres were granted. No explanation found. The 600-acre tract is believed to have been named Carter and the 300-acre tract, which could not be drawn or measured due to incomplete boundary course information, is believed to have been named Carter Bennett. This accounts for the large certified vs. actual acreage discrepancy.*

Cattline, Henry

The Middle Land 9/28/1666 – 40/23 acres. L10/178 SR7349
Location: B&TNH on the north side of the Severn River.
Persons mentioned: **Cornelius Howard** (assignor of land rights). **William Hopkins & Matthew Howard** (neighbors).

Note: The discrepancy between certified and actual acreage is extreme, even for this period. However, the boundary courses have been verified and the acreage is correct as shown above.

Chaffinch, John
The Neglect 3/17/1709 – 100/101 acres. LDD5i/550
SR7348
Location: B&TNH on the south side of the Patapsco River next adjoining a tract called Old Man's Folly.
Persons mentioned: None. *Note: This patent is included because the Cert and/or Survey date is within the targeted period.*

Champe, John
Champe's Adventure 8/8/1670 - 300/300 acres. L13/44
SR7355
Location: SRH on the west side of the South River at the lower end of Cattaile Meadow.
Persons mentioned: **George Yate & David Poole** (assignors of land rights). **Coll. William Burges** (neighbor).

Chandler, Thomas
Chandler's Grove 5/13/1664 – 100/100 acres. L6/329
SR7340
Location: HCH in the woods in back of the plantations of Herring Creek.
Persons mentioned: **John Sollers** (assignor of land rights). **William Hunt & Sammuel Chew** (neighbors).

Chathley, Thomas
Chathely's Well 3/15/1705 – 200/177 acres. LCDi/262
SR7376
Location: B&TNH on the south side of the Patapsco River at the head of Curtis Creek next adjoining a tract called Best Success.
Persons mentioned: None. *Note: The patent document places this tract in Baltimore County. I have included it here based*

on its location and proximity to Anne Arundel County tracts.

Cheney, Richard

    Cheney Hill 1/20/1659 100/83 acres. L4/439 SR7346
Location: SRH on the south side of the South River and on
the south side of Flatt Creek.
Persons mentioned: Charity (wife of Richard Cheney).

    Cheney's Neck 5/29/1663 – 110/109 acres. L5/294 SR
7347
Location: SRH adjoining the south side of the South River
and Cheney's Creek.
Persons mentioned: None.

    Cheney's Hazard 5/30/1663 100 acres. L5299 SR7347
Location: SRH near the plantation he now liveth upon.
Persons mentioned: None.

    Cheney's Purchase 5/30/1663 – 100/65 acres. L5/298
SR7347
Location: SRH on the south side of the South River on the
east side of Flat Creek.
Persons mentioned: None.

    Cheney's Resolution 5/29/1663 – 400/507 acres. L5/287
SR7347
Location: SRH on the south side of South River adjoining a
tract called Cheney's Rest.
Persons mentioned: None.

    Cheney's Rest 5/29/1663 – 300/300 acres. L5/295 SR7347
Location: SRH on the south side of the South River adjoining
Flatt Creek.
Persons mentioned: None.

Chew, Ann Ayres

    Unnamed Patent 8/6/1658 – 600/594 acres. LQ/99 SR7345

Location: HCH adjoining Capt. Edward Carter on Herring Creek Bay next adjoining Carter's Creek.
Persons Mentioned: William Ayres (father of Ann Ayres Chew). Samuel Chew (husband of Ann Ayres Chew). William Parker (neighbor).

Chew, Sammuel/Samuel/Samuell

Chew's Right 6/20/1665 – 300/300 acres. L7/635 SR7349
Location: HCH at the end of the *miles end* of the land he now liveth upon.
Persons mentioned: Ann Ayres Chew (wife). William Ayres (father in law). *Note: The patent document says that the tract lies at the "miles end" of the land he now liveth upon. No precise explanation of this was found.*

Sanetley 1/16/1664 – 450/450 acres. L7/203 SR 7349
Location: HCH on Herring Creek adjoining a tract named Gowery Banks.
Persons mentioned: Ann Chew (assignor of land rights & wife of Samuel Chew). William Ayres (father of Ann Chew). Thomas Ford & Nathan Smith (neighbors).

Chew's Resolution Mannor 11/1/1696 – 1,073/1,040 acres. L23i/306 SR7365
Location: B&TNH at Elk Ridge.
Persons mentioned: Edward Talbott (neighbor). *Note: This tract lies in present day Howard County.*

Chew's Vinyard 11/10/1695 – 1,024/998 acres. L23i/309 SR7465
Location: B&TNH at Elk Ridge adjoining a tract named Chew's Resolution Mannor.
Persons mentioned: Adam Shipley & John Dorsey (neighbors). *Note: This tract lies in present day Howard County*

Chilcott, James

The Addition 8/8/1670 – 90/111 acres. L14/24 SR7356
Location: SRH on the west side of the South River by a great branch *(of the Patuxent River)* adjoining tracts called West Puddington & Arnold Gray.
Persons mentioned: George Yate & David Poole (assignors of land rights). *Note: This grant conveyed two adjoining tracts.*

Chilcott's Increase 5/1/1672 – 18/18 acres. L16/575 SR7357
Location: SRH near the head of the South River adjoining a tract called Puddington.
Persons mentioned: George Yate (assignor of land rights).

Child, Abraham
Child's Reserve 1683 – 62/67 acres. L22/95 SR7363
Location: MNH on the south side of the Ann Arundell *(Severn)* River at the Round Bay.
Persons mentioned: None.

Chilton 9/10/1683 – 40/40 acres. LSDA/49 SR7369
Location: MNH on the south side of the Ann Arundell *(Severn)* River at Cypress Branch.
Persons mentioned: George Yate (Deputy Surveyor).
Thomas Browne (neighbor).

Clark, John
Clarkenwell 8/20/1665 - 100 acres. L8/144 SR730
Location: SRH on the south side of the South River adjoining Chandler's Creek.
Persons mentioned: Elizabeth Wattson (transported by Clark to this Province to inhabit. Richard Cheney (neighbor).
Note: The tract cannot be drawn and the actual acreage cannot be determined due to incomplete boundary course information in the patent document.

Clark, Matthew
Clarkston 2/28/1659 – 100/130 acres. L4/490 SR7346

Location: B&TNH on Dorrell's Creek at Clark's Point
Persons mentioned: None.

Clark, William

Clarke's Purchase 6/12/1688 – 90/61 acres. LNS2i/732
SR7371
Location: B&TNH on the south side of the Maggity River
near a marsh.
Persons mentioned: **Robert Proctor & John Gray** (assignors
of land rights).

Clark(e), Neal(e) *(Planter)*

Nealson 2/15/1659 – 100/100 acres. L4/433 SR7346
Location: MNH on the north side of the South River
adjoining the s'd river on the west and Broad Creek on the
east.
Persons mentioned: None.

Turkey Quarter 9/25/1663 – 150/176 acres. L5/598
SR7347
Location: MNH on the north side and near the head of the
South River next adjoining a tract called Wyatt's Ridge.
Persons mentioned: **James Wardner & Nicholas Wyatt**
(neighbors).

The Landing Place 9/25/1663 – 50/31 acres. L5/597
SR7347
Location: MNH on the north side of the South River next
adjoining a tract called Nealson.
Persons mentioned: **William Jones** (assignor of land rights).
Nathaniel Dolphin, & John Stimson (persons transported by
Clark(e) to this Province). *Note 1: Stimson later married
Clark(e)'s widow, **Rachel**. Note 2: The tract was sold to
Thomas Reynolds for 140 lbs sterling in 1704.*

Clarke's Inheritance 8/8/1670 – 400/394 acres. L14/33
SR7356

Location: SRH on the west side of the South River next adjoining a tract called The Indian Range.
Persons mentioned: Richard Cheney (neighbor).

Clark's Luck 6/1/1685 – 60/60 acres. NSBi/415 SR7370
Location: MNH on the north side of South River adjoining a tract called Hogg Neck.
Persons mentioned: Richard Beard (assignor of land rights). Edward Hope, Thobey Butler, James Wardner, & Henry Ridgely (neighbors).

Clarke's Enlargement 9/1/1687 – 265/286 acres. L14/33 SR7356
Location: MNH on the north side of the South River on the west side of Broad Creek.
Persons mentioned: Andrew Norwood & Robert Proctor (assignors of land rights). Henry Ridgely & John Hammond (neighbors).

Turkey Island 3/26/1696 – 200/188 acres. LCC4i/122 SR7375
Location: MNH on the south side of Rogue's Harbor Branch of the Patuxent River.
Persons mentioned: Richard Beard (assignor of land rights).

Clarke, Richard

Clark of the Councill 11/10/1701 – 191/191 acres. LDD5i/219 SR7378
Location: MNH on the north side of the North Branch of the Patuxent River.
Persons mentioned: Richard Clarke assigned this tract to Daniel Richardson (11/10/1701), who assigned the tract to Henry Hall (10/29/1706).

Elizabeth's Fancy 6/4/1702 – 225/211 acres. LCD5i/47 SR7378

Location: SRH on the south side of the South River next adjoining a tract called Clarke's Inheritance.
Persons mentioned: None.

Hunting Ridge 6/4/1702 – 122/136 acres. LDD5i/47 SR7378
Location: B&TNH on the north side of the North Branch of the Patuxent River at Clarke's Branch.
Persons mentioned: None. *Note: This tract was located in Baltimore County at the time of the patent/survey. I have included it because the land had been, and would again be, designated as Anne Arundel County before being absorbed into present day Howard County.*

Clarke's Walk 7/8/1702 500/540 acres. LDD5i/62 SR7378
Location: B&TNH in Elk Ridge on the Patuxent River.
Persons mentioned: None. *Note: The tract lies in present day Howard County.*

Clarkson, Robert
Horne Neck 9/20/1665 – 300/304 acres. L8/404 SR7350
Location: MNH on the south side of Severn River at Todd's Creek.
Persons mentioned: **Daniel Jennifer** (assignor of land rights).

Clarkson, Robert, Jr.
South Canton Res. 8/8/1680 – 200 acres. LCB2i/168 SR7366
Location: B&TNH on the south side of the Patapsco River at Rumbly Marsh.
Persons mentioned: **Thomas Taillor** and wife **Elizabeth**, former relict of **Thomas Sparrow. Robert Clarkson, Sr.,** & **George Holland** (persons involved in the assignment of rights to this tract).

Coape, George
Coape's Hill 8/10/1683 – 40/26 acres. LSDA/95 SR7369

Location: MNH in the woods adjoining a tract named Bright Seate.
Persons mentioned: **Henry Hanslap & Coll Thomas Taylor** (assignors of land rights). **Evan Davis & Edwin Price** (neighbors).

Cockey/Cockley, William

Cockey's Addition 8/10/1674 – 25/23 acres. LSDA/453 SR7369
Location: B&TNH by a branch adjoining other land owned by the William Cockey.
Persons mentioned: **Robert Jones & George Yate** (assignors of land rights). **Robert Davidge** (neighbor).

Cockley's Addition 8/5/1683 – 130/182 acres. LCB3i/305 SR7357
Location: B&TNH on the north side of the Maggity River next adjoining his own land.
Persons mentioned: **Henry Hanslap & Coll. Thomas Taylor** (assignors of land rights). **John Raffey & Robert Proctor** (neighbors).

Cuckold's Pointe 3/1695 – 100/123 acres. LWD/124 SR7372-1
Location: B&TNH on the north side of the Maggity River at Cuckold's Creek.
Persons mentioned: **George Holland** (Deputy Surveyor).

Cole, Thomas

Cole's Cliffs 10/27/1651 – 200 acres. AB&H/289 SR7344
Location: SRH next adjoining a tract called Todd.
Persons mentioned: **Thomas Todd** (neighbor). *Note 1: The tract was sold to **Patrick & Margaret Dunken** in 1663.* Note 2: The tract cannot be drawn and the actual acreage cannot be determined due to incomplete boundary course information in the patent document.

Coles Point 10/29/1665 – 50 acres. L9/192 SR7251
Location: SRH by Fishing Creek.
Persons mentioned: **George Puddington** (assignor of land rights). *Note: The tract cannot be drawn and the actual acreage cannot be determined due to incomplete boundary course information in the patent document.*

Collier, John

Collierby 2/9/1654 – 150 acres. LQ/400 SR7378
Location: SRH on the south side of the South River on the riverside.
Persons mentioned: **John Stringer** (assignor of land rights) **Ellis Brown** (neighbor). *Note 1: This is a "survey." The tract was patented by* **John Brewer** *in 1678. Note 2: The tract cannot be drawn and the actual acreage cannot be determined due to incomplete boundary course information in the patent document.*

Cossill 1/21/1659 – 200/196 acres. L4/501 SR7346
Location: MNH on the south Side of the Severn River on the south side of Todd's Creek.
Persons mentioned: None. *Note: In 1663, the tract was sold to* **Patrick & Margaret Dunken** *and by them to* **Robert Clarkson**. Upon Clarkson's death the tract was devised to his daughter **Mary**, the wife of **Samuel Young**.

Collier. William

The Gift 5/1/1676 – 170/115 acres. L19/295 SR7360
Location: HCH on Gott's Creek next adjoining a tract called Gordon.
Persons mentioned: **Edward Parrish, Robert Lockwood, & Thomas Harwood** (assignors of land rights). **George Pascall & William Horne** (neighbors).

Conant, Robert

Conant's Chance 7/17/1680 – 25/21 acres. LCB2/19 SR7366

Location: HCH by Herring Creek Branch.
Persons mentioned: George Holland (assignor of land rights). Anthony Salloway & John Burrage (neighbors).

Conaway, James *(Maryner)* **& Turner, Thomas** *(Planter)*
The Ridge 7/8/1699 – 471 acres. L12/259 SR7354
Location: B&TNH on the north side of the Severn River.
Persons mentioned: *From the Patent Document:* "Whereas we did grant on 2/16/1659, a Parcell of land called Swan Neck to **Edward Lloyd** for six hundred acres and whereas the s'd parcell was afsigned, vested, and settled in Thomas Turner excepting and reserving to **John Smith, Christopher Rowles,** and **Richard Horner** one hundred acres each, as appears on record. And whereas the s'd Turner hath alienated and sold unto the s'd James Conaway of London one half moiety to the land specified and whereas Thomas Turner hath due unto him four hundred seventy one acres, as appears on record. Doe hereby grant unto them the s'd Conaway and Turner that parcel of land resurveyed and now called The Ridge." *Note 1: Adjoins tracts owned by Christopher Rowles, William Crouch, & Robert Tyler. Note 2: The tract cannot be drawn and the actual acreage cannot be determined due to incomplete boundary course information in the patent document.*

Forked Neck 8/11/1670 – 50/37 acres. L14/183 SR7356
Location: B&TNH on the south side of the Maggity River next adjoining a tract called Brushy Neck.
Persons mentioned: **Robert Tyler** (neighbor).

The Addition 9/7/1688 – 400 acres. L12/135 SR7354
Note 1: This tract was conveyed by an abbreviated form of patent document that was occasionally used. No information concerning boundary courses or location is included. However, the Rent Rolls confirm that this tract was located in the Broad & Town Neck Hundred. Note 2: The tract cannot be drawn and the actual acreage cannot be determined due to incomplete boundary course information

in the patent document.

Constable, Henry
The Range 9/8/1687 – 240/263 acres. LNS2i/379 SR7371
Location: B&TNH on the south side of the Patapsco River
next adjoining a tract called The United Friendship.
Persons mentioned: None.

Covill, John
Covill 10/27/1651 – 200/200 acres. LAB&H/280 SR7344
Location: MNH adjoining Chesapeake Bay
Persons mentioned: William Durand (neighbor).

Cox, Christopher *(Planter)*
Coxes Forrest 8/10/1684 – 199/199 acres. LSDA/512
SR7369
Location: B&TNH in Ann Arundell County on Rock Creek of
the Patapsco River.
Persons mentioned: Robert Jones & George Yate (assignors
of land rights).

Coxes Range 11/15/1686 – 200/202 acres. L22/290
SR7363
Location: B&TNH on the south side of the Patapsco River on
the east side of Curtis Cr.
Persons mentioned: Thomas Lytfoot (assignor of land
rights). *Note: The patent/survey document places this tract
in Baltimore County. MSA Land Index #55 places it in Anne
Arundel County. I have included here it based on its
location.*

Coxes Enlargement 4/15/1689 – 200/200 acres. LC3/278
SR7377
Location: B&TNH on the east side of Curtis Creek.
Persons mentioned: None.

Cox, Edward
Coxby 2/18/1650 – 100/104 acres. LQ/397 SR7345

Location: SRH on the south side of the South River adjoining a tract called Collierby.
Persons mentioned: Joan (Coxes wife, transported by him to this Province here to inhabit). John Collier (neighbor).

Croker, Thomas & Merrica, Joshua

Parker's Encrease 12/26/1696 – 225/264 acres. LBB3B/2 SR7374

Location: B&TNH on Curtis Creek next adjoining a tract called Curtis Neck.

Persons mentioned: Henry Hale purchased the tract from Quinton Parker before it was patented. He devised the tract to Henry Hale, Jr. who, as the result of a resurvey, found an additional 25 acres of surplus land. After complying with the LOP's instructions *(to make a payment)* the tract was granted to Henry Jr., who assigned *(sold)* it to Croker & Merrica. *Note: The patent/survey document places this tract in Baltimore County. MSA Land Index #55 places it in Anne Arundel County. I have included it here based on its location.*

Cromwell, John & Richard

Cromwell's Adventure 7/1/1671 – 360/320 acres. L14/253 SR7356

Location: B&TNH on the south side of the Patapsco River at a branch of Courteous *(probably Curtis)* Creek.

Persons mentioned: George Yate (assignor of land rights). John Brown & Richard Mascall (neighbors).

Cromwell, Richard

Cromwell's Addition 9/8/1687 – 16/15 acres. LNS2i/557 SR7371

Location: B&TNH on the south side of Patuxent River on the west side of Curtis Creek.

Persons mentioned: Thomas Lytfoot (assignor of land rights). *Note: The patent/survey document places this tract in Baltimore County. MSA Land Index #55 places it in Anne*

Arundel County. I have included it here based on its location.

Cromwell, William

Phillip's Fancy 8/10/1684 – 61/60 acres. LIB&ILC/24 SR7368
Location: B&TNH on the south side of the Patapsco River on the west side of Deep Creek.
Persons mentioned: **George Holland** (assignor of land rights). **Franklin Smith** (neighbor).
Note: The patent/survey document places this tract in Baltimore County. MSA Land Index #55 places it in Anne Arundel County. I have included it here based on its location.

Crosley, William

Jerrico 6/1/1685 – 200/200 acres. L5/469 SR7347
Location: HCH between the branches of Herring Creek Bay and Lyon's Creek
Persons mentioned: **Charles Stevens, Elizabeth Jones, & Elizabeth Sidney** (persons transported to this Province by **Thomas Ford** who assigned the resulting land rights to William Crosley). **Nathan Smith & Robert Paca** (neighbors).

Cross, John

The Angle 9/11/1682 – 264/271 acres. L21/465 SR7362
Location: MNH on the north side of the South River at the head of Enlargement Creek
Persons mentioned: **Zephaniah Smith** (neighbor).

The Angle 10/5/1684 – 70/70 acres. LSDA/409 SR7369
Location: B&TNH on the north side of the Severn River next adjoining a tract named Bell's Haven.
Persons mentioned: **Henry Hanslap** (assignor of land rights). **Thomas Bell & John Taillor** (neighbors).

The Levell 10/5/1683 – 260/ 272 acres. LCB3i/510
SR7367
Location: MNH on the north side of the South River at
Enlargement Creek.
Persons mentioned: **Henry Hanslap** (assignor of land rights).
Zephaniah Smith (neighbor).

Crosses Forrest 10/10/1695 – 357/400 acres. LCDi/31
SR7356
Location: B&TNH at Elk Ridge by Ridgely's Great Branch
of the Patuxent River.
Persons mentioned: None. *Note: This tract lies in present
day Howard County.*

Crouch, William

> **Unnamed Patent 12/10/1650 – 3 Tracts totaling 500 acres.**
> LAB&H/263 SR7347
> Location: Tract 1 (300 acres) & Tract 2 (50 acres) are
> located in the B&TNH on the north side of Severn River.
> Tract 3 (150 acres) is located in the MNH on the south side
> of the Severn River near Marshes Creek.
> Persons mentioned: None. *Note: None of these tracts can be
> drawn or measured due to incomplete boundary course data
> in the patent document.*
>
> **Crouchfield 9/7/1659 – 150/122 acres.** L4/87 SR7346
> Location: MNH on the south side of the Severn River near
> Marsh's Creek.
> Persons mentioned: **Josias & Rachell** (children of **William
> Crouch** transported by him to this Province in 1650, to
> inhabit). *Note: Crouch also received, and used, land rights
> for other patents for transporting daughters **Mary,
> Elizabeth, Elizabeth, Elizabeth, John & John**. Either he
> had three daughters named Elizabeth and two sons named
> John or he claimed rights for Elizabeth three times and John
> twice for this tract and again for the following tract (North
> Crouchfield).*

North Crouchfield 9/7/1659 – 50/300 acres. L4/89 SR7346
Location: B&TNH on the north side of the Ann Arundell
(Severn) River.
Persons mentioned: Himself, **Mary,** his wife, and **Elizabeth**
and **John,** his children (persons transported by **Crouch** to this
Province to inhabit). *Note: The certified rights are for fifty*
acres and the grant was for three hundred acres (and the
tract measures exactly 300 acres). No explanation found.

Crouches Tryangle 12/20/1662 – 60/37 acres. L5/577
SR7349
Location: B&TNH on the north side of the Severn River next
adjoining a tract called North Crouchfield.
Persons mentioned: None.

Crouches Triangle Addition 8/20/1665 – 40 acres. L8/139
SR7350
Location: B&TNH on the north side of the Severn River next
adjoining a tract called North Crouchfield.
Persons mentioned: None. *Note: The tract cannot be drawn*
and the actual acreage cannot be determined due to
incomplete boundary course information in the patent
document.

Crouches Calf Pasture 10/25/1666 – 30 acres. L10/222
SR7352
Location: B&TNH on the north side of the Severn River
adjoining his own land.
Persons mentioned: **John Howard** (assignor of land rights).
Note: The tract cannot be drawn and the actual acreage
cannot be determined due to incomplete boundary course
information in the patent document.

Crouches Mill Dam 10/25/1666 – 70 acres. L10/220
SR7352
Location: B&TNH on the north side of Severn River
adjoining a tract called Swan Neck.
Persons mentioned: **John Howard** (assignor of land rights).

Edward Lloyd & James Smith (neighbors). *Note: The tract cannot be drawn and the actual acreage cannot be determined due to incomplete boundary course information in the patent document.*

Crouchley, Thomas

Crouchley's Choice 5/10/1676 – 200/185 acres. L19/342 SR7360
Location: WRH in Herring Creek Swamp.
Persons mentioned: George Yate & Edward Wheelock (assignors of land rights). John Baldwin & Ralph Boswell (neighbors).

Cumber, John

Cumberston 2/16/1659 – 600/552 acres. L4/513 SR 7346
Location: WRH on the north side of the West River and on the west side of Cedar Creek next adjoining a tract called Peake.
Persons mentioned: None.

Cumber's Ridge 8/5/1662 – 170/125 acres. L7/318 SR7349
Location: WRH in the swamp between Herring Creek and the Three Islands.
Persons mentioned: Emmanuel Drue *(probably Drew)* (assignor of land rights).

Cumberton 7/12/1667 – 200/147 acres. L19/595 SR7369
Location: WRH in the woods next adjoining a tract called Cumberstone.
Persons mentioned: Robert Franklin (assignor of land rights). Gustavis White, Nicholas Alderidge, William Wells, & Thomas King. (persons transported to this Province here to inhabit by Franklin).

Cumber, John, Jr.

Cumberston Grainge 12/2/1662 – 250/240 acres. L5/622
SR7347
Location: WRH on the north side of the West River next
adjoining a branch of Beaver Dam Creek.
Persons mentioned: None

Buck Stands 8/5/1664 – 80/87 acres. L7/316 SR7349
Location: HCH near the head of Gott's Branch.
Persons mentioned: **Emmanuel Drue** (assignor of land
rights). **Richard Gott** (neighbor).

Cusack, Michael

Garrett's Town 7/6/1684 59/59 acres. NWBi/414 SR7370
Location: MNH on the north side of the South River on the
east side of Broad Creek.
Persons mentioned: **George Yate & Thomas Richardson**
(assignors of land rights).

Wellfare 9/8/1687 – 104/103 acres. LNS2i/458 SR7371
Location: B&TNH on the south side of the Patapsco River
next adjoining a tract called Cusack's Forrest.
Persons mentioned: None. *Note: The patent document places
this tract in Baltimore County. I have included it here based
on its location and proximity to Anne Arundel County tracts.*

Daborne, Thomas

Daborne's Hope 9/18/1666 – 40/40 acres. L10/145
SR7352
Location: HCH in Herring Creek Swamp on the south side of
South Creek.
Persons mentioned: **Thomas Hooker & Thomas Thurstone**
(assignors of land rights). **William Alderidge & Richard
Talbott** (neighbors).

Daborne's Inheritance 10/10/1668 - 250/256 acres.
L12/517 SR7354
Location: HCH in Herring Creek Swamp in the main branch

of Broad Creek.

Persons mentioned: George Yate & James Connaway, Mariner (assignors of land rights). Thomas & Ann Carr (neighbors).

Darnall, Henry, Coll.

Unnamed Patent 12/11/1667 – 300 acres. LBB3/529 SR7374

Location: HCH on the east side of the Patuxent River at Lyon's Creek.

Persons mentioned: Francis Leafe (former owner). *Note: The tract cannot be drawn and the actual acreage cannot be determined due to incomplete boundary course information in the patent document.*

Portland Manor Part Of 7/26/1696 – 1,090/1,456 acres. LBB3B/537 SR7357

Location: HCH adjoining tracts called Portland Landing and Ann Arundell Mannor.

Persons mentioned: Jerome White (former owner).

St. Jeromes & Portland Landing Res. 8/6/1700 – 700/706 acres. LCDi/54 SR7346

Location: HCH adjoining tracts called Quicksale and Portland Mannor

Persons mentioned: Jerome White (former owner). *Note: This resurvey addresses two separate unadjoined tracts.*

Davidge, John

Davidge's Meadows 7/10/1701 – 121/134 acres. LDCi/237 SR7376

Location: MNH on the north side of the South River next adjoining tracts called Smith's Rest and Lusby.

Persons mentioned: Walter Smith & Robert Lusby (neighbors).

Davies/Davis, Thomas

Devise 2/22/1659 – 150/150 acres. L4/527 SR7346
Location: MNH next adjoining a tract called Warringston.
Persons mentioned: Sampson Warring (neighbor).

Davistone 10/17/1701 –240/240 acres. LDD5i/136 SR7359
Location: MNH on the south side of the Severn River next
adjoining a tract called Greeniston.
Persons mentioned: None.

Davis, Evan

Davis His Rest 9/10/1672 – 200/112 acres. L17/288
SR7359
Location: MNH on the south side of the Severn River.
Persons mentioned: Robert Wilson (assignor of land rights).
John Gray (neighbor).

Davis, Isaac

Davis' Pasture 6/1/1700 – 200/199 acres. LDD5i/13
SR7378
Location: B&TNH on the north side of the Patuxent River
next adjoining a tract called Batchellor's Delight and a
draught of Snowden's River.
Persons mentioned: James Carroll (Deputy Surveyor). *Note:
This tract was located in Baltimore County at the time of the
patent/survey. I have included it because the land had been,
and would again be, designated as Anne Arundel County
before being absorbed into present day Howard County.*

Davis, Robert

Elk Thickett Res. 5/20/1700 – 35/35 acres. LDD5i/6
SR7378
Location: SRH at the head of the South River on Hugging's
Path.
Persons mentioned: None. *Note: This is a survey. Patent not
found. On the same day the tract was assigned by Davis to
Walter Phelps.*

Davis, William

Hogg Neck 6/1//1672 70 acres. L16/514 SR7357
Location: BNTNH on the north side of the Severn River in a
neck of land called the Hogg Neck about one half mile from
the head of Homewood's Creek.
Persons mentioned: **Robert Ridgely & Robert Monfort**
(assignors of land rights). **William Sargeson & Henry
Moore** (persons transported to this Province by Monfort,
here to inhabit). *Note: The tract cannot be drawn and the
actual acreage cannot be determined due to incomplete
boundary course information in the patent document.*

Dawson, Abraham

Deep Creek Point 10/9/1663 – 100/100 acres. L6/110
SR7348
Location: B&TNH on the north side of Deep Creek of the
Magothy River.
Persons mentioned: None. *Note: Patent not found. However,
this tract is listed in the B&TNH Rent Rolls.*

Brushy Neck 9/20/1665 – 100/100 acres. L8/3976 SR7350
Location: B&TNH adjoining the Magothy River.
Persons mentioned: **Thomas Bradley** (assignor of land
rights). *Note: A marginal note on the patent document
identifies this tract as Deep Creek Point. Dawson did own a
tract of that name. However, the patent document clearly
identifies this tract as Brushy Neck.*

Dearing, John

The Choice 9/20/1665 – 50/25 acres. L10/161 SR73352
Location: B&TNH on the north side of the Severn River one
quarter mile from Eagle's Nest Bay.
Persons mentioned: **Christopher Rolls & John Howard**
(neighbors). *Note: The land rights used by Dearing for this
patent were earned by transporting himself to this Province
to inhabit.*

Dearing's Increase 9/2/1666 – 100/167 acres. L10/163

SR7352
Location: B&TNH on the north side of the Severn River and
on the northwest side at the head of Eagle's Nest Bay.
Persons mentioned: **Edward Parrish, Thomas Hooker, &
Thomas Thurstone** (assignors of land rights). **William
Hopkins** (neighbor). *Note: The following is from a marginal
note on the patent document: "This Patt delivered into the
office by* **John Dearing** *and the land herein lett fall it
running within the bounds of my Lord's Manor. Another
warrant issued for the same quantity of acres in the name of
the s'd John Dearing.
3 March 1667."*

Velmeade 1/11/1667 – 400/400 acres. L11/214 SR7353
Location: SRH on the south side of the South River adjoining
a tract called Hickory Hills.
Persons mentioned: **Charles Boetler, George Green, John
Blomfield, John Gillium & Francis Richardson** (assignors
of land rights. Also, all of these men transported themselves
into this Province here to inhabit). **Robert Franklin**
(neighbor).

Dearing's Encrease 6/20/1688 – 200/200 acres. L12/14
SR7354
Location: B&TNH on the north side of the Patapsco River.
Persons mentioned: **George Yate** (assignor of land rights).
*Note: Although this tract lies on the north side of the
Patapsco River, the patent document places it in Ann
Arundell Manor.*

Dearing's Gullier 6/20/1668 – 100/103 acres. L12/15
SR7354
Location: WRH in Herring Creek Swamp on the south side
of South Creek.
Persons mentioned: **Robert Franklin** (assignor of land rights).
John Barwell (neighbor).

DeLapp, Adam

Lappston 2/16/1659 - 300/283 acres. L4/509 SR7346
Location: SRH on the south side at the mouth of the South
River.
Persons mentioned: Thomas Emerson (assignor of land
rights). William Pennington (neighbor).

Lappston 8/5/1664 – 50/50 acres. L7/340 SR7349
Location: SRH adjoining his own tract called Lappston.
Persons mentioned: Phillip Allamby (assignor of land rights).

Devoir/ Devour/Deaver, Richard *(Planter)*
  Deaver's Purchase 12/17/1662 – 213/292 acres. L5/626
  SR7347
  Location: B&TNH on the north side of the Severn River near
  the town path and the meeting house.
  Persons mentioned: Capt. Edward Carter, Archer
  Arbuckle, & Phillip Thomas (former owners of the tracts
  that were "surveyed" into Deaver's Purchase).

  Rattlesnake Neck 8/10/1684 – 300/308 acres. LSDA/444
  SR7369
  Location: B&TNH on a creek of the Patapsco River called
  Rock Creek.
  Persons mentioned: Henry Hanslap (assignor of land rights).

  Altogether 8/14/1664 – 215/291 acres. L7/213 SR7349
  Location: B&TNH on the north side of the Severn River
  Persons mentioned: Edward Lloyd, Esq., Capt. Edward
  Carter, Archer Arbuckle, & Phillip Thomas (assignors of
  land rights).

  Barren Neck 8/4/1664 – 150 acres. L7/241 SR7349
  Location: B&TNH on the west side of Ferry Creek at the
  head of Strong's Cove. .
  Persons mentioned: **Gatry Cornelius, Hedrick Cornelius &
  _____Elliston.** (persons transported by **Richard Devoir** into
  this Province to inhabit). *Note: The tract cannot be drawn*

and the actual acreage cannot be determined due to incomplete boundary course information in the patent document.

Devoure's Range 8/24/1675 – 200/144 acres. L19/245 SR7360
Location: HCH in the woods about three miles from Herring Creek Bay.
Persons mentioned: **George Yate** (assignor of land rights). **Benjamin Wells & Thomas Ford** (neighbors).

Dodderidge, John *(Merchant)*
Dodderidge's Forrest 3/26/1696 – 200/223 acres. LC3i/365 SR7377
Location: MNH on the west side of the North Branch of the Patuxent River.
Persons mentioned: **Thomas Brown & Samuel Dryer** (neighbors).

Dorrell, Elizabeth
Long Neck 8/1/1665 – 50/50 acres. L8/107 SR7350
Location: B&TNH on the north side of the Magothy River next to Back Creek.
Persons mentioned: **Thomas Turner** (assignor of land rights).

Dorrell/Dorrill, Paul
Linnestone 8/1/1668 – 300/233 acres. L12/117 SR7354
Location: B&TNH in the mountains.
Note: This tract was granted via a seldom used and abbreviated form of patent document that generally does not include the names of other persons or information on the location or boundaries of the tract. The drawing was made from courses found in the Cert (L10/588) which states only that the tract was located in "Ann Arundell County in the mountains beginning at a bound Hickory."

Dorrell's Inheritance 8/1/1668 – 300/182 acres. L12/117 SR7354

Location: B&TNH
Note: This tract was granted in a seldom used and abbreviated form of patent document that generally does not include the names of other persons or information on the location or boundaries of the tract. In this instance the patent document does indicate that the tract was located in Ann Arundell Manor. The tract is not mentioned in the Rent Rolls. It has been included among the Broad & Town Neck Hundred patents only because all of the other Dorrell-owned Anne Arundel tracts were so located. Also, the certified/actual acreage discrepancy is extreme even for this period. The boundary courses, which were found in the Certification (L20/88 SR7361), have been verified and the "actual" acreage shown above is correct.

Dorrell's Luck 10/1/1687 – 76/87 acres. LNS2i/410
SR7372
Location: B&TNH on the north side of an island at the mouth of the Maggity River.
Persons mentioned: **Richard Beard** (assignor of land rights).
Thomas Hammond (neighbor).

Dorsey, Edward, Joshua, & John
Hockley in the Hole 8/20/1664 – 400/448 acres. L7/378
SR7349
Location: MNH on the south side of the Severn River.
Persons mentioned: **Samuel & Cornelius Howard** (neighbors). *Note: The present day Annapolis Water Works is located within the bounds of this tract.*

Dorsey, Edward, Maj.
Dorsey 9/9/1668 – 60 acres. L12/136 SR7354
Location: MNH
Persons mentioned: **George Yate & Capt James Connaway** (assigners of land rights). **Charles Calvert, Esq.** (witness).

Long Reach 11/10/1695 – 448/ 452 acres. LB23i/303

SR7346
Location: B&TNH in Elk Ridge.
Persons mentioned: **Sammuell Chew** (neighbor). *Note: This tract lies in present day Howard County.*

Major's Fancy 11/10/1685 – 186/187 acres. L23/257
SR7364
Location: BT&H *(possibly MNH. See note.)*
Persons mentioned: **Capt. Richard Hill** (neighbor). *Note: The patent document says that the tract is located between the South and Severn Rivers, adjoining a tract named Littleworth. The Maryland Rent Rolls (pg 224) confirms this location without mentioning an adjoining tract. The Rent Rolls, however, place the adjoining tract (Littleworth) on the north side of the Severn River in the Broad and Town Neck Hundred.*

Major's Choice 6/12/1688 – 599/584 acres. NS2i/717
SR7371
Location: B&THN in Elk Ridge between the hills of the Patuxent & Patapsco Rivers.
Persons mentioned: **John Edwards, Madame Ursala Burges, Coll. William Burges,** deceased (assignors of land rights). *Note: This tract is located in present day Howard County.*

Dorsey, John
Hockley in the Hole Res. 3/17/1683 – 845/770 acres. L22/36 SR7363
Location: MNH on the south side of the Severn River.
Persons mentioned: **Edward & Joshua Dorsey** (brothers & former owners). **George Yate** Deputy Surveyor). **Cornelius & Samuel Howard** (brothers & neighbors).

Hockley in the Hole Res. & Confirmation 7/5/1686 842 acres. LIB&ILC/225 SR7369
Location: MNH on the south side of the Severn River.

Persons mentioned: George Yate (Dep. Surveyor). **Samuel & Cornelius Howard** (neighbors). *Note: The tract cannot be drawn and the actual acreage cannot be determined due to incomplete boundary course information in the patent document.*

Dorsey's Adventure 1688 – 400/418 acres. LNS2i/733 SR7371
Location: B&TNH in Elk Ridge between the Patapsco & Little Patuxent Rivers.
Persons mentioned: **Adam Shipley** (neighbor). *Note: This tract was located in Baltimore County at the time of the patent/survey. I have included it because the land had been, and would again be, designated as Anne Arundel County before being absorbed into present day Howard County.*

Dorsey's Search 3/26/1696 – 479/395 acres. LC3i/ 353 SR7377
Location: B&TNH at Elk Ridge adjoining the Little Patuxent River.
Persons mentioned: **John Howard** (assignor of land rights). *Note: This tract was located in Baltimore County at the time of the patent/survey. I have included it because the land had been, and would again be, designated as Anne Arundel County before being absorbed into present day Howard County.*

Troy 11/10/1695 – 763/567 acres. L23/290 SR7364
Location: B&TNH at Elk Ridge.
Persons mentioned: **John Howard, Gent.** (assignor of land rights). *Note: This tract lies in present day Howard County.*

White Wine & Claret 6/6/1702 – 1400/1401 acres. LCDi/76 SR7376
Location: B&TNH on the west side of the Middle River of the Patuxent River next adjoining a tract called Doughoregan.
Persons mentioned: **Charles Carroll** (neighbor). *Note: This tract was located in Baltimore County at the time of the*

patent/survey. I have included it because the land had been, and would again be, designated as Anne Arundel County before being absorbed into present day Howard County.

Mt. Gilboa 6/10/1706 – 247/248 acres. Ldd5i/207 SR7378
Location: B&TNH on the east side of the North Branch of the Patuxent River next adjoining a tract called Pinkston's Delight.
Persons mentioned: None. Note *1: This patent is included because the Cert and/or Survey date is within the targeted period. Note 2: This tract was located in Baltimore County at the time of the patent/survey. I have included it because the land had been, and would again be, designated as Anne Arundel County before being absorbed into present day Howard County.*

Dorsey, Joshua

Dorsey's Addition 5/10/1680 – 50/50 acres. LNSBi/433 SR7370
Location: MNH on the east side of the main branch of Broad Creek.
Persons mentioned: None.

Dowell, Phillip

Phillip's Pillaged Lott 6/1/1700 – 100/101 acres. LWD239 SR7372
Location: SRH next adjoining the land of Soloman Sparrow.
Persons mentioned: **Soloman Sparrow** (neighbor).

Draper, Lawrence

Chelsy 3/26/1695 – 117/108 acres. LWD/132 SR7372-2
Location: MNH at Saughier's Creek.
Persons mentioned: None.

Mayden Croft 2/11/1688 – 98/139 acres. LNSBi/618 SR7370
Location: MNH on the north side of the South River adjoining Saugher's Creek & The Chesapeake Bay.

: **Thomas Richardson** (assignor of land rights).

Drew/Drue, Emmanuel *(Planter)*

Unnamed Cert 10/28/1652 - 300 acres. LAB&H/231 SR7344

Location: WRH on the west side of the West River at the mouth of Cedar Creek.

Persons mentioned: None. *Note 1: This tract was later patented by Jacob Duhaddaway and called Dort. Note 2: The tract cannot be drawn and the actual acreage cannot be determined due to incomplete boundary course information in the patent document.*

Swan Cove 8/20/1665 – 50 acres. L8/103 SR7350

Location: B&TNH on the east side of Ferry Creek adjoining land he now liveth upon.

Persons mentioned: **Thomas Harris** (transported into this Province by Drue here to inhabit). **Robert Burle & Ralph Hawkins** (neighbors). *Note: The tract cannot be drawn and the actual acreage cannot be determined due to incomplete boundary course information in the patent document.*

Dryer, Samuel

Dryer's Inheritance 3/10/1695 – 254/257 acres. LC3i.354 SR7377

Location: MNH on the west side of the North Branch of Patuxent River.

Persons mentioned: **Adam Shepley** (neighbor).

Duhaddaway, Jacob

Dort 9/14/1659 – 300 acres. L4/100 SR7346

Location: WRH on the west side of The West River near the mouth of Cedar Branch.

Persons mentioned: **John Browne** (assignor of land rights).

Dunken/Dunkin, Patrick

Wardrop Ridge 5/12/1663 100/75 acres. LCB3i/282
SR7367
Location: MNH on the south side of the Ann Arundell River
next adjoining a tract called Wardrop.
Persons mentioned: **Thomas Bland** (transported by Dunken
to this Province here to inhabit). *Note: in 1680 Dunken
obtained a Special Warrant to resurvey this tract
(LWC2/360 SR7340). The results of this resurvey were not
found.*

The Neglect 5/4/1683 – 30 acres. LCBi/280 SR7367
Location: MNH on the north side of the South River and on
the east side of Broad Creek.
Persons mentioned: **Thomas Bland** (assignor of land rights).
John Frissel (son-in-law of Dunkin, who received this from
Dunken as a gift in 1684). *Note: The tract cannot be drawn
and the actual acreage cannot be determined due to
incomplete boundary course information in the patent
document.*

Dunkin's Luck 9/11/1687 – 53/52 acres. LNS2i/399
SR7371
Location: MNH on the north side of the South River on the
east side of Hamilton Creek.
Persons mentioned: **John Dorsey** (assignor of land rights).

Dunkin's Chance 2/23/1709 – 100/102 acres. LDD5i/654
SR7378
Location: B&TNH on the west side of Curtis Creek next
adjoining a tract called Knavery Prevented.
Persons mentioned: **James Carroll** (assignor of land rights).
John Selby (neighbor). *Note: This patent is included
because the Cert and/or Survey date was within the targeted
period.*

Durand, Alice *(Spinster)*
　　Durand's Place 8/5/1664 – 100 acres. L7/255 SR7349

Location: B&TNH on the north side of the Severn River
adjoining Steer's Cove.
Persons mentioned: Henry Woolchurch & Richard Devons
(neighbors).

Duvall, John

Duvall's Delight 12/10/1695 – 1,000/1,374 acres.
LWD/132 SR7372-2
Location: SRH on the northeast side of the Patuxent River.
Persons mentioned: None. *Note 1: Another patent for
Duvall's Delight was found in LC3i/323 SR7377. Note 2:
The discrepancy between certified and actual acreage is
extreme, even for this period. However, the boundary
courses have been verified and the acreage is correct as
shown above.*

Duvall's Range Res. 11/10/1695 – 708/615 acres.
LB23i/293 SR7365
Location: SRH at the forke by the westernmost branch of the
Patuxent River.
Persons mentioned: None.

What You Will 6/1/1700 – 373/319 acres. LIB&ILC/344
SR7368-1
Location: MNH on the South Runn of the South River next
adjoining a tract called White's Hall.
Persons mentioned: **Jerome White** (neighbor).

Lugg Ox 7/9/1702 – 780/1,010 acres. LCDi/82 SR7376
Location: MNH on the west side of the North Branch of the
South River next adjoining a tract called White's Hall.
Persons mentioned: **Jerome White** (neighbor). *Note: The
discrepancy between certified and actual acreage is extreme,
even for this period. However, the boundary courses have
been verified and the acreage is correct as shown above.*

Honest Man's Lott 7/23/1704 – 110/107 acres. LCDi/220
SR7376

Location: MNH on the north side of the South River next adjoining a tract called Howard & Porter's Range.

Persons mentioned: The patent document states that the tract begins at a "bound Poplar tree near a gatepost by a roadside that leads from the house of **Richard Warfield** to **Mrs. Ruth Howard's** door."

Duvall, Lewis

Duvall's Pasture 5/10/1705 – 62/64 acres. LDD5i/208 SR7378

Location: SRH on the North Great Branch of the Patuxent River next adjoining a tract called Burges' Choice.

Persons mentioned: **Thomas Larkin** (Surveyor). *Note: According to the warrant, 144 acres were certified. Only 62 acres were granted. No explanation found.*

Middle Plantation Res. 10/10/1708 – 844/1,218 acres. LDD5i/510 SR7348

Location: SRH on the south side of the South River.

Persons mentioned: **Marin Duvall** (father of **Lewis**). **Benjamin Williams** (neighbor). *Note: The discrepancy between certified and actual acreage is extreme, even for this period. However, the boundary courses have been verified and the acreage is correct as shown above.*

Eversail 5/10/1709 – 200/211 acres. LDD5i/576 SR7378

Location: SRH in the forke of the Patuxent River next adjoining a tract called Littleton.

Persons mentioned: None.

Duvall, Marin & Young, William

Rich Neck 8/24/1665 – 200/207 acres. L8/147 SR7350

Location: SRH on the south side of the South River on the west side of Jacob's Creek.

Persons mentioned: **George Puddington & Ann Covell** (assignors of land rights). **John Clark** (neighbor).

Duvall, Marin

    Lavall 1658 – 100/100 acres. L4/259 SR7346
Location: SRH on the westernmost branch of the South River near the head.
Persons mentioned: **William Burges** (transporter of Duvall to this Province to inhabit). **John Covill** (owner of Duvall's indenture of servitude). **Tobias Butler** (assignor of land rights). **John Freeman** (neighbor). *Note: Duvall, a prisoner during the English Civil War being held in Scotland was transported into this Province by Burges who assigned (sold) his service indenture to John Covill.*

    Middle Plantation 9/4/1664 – 600/585 acres. L7/451 SR7349
Location: SRH on the southwest side of the South River.
Persons mentioned: **John Ewan, Thomas Pierson, & Andrew Skinner** (assignors of land rights).

    Duvall's Addition 8/8/1670 – 154/169 acres. L14/22 SR7356
Location: MNH on the west side of the South River next adjoining a tract called Middle Plantation.
Persons mentioned: **George Yate & David Poole** (assignors of land rights).

    Duvall's Range 9/10/1672 – 200/198 acres. L17/291 SR7358
Location: MNH on the east side of the North Branch of the Patuxent River.
Persons mentioned: **George Yate, Thomas Taylor, & Jerome White. Esq.** (assignors of land rights).

Eagleston, Bernard

    Eagleston's Range 9/23/1680 – 200/200 acres. LCDi/55 SR7366

Location: B&TNH on the north side of the Severn River at Cypress Swamp.
Persons mentioned: **George Yate** (assignor of land rights). **Edward Phillips** (neighbor).

Ebden, William

Hockley 8/8/1670 – 100/92 acres. L14/8 SR7356
Location: B&TNH on the south side of the Patapsco River beginning at the northwest bound tree of a tract called Foster's Fancy.
Persons mentioned: **George Yate** (assignor of land rights).

Edge, Daniel

The Advance 5/10/1676 – 42/42 acres. L19/245 SR7360
Location: MNH between the South and Severn Rivers at Norwood's Creek.
Persons mentioned: **John Norwood** (neighbor).

Edge's Addition 9/10/1684 – 50/42 acres. LSDA/456 SR7369
Location: MNH between the South and Severn Rivers.
Persons mentioned: **Robert Jones & George Yate** (assignors of land rights).

Edwards, John

Edward's Neck 5/4/1688 – 100/92 acres. L11/354 SR7353
Location: MNH on a pointe at the mouth of Fishing Creek.
Persons mentioned: None.

Efford, John & Goodrick, Henry

Efford's Chance 10/20/1677 – 150/210 acres. L11/220 SR7353
Location: B&TNH on the south side of the Patapsco River.
Persons mentioned: **George Yate, Edward Dorsey, & Ann Covell** (assignors of land rights). *Note: The discrepancy between certified and actual acreage is extreme, even for this period. However, the boundary courses have been*

verified and the acreage is correct as shown above.

Efford, Will
>Efford's Delight 10/10/1704 – 180/191 acres. LCDi/180
>SR7376
>Location: MNH in the forke of the Patuxent River to the
>north of a tract called Robin Hood's Forrest.
>Persons mentioned: **Richard Snowden, Jr., & James
>Carroll** (assignors of land rights).

Emmerson, Thomas
>Unnamed Patent 8/27/1658 – 100 acres. LQ/101 SR7345
>Location: SRH near the Road River adjoining Grosses
>Valley.
>Persons mentioned: **Thomas Howell** (assignor of land rights).
>*Note: The tract cannot be drawn and the actual acreage
>cannot be determined due to incomplete boundary course
>information in the patent document.*

Emmerton, Humphrey
>Emmerton's Addition 6/25/1680 – 20/12 acres. LCB2i/39
>SR7366
>Location: HCH by the Main Branch of Lyon's Creek.
>Persons mentioned: **George Holland** (assignor of land
>rights). **Francis Holland, Richard Hall, & William Hunt**
>(neighbors).
>
>Emmerton's Range 6/28/1680 – 130/132 acres. LCB2i/42
>SR7366
>Location: HCH adjoining a tract called Broadnashly
>*(Browton Ashley).*
>Persons mentioned: **George Holland** (assignor of land
>rights). **Francis Holland** (neighbor).

Essen, John
>Scotland 9/8/1659 – 600 acres. LAB&H/98 SR7344
>Location: B&TNH on Fishing Creek near the head of

Scotcher's Creek.

Persons mentioned: **Richard Ewen** (assignor of land rights obtained for transporting **John, Susan, & Ann**, his children & **Wiliam Davis, John King, & James Brown** into this Province here to inhabit). **Robert Short** (neighbor). *Note: The tract cannot be drawn and the actual acreage cannot be determined due to incomplete boundary course information in the patent document.*

Everet, Richard

Stony Hills 1/10/1695 – 36/26 acres. LWD/126 SR7372-2
Location: MNH adjoining **John Howard.**
Persons mentioned: **Charles Hopkins** (assignor of land rights). *Note: Another patent for this tract was found in LC3i/328 SR7377.*

Ewen, Richard Maj.

Unnamed Cert 5/11/1652 – 600 acres. LAB&H/278 SR7344
Location: B&TNH on Fishing Creek by a swamp of a creek called Scotcher's Creek.
Persons mentioned: **Robert Short** (neighbor). *Note 1: The tract was patented by **John Essen** as Scotland in 1659. Note 2: The tract cannot be drawn and the actual acreage cannot be determined due to incomplete boundary course information in the patent document.*

Duke's Cove 9/15/1659 – 350/314 acres. L4/113 SR7346
Location: B&TNH on pointe by a branch of the Patapsco River called The Westernmost Branch.
Persons mentioned: **Sophia, Elizabeth, & David** (wife & children of **Ewen** transported by him to this Province here to inhabit). *Note 1: Prior to 6/1661, Ewen sold the tract to **Paul Kinsey** of Anne Arundel County. Upon Kinsey's death a Patent of Confirmation was granted to his orphaned son and Heir **Paul Kinsey, Jr.** (L14/245 SR7356). Note 2: MSA Land Record #55 iidentifies this as "Dake's" Cove.*

The Barren Neck 9/9/1663 – 150 acres. L5/49 SR7347
Location: WRH on the north side of the West River.
Persons mentioned: **William Hadwell, Thomas Milliard, & Mary Waters** (persons transported to this Province to inhabit by **Richard Ewen** in 1661. **George Skipworth** (neighbor).
Note: The tract cannot be drawn and the actual acreage cannot be determined due to incomplete boundary course information in the patent document.

Ewen Upon Ewenton 7/3/1668 – 400/400 acres. L10/378 SR7352
Location: WRH on the north side of the West River adjoining Miles' Branch.
Persons mentioned: **Thomas Miles** (neighbor).

Ewen's Addition 8/4/1664 – 90/78 acres. L7/240 SR7349
Location: WRH on the north side of the West River adjoining a tract called Ewen Upon Ewenton.
Persons mentioned: **Richard Talbott & Fernando Batten** (neighbors).

Faulkner, Martin
>**Martin's Nest 9/23/1680 – 150/147 acres.** LCB2i/64 SR7366
>Location: B&TNH on the north side of the Ann Arundell *(Severn)* River.
>Persons mentioned: **George Yate & Coll. William Burges** (assignors of land rights).

Filer, Robert
>**Brushy Neck 10/19/1663 – 100/95 acres.** L6/100 SR7348
>Location: B&TNH on the north side of the Severn River.
>Persons mentioned: **Thomas Turner** (neighbor).

Floyd, James
>**Floyd's Beginning 8/8/1684 – 230/222 acres.** LSDA/513 SR7369

Location: B&TNH on Bodkin Creek of the Patapsco River.
Persons mentioned: **Robert Jones & George Yate** (assignors of land rights).

Floyd's Adventure 3/10/1695 – 320/321 acres. LC3/308
SR7377
Location: B&TNH on Bodkin Creek next adjoining a tract called Milford.
Persons mentioned: **Charles Stevens & Richard Beard** (assignors of land rights). **John North & James Smith** (neighbors).

Floyd, John
Floyd's Chance 6/5/1687 – 60/60 acres. LIB&ILC/272
SR7378-2
Location: B&TNH on the south side of the Maggity River.
Persons mentioned: **Lawrence Draper & John Gray** (assignors of land rights). **William Luffman** (neighbor).

Ford/Forde, Thomas:
Fordston 2/20/1659 – 120/150 acres. L4/517 SR7346
Location: WRH on the south side of the West River at the head of Cumber's Branch.
Persons mentioned: **John Cumber** (neighbor).

Dinah Ford Beaver Dam 9/21/1663 – 400/400 acres.
L5/594 SR7347
Location: HCH near Herring Creek next adjoining a tract called Padgett.
Persons mentioned: **Richard Ensill, Samuell Chew, Giles Allen** (assignors of land rights). **William Padgett** (neighbor).

Gowrey Banks 9/25/1663 – 600/600 acres. L5/596 SR7347
Location: HCH in the woods on the west side of the plantations of Herring Cr. Bay.
Persons mentioned: **Giles Allen, William Hill, Robert Lloyd, William Suggs, &Thomas Bosley** (persons involved

in the assignment of land rights for this tract). **Robert Morley & John Gray** (neighbors).

Forde's Folly 5/1/1676 – 170/171 acres. L19/328 SR7360
Location: HCH on Herring Creek adjoining a tract called Holloway's Encrease.
Persons mentioned: **George Yate & Richard Harris** (assignors of land rights). **George Pascall** (neighbor).

Foster, Richard & Lewis, John

Foster & Lewis 9/10/1666 – 100/102 acres. L10/165 SR7352
Location: SRH on the south side of the South River and on the west side of Jacob's Creek.
Persons mentioned: **George Yate** (assignor of land rights). **Richard Cheney** (neighbor).

Foster, John

Foster's Point 5/1/1672 – 50/45 acres. L16/575 SR7357
Location: SRH on the south side of the South River at the head of Flatt Cr.
Persons mentioned: **Mary Foster** (wife). **Richard Cheney** (neighbor). *Note: The land rights used for this patent were due Mary Foster for completing her time of service.*

Foster, Joseph

Foster's Fancy 6/29/1669 – 100 acres. L12/311 SR7354
Location: B&TNH on the south side near the head of the Patapsco River.
Persons mentioned: **George Yate, Gent** (assignor of land rights and Deputy Surveyor). **Jerome White, Esq.** (Surveyor Generall).

Foster, Richard

The Conclusion 9/25/1666 – 50/32 acres. L10/152 SR7352
Location: SRH on the east side of Flatt Creek.

Persons mentioned: **Richard Beard** (assignor of land rights).
Richard Cheney, John Wheeler, & Marin Duvall
(neighbors).

Francis, Thomas, Capt
Francis His Addition 9/10/1664 – 42/42 acres. L15/267
SR4327
Location: SRH on Nettlefold's Branch next adjoining a tract
called Shaw's Folly.
Persons mentioned: **George Yate** (assignor of land rights).
John Shaw (neighbor).

Brushy Neck Res. 10/7/1683 – 390/390 acres. L22/106
SR7363
Location: MNH on north side of the South River adjoining
Todd's & Clarkson's Creeks.
Persons mentioned: **George Yate** (Deputy Surveyor) &
Vincent Long (Surveyor Generall).

Franklin, Robert & Beard, Richard
The Indian Range 9/20/1665 – 250/217 acres. L16/239
SR7357
Location: SRH on the south side of the South River adjoining
a branch of the Patuxent River.
Persons mentioned: **George Yate & John Dartford**
(assignors of land rights). **Francis Clarke, James Blunt,
Sarah Oberton, Stephen Harper,** & himself (persons
transported to this Province by John Dartford).

Franklin, Robert
Hickory Hills 1667 – 550/320 acres. L11/213 SR7353
Location: SRH about four miles from the South River
adjoining a tract called The Friend's Choice.
Persons mentioned: **Capt. William Burges, George
Nettlefold, George Yate, Thomas Cole, Robert Simkin**
(assignors of land rights). Himself, **William Stimson, Ann**

Hatt, & Augustine Skinner (persons transported by Robert Franklin to this Province here to inhabit).

Franklin's Enlargement 8/8/1670 – 240/374 acres. L14/9 SR7356
Location: SRH in the woods next adjoining a tract called The Indian Range.
Persons mentioned: **George Yate & David Poole** (assignors of land rights). **Richard Beard & Neal Clark** (neighbors).

Ann Arundell Manour Part Of - 6/16/1674 - 300/302 acres. L15/23 SR4327
Location: HCH on Beaver Dam Branch.
Persons mentioned: **Charles Calvert, Esq.** (Captain Generall, Governor, & Lord Prop.).
John Cumber & Alexander Gordon (neighbors).

Franklin, Robert, Jr.
Robert's Luck 2/27/1671 – 24/35 acres. L15/694 SR4327
Location: HCH at the mouth of Herring Creek.
Persons mentioned: **George Holland** (assignor of land rights). **Wm. Collier** (neighbor).

Freeborne, Thomas
Freeborne's Enlargement 10/10/1695 – 80/81 acres. L23/260 SR7364
Location: MNH on the north side of the South River next adjoining a tract called Baldwin's Addition.
Persons mentioned: **Daniel Ellet** (assignor of land rights). **John Baldwin** (neighbor).

Freeborne's Progress 12/10/1695 – 600/648 acres. LC3i/322 SR7377
Location: B&TNH at Elk Ridge by the Patuxent River.
Persons mentioned: **Major Dorsey, Samuel Chew, & John Dorsey** (neighbors). *Note: This tract lies in present day Howard County.*

Freeman, John

Free Manston 2/15/1659 – 150/127 acres. L5/127 SR7347
Location: SRH on the west side of the South River near the head.
Persons mentioned: None. *Note: A note in the margin of the patent document identifies this tract as Freeman's Neck. MSA Land Index #54 uses both names. However, the "text" of the patent document identifies the tract as Free Manston.*

Freeman's Fancy 5/27/1663 – 300/250 acres. L5/289 SR7347
Location: SRH near the head of the South River adjoining a tract called Free Manston.
Persons mentioned: None. *Note: Upon his death,* **Freeman** *devised the tract to his wife* **Elizabeth** *who, later, became the wife of* **Robert Proctor**).

Friend, Joseph & Cook, William

The Friendship 8/5/1679 – 160/161 acres. L15/905 SR4327
Location: B&TNH on the south side of the Maggity River at the mouth of Tyler's Cove.
Persons mentioned: **George Yate** (assignor of land rights). **Robert Tyler & William Luffman** (neighbors).

Frissell, John

Knavery Discovered 11/1/1701 – 400/384 acres. LDD5i/37 SR7378
Location: B&TNH among the westernmost branches of Curtis Creek.
Persons mentioned: **Hugh Merrica** (neighbor). *Note: The patent/survey document places this tract in Baltimore County. MSA Land Index #55 places it in Anne Arundel County. I have included it here based on its location.*

Frizzell, William

The Adventure 9/13/1663 – 50/43 acres. L5/574 SR7347
Location: MNH on north side of the South River on the east
side of Broad Creek.
Persons mentioned: Nicholas Wyatt (neighbor). *Note: The
tract was purchased by John Hammond on 6/26/1670 (BC
& GS/45), and purchased again by Henry Ridgely in
6/1677.*

Chance 8/8/1664 – 100/100 acres. L7/342 SR7349
Location: MNH on the north side of the South River and the
east side of Green Ginger Cr.
Persons mentioned: Ann Potter (wife of Wm. Frizzell who
was transported by him into this province here to inhabit).

The Friendship 8/20/1683 - 30 acres. LCBi/484 SR7367
Location: MNH on the north side of the South River and on
the east side of Broad Creek.
Persons mentioned: George Yate (assignor of land rights).
*Note: The tract cannot be drawn and the actual acreage
cannot be determined due to incomplete boundary course
information in the patent document.*

Fuller, Mary
Fuller's Luck 1/8/1701 – 80/73 acres. DD5i/517 SR7378
Location: B&TNH on the south side of the Maggity River at
the mouth at Bodkin's Cove.
Persons Mentioned: Edward Fuller (former owner and father
of Mary).

Fuller, William, Capt.
Unnamed Cert 10/27/1651 – 100 acres. LAB&H/263
SR7344
Location: MNH on the south side of the Severn River next
adjoining a tract called Fuller's Point.
Persons mentioned: Phillip Thomas (neighbor). *Note: The
tract cannot be drawn and the actual acreage cannot be
determined due to incomplete boundary course information
in the patent document.*

Unnamed Patent 8/3/1658 – 300/300 acres. LQ/82 SR7345
Location: B&TNH
Persons mentioned: William Jones (neighbor).

Broad Creek 2/16/1659 – 200 acres. L4/197 SR7346
Location: B&TNH on the north side of Severn River on the
north side of Sassafras Creek.
Persons mentioned: William Blay (neighbor). *Note: The tract
cannot be drawn and the actual acreage cannot be
determined due to incomplete boundary course information
in the patent document.*

Fuller 2/17/1659 – 150 acres. L4/486 SR7346
Location: B&TNH on the north side of the Severn River on
the north side of Homewood's Creek and on the west side of
Scotcher's Creek.
Persons mentioned: None. *Note: The tract cannot be drawn
and the actual acreage cannot be determined due to
incomplete boundary course information in the patent
document.*

Gadsby, John
Gadsby's Adventure 10/10/1694 – 33/33 acres. LWD/115
SR7372-2
Location: B&TNH on the north side of the Ann Arundell
(Severn) River next adjoining a tract called Hopkins Fancy.
Persons mentioned: Daniel Elliot (assignor of land rights).
Christopher Randall, John Gray, John Wheeler, &
Richard Beard, Jr. (neighbors).

Gaither/Gater/Gather), John & Proctor, Robert
Abingdon 9/20/1664 – 875/876 acres. L7/387 SR7349
Location: MNH at the head of the South River near the main
branch of the South Runn.
Persons mentioned: None

Gaither/Gater/Gather, John

Gater's Range 9/10/1675 – 200/147 acres. L17/293 SR 7358
Location: SRH on the west side of the North Runn of the South River.
Persons mentioned: George Yate, Thomas Taylor, Jerome White, Esq. (assignors of land rights).

Roundabout Hill 9/1/1687 – 120/121 acres. LNS2i/396 SR7371
Location: SRH on the west side of the South Runn of the South River next adjoining a tract called Free Manston.
Persons mentioned: Robert Proctor (assignor of land rights).

Poll Cat Hill 9/1/1687 – 391/373 acres. LNS2i/380 SR7371
Location: SRH at the forke on the North Great Branch of the Patuxent River.
Persons mentioned: John Stimson & Richard Beard (assignors of land rights).

Abindgon Part Of 8/27/1699 – 364/364 acres. DD5i/44 SR7378
Location: MNH on the south side of a branch of the North Branch of the South River.
Persons mentioned: James Finley, Jerome Finley, & Robert Proctor (former owners).

Gaither, John, Jr.

Abingdon Res. 5/10/1701 – 364/382 acres. LWD/375 SR732
Location: MNH on the south side of a branch of the North Runn of the South River.
Persons mentioned: John Gaither *(the elder)*& Robert Proctor (original owners). Coll. Henry Darnall (Surveyor Generall).

Galloway, Richard
> Galloway 12/4/1662 – 250/231 acres. L5/623 SR7347
> Location: WRH on the north side of the West River at the head of Galloway's Creek
> Persons mentioned: **James Bonner & James Watkins** (neighbors).

Galloway, Richard, Jr.
> The Gift 6/10/1676 – 125/113 acres. L19/313 WR7360
> Location: WRH on the northwest side of the West River in the woods.
> Persons mentioned: **Richard Galloway**, *the elder* (father). **George Yate** (Deputy Surveyor). **John Watkins, Thomas Hooker, & Samuel Galloway** (neighbors).

Galloway, Samuel
> The Favor 6/10/1676 – 125/128 acres. L19/313 SR7360
> Location: WRH on the northwest side of the West River near the head of Galloway's Cr.
> Persons mentioned: **Richard Galloway**, *the elder* (father). **George Yate** (Deputy Surveyor). **James Bonner, John Watkins, & Thomas Hooker** (neighbors).

Galloway, William
> Clinke 1/18/1659 – 100/100 acres. L4/440 SR7346
> Location: MNH on the south side of the Severn River at Galloway's Creek.
> Persons mentioned: **Lucy Child** (Galloway's wife who received fifty acres of land for completing her time of service). *Note: Lucy Child was transported to this Province by **John Norwood** in 1658.*

> Clinke 1/18/1659 – 150 acres. L4/427 SR7346
> Location: MNH on the western branch of the South River.
> Persons mentioned: **Lucy** (**Galloway's** wife who received fifty acres of land for completing her time of service in this Province). *Note: a marginal notation on the patent*

document states, "This Patent is written Folio 456 over again because the certificate was mistaken."

Gardner, Christopher

Gardner's Folly 9/20/1665 – 100 acres. L9/275 SR7351
Location: WRH in a swamp between the Three Islands and Herring Creek.
Persons mentioned: **George Yate** (assignor of land rights). **Armigill Greenwood** (neighbor). *Note: The tract cannot be drawn and the actual acreage cannot be determined due to incomplete boundary course information in the patent document.*

Gardner's Chance 5/1/1672 – 40 acres. L14/523 SR7365
Location: WRH on South Creek.
Persons mentioned: **Robert Wilson** (assignor of land rights). **Richard Talbott & Anthony Holland** (neighbors). *Note: The tract cannot be drawn and the actual acreage cannot be determined due to incomplete boundary course information in the patent document.*

Gardner, Edward & Warfield, Richard

Gardner's Warfield 8/10/1669 – 60/62.5 acres. L12/328 SR7354
Location: MNH on the north side of the North Runn of the South River.
Persons mentioned: **George Yate** (assignor of land rights.) **Nicholas Wyatt** (neighbor).

Gardner, Edward

The March 6/11/1687 – 110/113 acres. LNS2i/280 SR7371
Location: MNH near head of Ann Arundell *(Severn)* River next adjoining a tract called Howard & Porter's Fancy.
Persons mentioned: **George Yate & Coll William Burges** (assignors of land rights).

Gardner, Mary

Luck 1689 – 155/156 acres. LNS2i/169 SR7371
Location: B&TNH on the south side of the Maggity River
next adjoining a tract called Betty's Choice.
Persons mentioned: Richard Beard (assignor of land rights).
Richard Bayley & Richard Moss (neighbors).

Garrett, Amos

Providence 8/10/1710 – 200/200 acres. LDD5i/663
SR7378
Location: MNH on the south side of the Severn River at
Round Bay next adjoining a tract called Norwood's Fancy.
Persons mentioned: William Crouch & John Howard
(assignors of land rights). *Note: This tract was surveyed, but
not patented, as Orphans Addition by Elizabeth Sisson on
5/21/1666 (L9/465 SR7351). The following preceded the
above patent on the page referenced: "... Wee, Thomas
Brown and Elizabeth, his wife, formerly Elizabeth Sisson,
doe assign, sell, and make over to Amos Pierpoint all right,
title, and interest in a certaine survey dated 5/21/1666, for
two hundred acres of land called The Orphan's Addition."*

Gassaway, Nicholas

Poplar Ridge 8/5/1654 – 150/144 acres. L7/269 SR7349
Location: MNH on the north side of the South River.
Persons mentioned: George Saughier & Robert Loyd
(assignors of land rights). Capt. Thomas Besson (neighbor).

The Addition 9/8/1688 – 70 acres. L12/135 SR7354
Location: SRH
Persons mentioned: George Yate & James Connaway
(assignors of land rights). Charles Calvert Esq. (witness).
*Note: The tract cannot be drawn and the actual acreage
cannot be determined due to incomplete boundary course
information in the patent document.*

Gates, Ann

White's Ford 7/20/1693 – 800 acres. L23i/147 SR7365
Location: SRH at the head of the South River adjoining a tract called Whites Ford Part Of.
Persons mentioned: Charles Baltimore (Lord Proprietor). Jerome White, Esq. (former Owner *(see White's Hall)*. Joseph Gates (father of Ann & Husband of Jane). *Note: The tract cannot be drawn and the actual acreage cannot be determined due to incomplete boundary course information in the patent document.*

Gates, Jane

White's Ford Part Of 7/20/1693 – 1,000 acres. L23i/147 SR7365
Location: SRH near the head of the South River adjoining a tract called White's Ford.
Persons mentioned: Joseph Gates (husband of Jane and father of Ann). *Note: The tract cannot be drawn and the actual acreage cannot be determined due to incomplete boundary course information in the patent document.*

Gates, Thomas, Ensign

Gatenby 1658– 100/121 acres. LQ/392 SR7345
Location: MNH on the north side of the South River on the north side of Dorsey's Creek.
Persons mentioned: Michael Bellot & John Holloway heirs of Thomas Gates. *Note: The land rights used for this tract were due Gates for transporting himself to this Province to inhabit on 7/8/1649.*

Gibbs, Edward

Ironstone Hill 6/12/1687 – 115/115 acres. LNS2i/731 SR7371
Location: B&TNH on the south side of the Maggity River.
Persons mentioned: Richard Beard (assignor of land rights). Henry Woolchurch, Mary Gardner, Alexander Gardner & Richard Moss (neighbors).

Gibbs, William

Gibbs His Folly 6/15/1685 – **200/198 acres.** LNSBI/312 SR7374

Location: B&TNH on the south side of the Maggity River next adjoining a tract called Sutton's Choice.

Persons mentioned: **William Michall** (assignor of land rights). **Thomas Sutton** (neighbor).

Goldsbury, Robert

Goldsbury's Choice 6/1/1672 – **128/128 acres.**

Location: WRH in Herring Creek Swamp next adjoining a tract called Greenwood.

Persons mentioned: **Charles Boetler** (assignor of land rights). **Armigill Greenwood** (neighbor).

Goodrick, Henry

The Middle Neck 6/20/1668 – **150/150 acres.** L12/17 SR7354

Location: B&TNH on the south side of the Patapsco River and on the west side of Curtis Creek.

Persons mentioned: None.

The Range 6/20/1668 – **100/49 acres.** L12/19 SR7354

Location: B&TNH on the south side of the Patapsco River and on the west side of Curtis Creek.

Persons mentioned: None. *Note: The discrepancy between certified and actual acreage is extreme, even for this period. However, the boundary courses have been verified and the acreage is correct as shown above.*

Gordon, Alexander:

Gordon 2/20/1659 – **300/300 acres.** L4/518 SR7346

Location: HCH on the north side of a branch of Herring Creek called Gott's Creek.

Persons mentioned: **Thomas Forde** (neighbor).

Gossum, Patrick

Townhill Choice 6/20/1652 – 180 acres. LAB&H/295
SR7344
Location: SRH on the south side of the South River adjoining
a tract called Townhill.
Persons mentioned: **Edmund Townhill** (neighbor). *Note: The
tract cannot be drawn and the actual acreage cannot be
determined due to incomplete boundary course information
in the patent document.*

Goswell/Goznell, William

Goswell's Adventure 2/10/1684 – 199/199 acres.
LIB&ILC/140 SR7368
Location: B&TNH in Ann Arundell County on Rock Creek of
the Patapsco River.
Persons mentioned: **George Yate** (assignor of land rights).

Goznell's Choice 11/10/1695 – 250/250 acres. LB23i/295
SR7365
Location: B&TNH on the south side of Curtis Creek.
Persons mentioned: **Philemon Smith** (neighbor).

Gott, Richard

Ram Gott Swamp 2/20/1659 – 600/621 acres. L4/519
SR7346
Location: HCH on the north side of Herring Creek next
adjoining Herring Creek Bay.
Persons mentioned: None

Gover, Robert:

Gover's Ferin 7/12/1677 – 419/429 acres. LCB3i/283
SR7367
Location: HCH next adjoining the west line of a tract called
Browton Ashley.
Persons mentioned: **David Brosn, Robert Homewood,
Elizabeth Holt,** and **Grace Dennis** (persons transported into
this Province here to inhabit). **George Yate** and **Coll.
William Burges** (assignors of land rights). **Francis Holland**

(neighbor).

Gover's Hills 7/8/1680 – 70/62 acres. LCB2i/20 SR7366
Location: HCH next adjoining the west line of a tract called
Well's Hills.
Persons mentioned: **George Yate & Coll. William Burges**
(assignors of land rights).

Gover's Venture 5/21/1679 – 295/295 acres. L15/890
SR4327
Persons mentioned: **George Holland** (assignor of land
rights). **Francis Holland** (neighbor).

Grammar/Grammer/Gramer, John
The School House 10/25/1659 – 100/93 acres. L16/135
SR7357
Location: HCH on the north side of the Patuxent River near
Island Creek.
Persons mentioned: **John Pawson,** merchant (assignor of land
rights). **John Howerton** (neighbor). *Note: Although the
grant is to Grammer, the rights are based, in part, on the
rights of Lawrence Ward. There is no mention of a transfer
of Ward's rights to Grammar.*

Grammar's Chance 5/12/1666 - 350/350 acres. L10/278
SR7352
Location: HCH near Lyon's Creek.
Persons mentioned: **Josias Towgood** (neighbor).

Grammar's Parrott 7/1/1667 – 400/423 acres. L10/562
SR7352
Location: HCH on the east side of the Patuxent River near the
mouth of Lyon's Creek.
Persons mentioned: **William Parrott** (former owner).

Grange, John

    The United Friendship 3/1/1671 – 300/425 acres. L14/434 SR7356

    <u>Location:</u> B&TNH on the south side of the Patapsco River by a small branch.

    <u>Persons mentioned:</u> **George Yate** (assignor of land rights). *Note 1: According to the patent document, George Yate obtained the rights to this acreage on 9/11/1671, about six months before the patent date. A transfer of rights to Grange is not mentioned. No explanation found. Note 2: The discrepancy between certified and actual acreage is extreme, even for this period. However, the boundary courses have been verified and the acreage is correct as shown above.*

Gray, John & Jones, William

    The Friend's Choice 8/8/1670 – 340/320 acres. L14/12 SR7356

    <u>Location:</u> SRH on the south side of the South River adjoining a tract called Hickory Hills.

    <u>Persons mentioned:</u> **George Yate & David Poole** (assignors of land rights). **Robert Franklin** (neighbor).

Gray, John

    Haslenut Ridge 9/20/1665 –200/196 acres. L8/392 SR 7350

    <u>Location:</u> SRH on the south side of the South River at the head of the Rode River.

    <u>Persons mentioned:</u> **Richard Ewen** (assignor of land rights). **Nicholas Gassaway** (neighbor).

    Beaver Dam Neck 6/10/1671 – 100/100 acres. L14/225 SR7356

    <u>Location:</u> West Side of the Rode River adjoining Muddy Creek.

    <u>Persons mentioned:</u> None.

    The Addition 9/10/1672 – 300 acres. L17/292 SR7358

Location: SRH on the south side of the South River on a plaine by a great marsh.
Persons mentioned: **George Yate, Thomas Taylor, & Jerome White Esq.** (assignors of land rights). *Note: The tract cannot be drawn and the actual acreage cannot be determined due to incomplete boundary course information in the patent document.*

Gray's Range 5/1/1676 – 100/80 acres. L19/303 SR7360
Location: B&TNH on the north side of the Maggity River next adjoining a tract called Gray Sands.
Persons mentioned: George Yate (assignor of land rights).

Gray's Increase 7/6/1681 – 300/361 acres. LCB2i/147 SR7366
Location: B&TNH on the north side of the Ann Arundell *(Severn)* River next adjoining a tract called Martin's Nest.
Persons mentioned: **George Yate, Coll. William Burges, & William Jones**, deceased (assignors of land rights). **Martin Faulkner, Christopher Randall, & Henry Lewis** (neighbors).

Gray's Chance 1/15/1684 – 64/65 acres. L22/230 SR7363
Location: SRH on the south side of the South River at Jacob's Creek next adjoining a tract called Cheney Hills.
Persons mentioned: **John Dorsey** (assignor of land rights). **Richard Cheney** (neighbor).

Gray's Land 2/15/1684 – 17/17 acres. L22/220 SR7363
Location: SRH on the north side of Jacob's Creek adjoining a tract called The Conclusion.
Persons mentioned: **Richard Foster** (neighbor).

Gray's Lott 6/1/1687 – 239/198 acres. LIB&ILC/283 SR7268
Location: B&TNH on the north side of the Maggity River next adjoining a tract called Pawson's Plaine.

Persons mentioned: **Robert Proctor** (assignor of land rights).
Thomas Homewood & **Thomas Turner** (neighbors).

Gray's Land 2/11/1688 – 361/361 acres. LNSBi/622
SR7370
Location: B&TNH on the south side of Marly's Ridge
Branch.
Persons mentioned: **Thomas Richardson** (assignor of land
rights).

The Happy Choice 6/12/1688 – 331/331 acres. L22/98
SR7363
Location: B&TNH near the head of Rock Creek of the
Patapsco River.
Persons mentioned: None.

Greene, George

Greenes Town 6/29/1673 – 50/50 acres. L17/507 SR7358
Location: SRH on the south side of the main branch of The
Flatt Creek.
Persons mentioned: **William Wheatly** of London, Marriner &
Robert Wilson (assignors of land rights). **George Yate**
(Deputy Surveyor). **Baker Brooke. Esq.** (Surveyor
Generall). **Richard Cheney** (neighbor).

Green, John

Greenbury 8/6/1664 – 50/47 acres. L7/320 SR7349
Location: B&TNH on the north side of the Severn River.
Persons mentioned: **William Hills** & **John Askew**
(neighbors).

Green's Beginning 10/5/1683 – 70 acres. LCB3i/513 SR
7367
Location: SRH in the forke of Nettlefold's Creek next
adjoining a tract called Elke Thickett.
Persons mentioned: **Henry Hanslap** (assignor of land rights).
Archer Arbuckle, William Brewer, George Walker, &

Gabriel Parrott (neighbors). *Note: The tract cannot be drawn and the actual acreage cannot be determined due to incomplete boundary course information in the patent document.*

Greenbury, Nicholas

Greenbury's Forrest 6/29/1680 – 450/409 acres. L20/400 SR7361
Location: B&TNH between the Ann Arundell *(Severn)* & Magothy Rivers by Cattaile Creek next adjoining a tract called Howard's Folly.
Persons mentioned: **George Yate** & **Richard Painter** (assignors of land rights).

Middle Burrow 6/12/1688 – 11/5 acres. LNSBi/513 SR7370
Location: B&TNH on the north side of the Ann Arundell *(Severn)* River next adjoining a tract called Altogether.
Persons mentioned: **Charles Gorsuch** (assignor of land rights).

Greenwood, Armigill

Greenwood 9/20/1665 – 150/135 acres. L8/393 SR7358
Location: HCH on the north side of Broad Creek running out of Herring Creek Bay
Persons mentioned: **Christian Greenwood** (wife), **James White** (assignor of land rights). *Note: (From L7/531 SR7347). On 11/20/1662, Armigill Greenwood received a warrant for one hundred acres of land for transporting himself and Christian, his wife, to this province to inhabit. A marginal note states that these rights had been certified twice before (Folios 488, and 358 of the same Liber). Both Folios substantiate this and indicate that Greenwood received 100-acre warrants on each occasion. No explanation found.*

Greniston, James

Greniston 5/22/1683 – 700/724 acres. LSDA/353 SR7369

Location: B&TNH about four miles from the Ann Arundell *(Severn)* River.

Persons mentioned: **Henry Hanslap & Coll. William Burges** (assignors of land rights). **Thomas Brown** (neighbor). *Note: This followed the above patent (same reference): "Know all men by these presents that I James Greeniston for a valuable consideration received in hand do hereby bargain, sell, and assign over unto **Nicholas Painter** of the County of Ann Arundell all right, title, and interest in the within mentined Certification of 700 acres of land called Greeniston to have and hold by him and his heirs forever."* Signed: James Greniston 12/5/1682 (L21/483 SR7362).

Gresham, John
> Fortune 4/16/1687 – 54/61 acres. L22/316 SR7363
> Location: SRH on the northeast side of the Rode River.
> Persons mentioned: **Richard Beard** (assignor of land rights). **Edward Selby** (neighbor).

Griffith, William
> Griffith's Lott 11/10/1695 – 197/192 acres. L23/256 SR7364
> Location: MNH
> Persons mentioned: **Henry Ridgely** (assignor of land rights). **William Ridgely** (neighbor).

Grimes, William & Shepheard, Nicholas
> The Friend's Choice 9/19/1672 – 100/92 acres. L17/298 SR7358
> Location: MNH on the south side of the Ann Arundell *(Severn)* River at Spring Branch.
> Persons mentioned: **George Yate, Thomas Taylor, & Jerome White, Esq.** (assignors of land rights).

Grimes, William
> Grimeston 8/25/1665 – 100 acres. L8/153 SR7350

Location: MNH on the south side of the Severn River on the South Br. of Plum Creek.
Persons mentioned: **Thomas Bradley** (assignor of land rights). *Note: The tract cannot be drawn and the actual acreage cannot be determined due to incomplete boundary course information in the patent document.*

Grime's Addition 9/10/1672 – 100/81 acres. L17/291 SR7358
Location: MNH on the south side of the Ann Arundell *(Severn)* River at Plum Creek.
Persons mentioned: **George Yate, Thomas Taylor, & Jerome White, Esq.** (assignors of land rights). *Note: The tract was sold to **John Farthing** for 4,100 lbs of tobacco in 1697 (WH4/242).*

Grimes Enlargement 10/10/1695 – 187/186 acres. LWD/105 SR7372-2
Location: MNH on the south side of the Severn River next adjoining a tract called Salmon's Hill.
Persons mentioned: **John Norwood, Charles Stevens, Daniel Elliott** (assignors of land rights). *Note: The tract was sold by **William & Ann Grimes** to **Amos Garret** in 1709 (PK/84).*

Grosse, Roger
Unnamed Patent 8/15/1658 – 600 acres. LQ/90 SR7345
Location: SRH by a marsh near the head of the Road River.
Persons mentioned: **Edward Lloyd** (assignor of land rights). *Note: The tract cannot be drawn and the actual acreage cannot be determined due to incomplete boundary course information in the patent document.*

Gross, Nicholas
Eagle's Nest 6/1/1681 – 40/41 acres. LCB2/177 SR7366
Location: HCH near Herring Creek Bay at the mouth of Broad Creek.

Persons mentioned: George Yate (assignor of land rights).
Thomas Dabourne (neighbor).

Gross, Thomas

Grosses Increase 6/1/1685 – 180/182 acres. LNS2i/116
SR7371
Location: MNH on the north side of the South River next
adjoining a tract called Wardrop Ridge.
Persons mentioned: None.

Gudgeon, Lawrence & Robert.

Burntwood Common 6/1/1685 – 50/55 acres. L19/350
SR7360
Location: MNH on a branch of the Ann Arundell *(Severn)*
River called Rockhold's Creek.
Persons mentioned: George Yate (assignor of land rights).
*Note: The tract was conveyed to John Rockhold
(5/16/1687), and willed, by him, to his son Jacob Rockhold
(2/17/1698).*

Orphan's Addition 5/10/1685 – 85/90 acres. LNSBi/150
SR7370
Location: MNH between the South & Severn Rivers in the
main branch of Broad Creek.
Persons mentioned: George Yate (assignor of land rights).

Gudgeon, Robert

Burntwood 5/1/1676 – 100/176 acres. L19/350 SR7360
Location: MNH lying between the branches of the South and
Ann Arundell *(Severn)* Rivers.
Persons mentioned: Thomas Hedge (assignor of land rights).
Larrance Richardson (neighbor). *Note: In 1692, the tract
was sold to Thomas Blackwell who bequeathed it to his son-
in-law and daughter John & Comfort Dorsey.*

Guisse, John

Littleworth 6/10/1706 - 100/99 acres. LCDi/277 AR7376

Location: B&TNH on the south side of the Patapsco River at the head of Stoney Runn.
Persons mentioned: None. *Note 1: This patent is included because the Cert and/or Survey was within the targeted period (2/28/1704). Note 2: The patent/survey document places this tract in Baltimore County. MSA Land Index #55 places it in Anne Arundel County. I have included it here based on its location.*

Gullock, Thomas

Gullock's Folly 5/29/1679 – 85/52 acres. L20/253 SR7361
Location: HCH in the woods between Herring Creek and the Patuxent River.
Persons mentioned: **George Yate** (assignor of land rights).
William King (neighbor).

The Vale of Pleasure 6/1/1685 – 46/48 acres. LNSBi/216 SR7338
Location: HCH on the east side of the Patuxent River in the woods next adjoining a tract called Birkhead's Chance.
Persons mentioned: **Robert James** (assignor of land rights).
Nicholas Terratt (neighbor).

Hall, Christopher

Hall's Inheritance 8/8/1670 – 180/184 acres. L14/43 SR7356
Location: SRH on the north side of the Rode River adjoining a tract called Shaw's Folly.
Persons mentioned: **Nicholas Gassaway & George Nettlefold** (neighbors).

Hall, Henry *(Minister)*

Hall's Palace 11/10/1695 – 300/300 acres. LC3i/65 SR7377
Location: B&TNH by Curtis Creek.
Persons mentioned: None

Batchellor's Choice 12/24/1699 - 100/100 acres. LDD5/42
SR7348
Location: HCH adjoining his LOPs Manor.
Persons mentioned: Coll. Henry Darnall (Surveyor
Generall). William Cole (neighbor).

Hall, John:

Marshe's Seat 2/17/1661 150/147 acres. L5/51 SR734
Location: HCH on west side of Herring Creek Swamp near
West Creek.
Persons mentioned: Thomas Marsh, merchant (assignor of
land rights). *Note: West Creek was also called Parker's
Creek.*

Gadd's Hill 6/12/1688 – 140/218 acres. LNSBi/558
SR7370
Location: HCH on Herring Creek, adjoining Parker's Branch
(aka West Creek).
Persons mentioned: James Mills and George Holland
(assignors of land rights). James Maxfield (neighbor). *Note:
The discrepancy between certified and actual acreage is
extreme, even for this period. However, the boundary
courses have been verified and the acreage is correct as
shown above.*

Hall, Josias

Hall's Parcel 8/10/1683 – 100/103 acres. LSDA/66
SR7369
Location: B&TNH on the north side of the Maggity and on
the east side of Bayly's Creek.
Persons mentioned: Coll. Thomas Taylor (assignor of land
rights).

Hallit, Jacob

Hallit's Lott 9/1/1680 – 50/50 acres. LCB2i/17 SR7366
Location: B&TNH on the north side of the Maggity River.

Persons mentioned: George Holland (assignor of land rights). Richard Bayly & George Sturton (neighbors).

Hammond, John, Maj./Coll.

Rich Neck 3/20/1684 – 284/279 acres. L22/183 SR7363
Location: B&TNH on the east side of the northmost Great Branch of Patuxent River at Huntington.
Persons mentioned: **Richard Beard & Gabriel Parrott** (assignors of land rights). *Note: This tract is located in present day Howard County.*

The Addition 1/5/1687 – 22/20 acres. LIB&ILC/315 SR7368-1
Location: MNH on the south side of Ann Arundall *(Severn)* River next adjoining a tract called Mountain Neck.
Persons mentioned: **Thomas Hammond** (neighbor).

Hammond's Pasture 2/11/1688 – 118/116 acres. LNSBi/623 SR7370
Location: MNH on the north side of the South River at the mouth of Green Gingerville Cr.
Persons mentioned: **Thomas Richardson** (assignor of land rights). **Thomas Roper & Thomas Jeffe** (neighbors).

Hammond's Forrest 5/1/1696 – 362/382 acres. LWD/141 SR7372-2
Location: MNH at the head of branches of the Ann Arundell *(Severn)* River.
Persons mentioned: None. *Note: on the back of the Cert was written: "On this tract was one twenty foot dwelling house built and a parcel of land cleared but not tended."*

Hammond, Thomas

Mountain Neck 8/24/1665 - 190/211 acres. L8/115 SR7370
Location: MNH on the south side of the Ann Arundell *(Severn)* River at Hammond's Creek

Persons mentioned: None. *Note: Two unadjoined (but "neighboring") tracts were granted.*

Hanslap, Henry

Ayne 8/2/1683 – 400/401 acres. LSDA/408 SR7369
Location: MNH on the eastern side of the North Branch of The Patuxent River.
Persons mentioned: **Marin Duvall, Edwin Price, & Jerome White** (neighbors).

Hanslap's Range 7/11/1681 – 300/200 acres. LCB2i/211 SR7366
Location: B&TNH on the north side of the Severn River adjoining tracts called Phelps Encrease and Sewell's Encrease.
Persons mentioned: **Walter Phelps & Henry Sewell** (neighbors).

Come By Chance 11/30/1682 – 214/179 acres. L21/513 SR7362
Location: MNH on the north side of the South River by a branch.
Persons mentioned: **Zephaniah Smith & Walter Smith** (neighbors). *Note: On the same day, **Hanslap** assigned (sold) this tract to **George Yate** (same reference).*

Harbitt, Elinor

Harbitt's Clear 3/6/1696 – 146/147 acres. LWD/127 SR7372-1
Location: B&TNH at Elk Ridge.
Persons mentioned: **John Dorsey** (assignor or land rights and neighbor). *Note: Another patent can be found in LC3i/347 SR7377. The second patent uses all of the following spellings for the owner's name: Harbitt, Harbott, Herbert. Note 2: This tract lies in present day Howard County.*

Harding, Matthew

The Locust Thickett 12/23/1688 – 300/320 acres. L18/306
SR7359
Location: MNH on the east side of the Patuxent River at a
small cove.
Persons mentioned: **Henry Darnall** (assignor of land rights).
Jerome White Esq. (Surveyor General of Maryland)

Harness, Isaac

Harnesses Range 9/6/1670 – 250/263 acres. L14/104
SR7356
Location: MNH near the South Runn of the South River next
adjoining a tract called White's Hall.
Persons mentioned: **Robert Wilson & Jerome White, Esq.**
(assignors of land rights).

Harness, Jacob

Harnesses Gift 5/27/1684 – 51 acres. L22/33 SR7363
Location: MNH on the north side of The South River.
Persons mentioned: **Robert Jones** (assignor of land rights).
George Yate (Deputy Surveyor). *Note: The tract cannot be
drawn and the actual acreage cannot be determined due to
incomplete boundary course information in the patent
document.*

Harness, William

Harness 10/27/1652 400 acres. LQ/236 SR7345
Location: MNH on the north side of the South River at the
mouth of Harness Branch.
Persons mentioned: **Susan,** wife **& William & Isaac,** sons,
transported by William Harness (the elder) to this Province to
inhabit. *Note 1: The tract was sold to **Joseph Hill**
(3/8/1701) by **Jacob Harness** (son of William) and his wife
Elinor. Excluded from the sale was the," ...six or eight foot
square wherein William Harness, deceased lies interred."
(Abstracts of Ann Arundell County Land Records,Vol. 2,
page 29). Note 2: The tract cannot be drawn and the actual
acreage cannot be determined due to incomplete boundary
course information in the patent document.*

Harris, John

Harrisses Beginning 11/110/1695 122/139 acres. L23/267 SR7364

Location: B&TNH at Hunting Town.

Persons mentioned: Henry Ridgely (assignor of land rights).

Note: This tract is located in present day Howard County.

Harris, William

Harris His Mount 1677 – 100 acres. L11/211 SR7353

Location: MNH on the north side of the South River.

Persons mentioned: John Wheeler (assignor of land rights). Mary Bark (person transported by Wheeler to this Province to inhabit). John Baldwin (neighbor). *Note 1: Upon the death of Harris, his widow, Elizabeth Harris, sold the tract to John Summerland for 4,000 lbs of tobacco (MSA Tract Index #73). Note 2: The tract cannot be drawn and the actual acreage cannot be determined due to incomplete boundary course information in the patent document.*

Harrison, Richard

Grammar's Chance Res. 1699– 633/621 acres. LDD5/724 SR7378

Location: HCH in the Main Branch of Lyon's Creek.

Persons mentioned: John Grammar (original owner).

Harrison's Lott 6/12/1688 – 13/11 acres. LNSBi/521 SR7370

Location: HCH near Herring Creek.

Persons mentioned: Madame Ursala Burges (widow of William Burges, administrator of his estate, future wife of Dr. Mordecai Moore, and assignor of land rights). Richard Wells (neighbor).

Harrison's Enlargement to Grammar's Chance 6/1/1699 – 425/426 acres. LCC4i/155 SR7375

Location: HCH near Lyon's Creek.

Persons mentioned: **George Burges** (assignor of land rights). *Note 1: The patent document is not entirely clear on whether the tract is located in Calvert or Anne Arundel County. However, it does state that the patent is to be "held in the Mannor of Ann Arundell" and the Anne Arundel County Rent Rolls of 1651-1774 (SR7346) and 1707, include this tract in the Herring Creek Hundred of Ann Arundell County.*

Harsbottle, John

The Tryall 10/22/1698 – 165/165 acres. LCC4i/96 SR7375
Location: B&TNH on the south side of the Maggity River by the bayside at the mouth of Short's Creek.
Persons mentioned: **Edward Jones,** deceased (former owner). **Joshua Jones** (son & heir of Edward Jones and seller of this tract to Harsbottle).

Harwood, Robert

Unnamed Certification 11/26/1659 – 100 acres.
LAB7H/266 SR7344
Location: WRH adjoining the Road River near Three Island Bay.
Persons mentioned: None. *Note 1: This tract was named Harwood and patented by* **Richard Wollman** *in 1664. Note 2: The tract cannot be drawn and the actual acreage cannot be determined due to incomplete boundary course information in the patent document.*

Hasslin, Jeremy

Hasslin 8/4/1658 – 200/200 acres. LQ/87 SR7345
Location: SRH on the south side of the South River at the mouth of Hasslin's Creek.
Persons mentioned: None.

Hawkins, John

Bolealmanack 5/15/1668 – 100/87 acres. L11/406 SR7355
Location: B&TNH on the south side of the Patapsco River
Persons mentioned: None.

Hawkins, Ralph *(Planter)*

Hawkins 0/17/1652 – 500 acres. LAB&H/280 SR7344
Location: B&TNH near the Maggity River.
Persons mentioned: Richard Ewen (neighbor). *Note: The tract cannot be drawn and the actual acreage cannot be determined due to incomplete boundary course information in the patent document.*

Little Hawkins 9/11/1652 – 150/141 acres. LAB&H/200 SR7344
Location: B&TNH on the south side of the Maggity River at the mouth of Deep Creek.
Persons mentioned: Richard Young (neighbor).

Hawkins' Habitation 8/12/1665 – 100/55 acres. L8/101 SR7350
Location: B&TNH on the north side of the Severn River in a neck of land called The Broad Neck at the head of Hawkin's Branch.
Persons mentioned: None. *Note: See Hawkins Habitation Resurveyed – William Bladen.*

Hawkins' Neck 8/12/1665 – 100/100 acres. L8/100 SR7350
Location: B&TNH on the south side of the Maggity River at the mouth of a pond.
Persons mentioned: Henry Woolchurch (neighbor). *Note: The Rent Rolls and MSA Land Index #54 identify this tract as Ralph's Neck. However, the patent document identifies it as Hawkins' Neck.*

Hawkins, William

Hawkins His Range 9/10/1679 – 100/97 acres. L20/349 SR7361
Location: B&TNH on the south side of Rock Creek of the Patapsco River beginning at the mouth of Muddy Pond.
Persons mentioned: George Yate & William Burges (assignors of land rights).

Hawkins His Choice 8/10/1684 – 134/139 acres.
LIB&ILC//30 SR7368-1
Location: B&TNH next adjoining a tract called Hawkins His Range.
Persons mentioned: **Robert Jones & George Yate** (assignors of land rights).

Hawkins His Addition 11/10/1695 – 203/199 acres.
LWD/143 SR7372
Location: B&TNH next adjoining tracts called Hawkins Choice, White's Addition, and Hawkins Range.
Persons mentioned: **P. Smith** (assignor of land rights).
Matthew Howard (neighbor). *Note: The patent document places this tract in Baltimore County. I have included it here based on its location and proximity to Anne Arundel County tracts.*

Haywood, John
The Woodyard 6/10/1671 – 150/159 acres. L14/241
SR7356
Location: MNH on the south side of the Severn River at the Round Bay.
Persons mentioned: **Matthew Howard & Cornelius Howard** (assignors of land rights).

Heath, James
Heath's Meadow 9/13/1700 – 17/12 acres. LDD5i/261
SR7378
Location: HCH on the east side of the Main Branch of Lyon's Creek next adjoining a tract called Burrage.
Persons mentioned: None.

Heath's Purchase 4/20/1702 – 32 acres. LDD5i/180
SR7378
Location: HCH next adjoining a tract called Burrage's End.
Persons mentioned: **Thomas South** (neighbor). **Thomas Larkin** (Deputy Surveyor). *Note: The tract cannot be drawn*

*and the actual acreage cannot be determined due to
incomplete boundary course information in the patent
document.*

Heath's Landing 2/2/1704 - 138/165 acres. LDD5i/242
SR7378
Location: HCH adjoining other land owned by **James Heath.**
Persons mentioned: **Edward Selby, George Pascall,
Abraham Nailor, Christopher Vernon, John Jones** (former
owners of this tract).

Pascall's Purchase Surplus 4/20/1705 – 374/373 acres.
LDD5i/147 SR7378
Location: HCH on the west side of Herring Creek near The
West Creek.
Persons mentioned: **Thomas Larkin** (Deputy Surveyor).
Thomas Marsh (neighbor).

Heathcote, Nathaniel
Peake 4/11/1678 – 152/159 acres. L20/56 SR7351
Location: WRH in the woods next adjoining a tract called
Bonnerston.
Persons mentioned: **James Bonner** (former owner). **Walter
Carr & John Cumber** (neighbors).

Prop's Gift 7/3/1680 – 95/95 acres. L20/105 SR7361
Location: WRH
Persons mentioned: **William Richardson** (former owner).
Richard Talbott (neighbor).

Hedge, Thomas
Hedge Park 5/29/1675 – 94/76 acres. L8/381 SR7359
Location: SRH on a Creek of the Rode River called
Harwood's Creek next adjoining a tract called Margaret's
Fields.
Persons mentioned: **Adam DeLapp & Thomas Lynecomb**
(neighbors).

Herring, Bartholemew

Unnamed Cert 9/29/1652 – **100/100 acres.** LAB7H 318
SR7344
Location: WRH on the west side of the Rode River.
Persons mentioned: None.

Herring 9/28/1654 – 100/100 acres. LAB&H/318 SR7344
Location: WRH on the west side of a branch of the Rode
River called Herring's Cr.
Persons mentioned: None.

Herring, John

Herring's Purchase 1/26/1684 – 205 acres. L22/194
SR7363
Location: MNH at the forke of Patuxent River on the
northeast side of the Southwest Br.
Persons mentioned: **John Dorsey** (assignor of land rights).
*Note: The tract cannot be drawn and the actual acreage
cannot be determined due to incomplete boundary course
information in the patent document.*

Hill, Abel

Turkey Island 3/30/1667 – 33/33 acres. L19/475 SR7360
Location: HCH on the east side of Beaver Dam Branch.
Persons mentioned: **George Pascall** (former owner).
Alexander Gordon & Robert Franklin (neighbors).

Hillington 3/20/1683 – 50 acres. LCB3i/204 SR7367
Location: HCH in the woods on the east side of Beaver Dam
Creek.
Persons mentioned: **Thomas Ford** (neighbor). *Note: The
tract cannot be drawn and the actual acreage cannot be
determined due to incomplete boundary course information
in the patent document.*

Hill, Clement

Long Lane 9/18/1698 – 22/23 acres. LCC4i/7 SR7375
Location: HCH on the south side of Portland Manor

adjoining a tract called Talbott's Hill.
Persons mentioned: Coll Henry Darnall & Clement Hill, Jr.
(assignors of land rights).

Hill, Clement, Jr.

Hill's Chance 9/18/1698 – 215/199 acres. LCC4i/32
SR7375
Location: WRH on the east side of Ann Arundell Mannor
next adjoining a tract called Talbott's Angles.
Persons mentioned: Coll. **Henry Darnall** (assignor of land
rights and former Surveyor Generall). *Note: On 9/12/1698,
Hill assigned a warrant for 215 acres of land to Darnall. On
9/14/1698, the rights for what appears to be an additional
215 acres of land was assigned by Hill to Darnall out of a
warrant received by Hill on 8/30/1698. This 215-acre tract
was also surveyed, by Hill (in his capacity as Surveyor
Generall of the Western Shore of the Province of Maryland)
for Darnall on 9/14/1998. On 9/20/1698, Darnall assigned
rights to this tract to Hill, who had already patented it (two
days earlier) on 9/18/1698.*

Batia Purchase 9/18/1698 - 53/52 acres. LCC4i/8 SR7375
Location: HCH adjoining the south line of Portland Manor.
Persons Mentioned: Coll. **Henry Darnall** (former Surveyor
Generall.) *Note: The rights to 53 acres were assigned by
Hill to Darnall and this 53-acre tract was surveyed for
Darnall (by Hill) on 9/14/1698. On 9/18/1648, Hill, acting
as Surveyor Generall of the Western Shore of the Province
of Maryland, assigned a warrant for 53 acres of land to
Darnall. On 9/20/1698, Darnall assigned all rights to the
Cert & Survey for this 53-acre tract to Hill who had already
patented it (two days earlier) on 9/18/1698.*

Hill, Richard, Capt.

Littleworth 4/1/1666 – 132/133 acres. LIB&ILC/180
SR7369
Location: B&TNH on the north side of the Ann Arundell
(Severn) River.

Persons mentioned: **Robert Proctor** (assignor of land rights).

Beasley's Neck 2/3/1673 – 150/162 acres. L15/347
SR4327
Location: MNH at the mouth of the Ann Arundall *(Severn)*
River.
Persons mentioned: **George Yate & Baker Brook**
(surveyors). **Francis Beasley** (original owner). **John Beasley**
(son and heir of Francis Beasley, deceased). *Note: The
humble petition of Richard Hill sheweth that on 3/18/1672,
the petitioner purchased of John Beasley, son and heir of
Richard Beasley, a tract called Beasley's Neck for 250
acres. Upon resurvey it was found to be 159 acres. Your
petitioner requests rights for the balance of 90 acres.
Petition granted. (L15/480).*

Beazley's Neck Res. 5/10/1676 – 159/158 acres. L19/275
SR7360
Location: MNH on the south side of Beazley's Creek.
Persons mentioned: **Francis Beazley & John Beazley**
(former owners).

Mill Meadow 10/5/1683 – 240/247 acres. LSDA/260
SR7369
Location: MNH at the head of the Ann Arundell River
(Severn) adjoining a tract called Henry's Encrease.
Persons mentioned: **Henry Hanslap** (assignor of land rights).
Henry Sewell & Adam Shipley (neighbors).

Tolly's Point Res. 4/16/1684 – 140/141 acres. LSDA/319
SR7369
Location: MNH adjoining The Chesapeake Bay at Tolley
Point.
Persons mentioned: **William Durand & Thomas Tolley**
(former owners). **George Yate** (Deputy Surveyor). **George
Talbott, Esq.** (Surveyor Generall).

The Addition 6/1/1687 – 60/60 acres. NS2i/321 SR7371
Location: MNH on the south side of Todd's Creek adjoining
a tract called Horne Neck.
Persons mentioned: **Robert Clarkson** (neighbor).

The Angle 6/5/1687 – 7/7 acres. LIB&ILC/305 SR7368-1
Location: MNH on the south side of the Ann Arundell
(Severn) River at Dorsey's Creek.
Persons mentioned: None. *Note: This tract is within the
bounds of the Town of Annapolis (Rent Rolls pg. 220).*

Hills, William
Soloman's Desire 9/19/1666 – 10 acres. L10/149 SR7352
Location: B&TNH on the north side of the Severn River
adjoining his own land.
Persons mentioned: **George Yate** (assignor of land rights).
*Note: The tract cannot be drawn and the actual acreage
cannot be determined due to incomplete boundary course
information in the patent document.*

Holeman, Abraham
Holeman's Hope 6/15/1650 – 100 acres. LAB&H/43
SR7344
Location: BNTNH adjoining The Chesapeake Bay on the
east.
Persons mentioned: None. *Note 1: A patent was not found.
However, this tract is shown in the Rent Rolls. Note 2: The
tract cannot be drawn and the actual acreage cannot be
determined due to incomplete boundary course information
in the patent document.*

Woodham 8/6/1664 – 110/84 acres. L7/328 SR7349
Location: B&TNH on the north side of the Severn River on
the north side of Broad Creek.
Persons mentioned: **James Southard** (assignor of land
rights). **Robert Priest** (transported by Southard to this

Province here to inhabit). **John Gary** *(could be Gray),*
Richard Young, & **Edward Blay** (neighbors).

Holland, Anthony

> **Great Bonnerston Res. 7/10/1671 – 100 acres.** L16/266
> SR7357
> Location: WRH on the south side of the West River on the
> north side of Bonner's Branch.
> Persons mentioned: **James Bonner, Thomas Hooker, John
> Hawkins, William Aldrich,** & **John Gray** (former owners).
> *Note: The tract cannot be drawn and the actual acreage
> cannot be determined due to incomplete boundary course
> information in the patent document.*

> **Holland's Charge 4/30/677 – 100/101 acres.** L20/83
> SR7361
> Location: WRH on the south side of the West River in
> Herring Creek Swamp next adjoining Bonner's Creek and
> The South Creek.
> Persons mentioned: **James Bonner** (original owner).

> **Holland's Addition 4/9/1677 – 28/27 acres.** L19/478
> SR7360
> Location: WRH on the south side of the West River in
> Herring Creek Swamp.
> Persons mentioned: **Christopher Gardner** (neighbor).

> **Holland's Choice 5/12/1679 – 580/585 acres.** L15/877
> SR4327
> Location: B&TNH on the south side of the Patapsco River on
> the east side of Holly Runn adjoining Galloway's Runn.
> Persons mentioned: **George Yate** (assignor of land rights).

> **Holland's Range 5/13/1679 – 120/114 acres.** L15/878
> SR4327
> Location: HCH in Herring Creek Swamp next adjoining a
> tract called Greenwood.

<u>Persons mentioned:</u> George Yate (assignor of land rights).
Armigill Greenwood, Robert Gouldsbury, & Thomas
Daborne (neighbors).

Holland, Francis
Holland's Hills 7/29/1664 – 190/181 acres. L7/164
SR7349
<u>Location:</u> HCH to the west of Herring Creek Bay.
<u>Persons mentioned:</u> **Mary Holland** (wife), **Francis Holland**
(son), & **Mary Blackwell** (persons transported by Holland
into this Province to inhabit). **Capt. Edward Carter,**
Richard Wells, & **William Hunt** (neighbors).

Browton Ashley - 7/9/1664 – 950/1,123 acres. L7/180
SR7349
<u>Location:</u> HCH in the woods beginning at a bound
Pokehikary of Cooper's Neck.
<u>Persons mentioned:</u> **Tomas Dobbs, Dennis English, Richard**
Carver, Bryan Taylor, John Bee, Sammuel James
Strahan, Abigaill Attwell, Francis Baker, Andrew Baker,
Joseph Good, Robert Morgan, Anthony Stockeley, John
Courde, Nathan Smitz, John Hawes, and **Randall William**
Ellis (persons transported by **Francis Holland** into this
Province here to inhabit). **Richard Wells, Anthony**
Salloway, and **William Hunt** (neighbors). *Note 1: The*
boundary courses specified in the patent document differ
from those specified in the Cert (L12/528 SR7254). The tract
was drawn and measured from the courses found in the
Cert. Note 2: The following authorization to resurvey was
found in L12/318 SR737. " Whereas Francis Holland of the
County of Ann Arundell had surveyed for him a parcell of
land called Browton Ashley lying in the s'd County on the
west side of the plantations of Richard Wells and Anthony
Salloway, in the woods, for nine hundred fifty acres. And
whereas the s'd Francis hath delivered into the Secretary's
Office the grant which, upon examination, of the sheweth
that manifest error hath happened. Therefore, resurvey

according to the ancient bounds of the same. First sett forth for the s'd Francis a true copy whereof is here sent and returned. The contents of the same shall remain upon (completion) of the s'd resurvey wanting of the s'd quantity lay out in any part of this Province and whereas possible you may adjoin to the s'd land not formerly taken up nor reserved with convenient speed." Dated 7/6/1669.

Browton Ashley Res. 8/20/1670 – 950 acres. L13/50 SR7355
Location: HCH beginning at a marked Pokihikary of a tract called Cooper's Neck.
Persons mentioned: **Richard Wells, Anthony Salloway,** and **William Hunt** (neighbors).
Note 1: MSA Land Indices #54 & #55 have no record of a tract owned by Richard Wells (or any other person) called Cooper's Neck. Note 2: The tract cannot be drawn and the actual acreage cannot be determined due to incomplete boundary course information in the patent document.

The Addition 5/1/1672 – 95/76 acres. L14/516 SR7356
Location: HCH adjoining Bennettt's Island and the South Creek
Persons mentioned: **Charles Boetler** (assignor of land rights). **Richard Wells & John Burrage** (neighbors).

Holland's Addition 6/12/1678 – 47/42 acres. LNSBi/539 SR7370
Location: HCH on Herring Creek next adjoining a tract called Carter.
Persons mentioned: **Ursala Burges** (wife and administrator of Col. William Burges'estate). **Coll William Burges,** deceased (assignor of land rights). **Richard Harrisson & Richard Wells** (neighbors).

Holland, George
        The Oblong 5/30/1683 – 70/61 acres. LSDA/236 SR7369

Location: HCH next adjoining a tract called Hunt's Hills
Persons mentioned: Nicholas Nicholson & James Miller
(assignors of land rights). Francis Holland & Robert Paca
(neighbors).

Holloway, Oliver

Holloway's Purchase 5/13/1664 – 100 acres. L6/315
SR7378
Location: HCH on Herring Creek next adjoining The West
Creek.
Persons mentioned: Richard Bennett (assignor of land
rights). *Note: The tract cannot be drawn and the actual
acreage cannot be determined due to incomplete boundary
course information in the patent document.*

Holloway's Encrease 5/1/1676 - 54/55 acres. L19/327
Location: HCH on Gott's Creek.
Persons mentioned: Edward Parrish, Robert Lockwood, &
Thomas Harwood (assignors of land rights). Thomas Forde
(neighbor).

Homewood, James

Homewood's Lott 9/16/1652 - 394 acres. LAB&H/294
SR7344
Location: B&TNH at the mouth of the Maggity River.
Persons mentioned: None. *Note: The tract cannot be drawn
and the actual acreage cannot be determined due to
incomplete boundary course information in the patent
document.*

Homewood's Outlett 3/24/1684 – 60/62 acres. LNS2i/403
SR7371
Location: B&TNH on the north side of the Maggity River
adjoining Homewood's Creek.
Persons mentioned: Richard Beard (assignor of land rights).

Homewood's Inlargement 3/26/1686 – 100/99 acres.
LC3/761 SR7377
Location: B&TNH on the south side of the Maggity River
next adjoining a tract called Homewood's Outlett.
Persons mentioned: Edward Dorsey (assignor of land rights).
Josias Hall (neighbor).

Homewood, John *(Planter)*
　　Unnamed Pattent 9/21/1663 – 210 acres. L5/573 SR7347
　　Location: B&TNH on the east side of Gray's Creek in
　　Homewood's Swamp.
　　Persons mentioned: Thomas Homewood & John Essen
　　(persons transported by Homewood into this Province here to
　　inhabit). *Note 1: One day earlier Thomas Homewood
　　claimed rights for transporting John. See Unnamed Patent
　　Thomas Homewood (9/20/1663). Note 2: The tract cannot
　　be drawn and the actual acreage cannot be determined due
　　to incomplete boundary course information in the patent
　　document.*

　　Wadlington 8/25/1664 – 150/138 acres. L7/303 SR7349
　　Location: B&TNH on the north side of the Severn River by
　　Homewood's Creek.
　　Persons mentioned: None.

　　Homewood's Purchase 8/20/1664 – 260/221 acres.
　　L7/382 SR7349
　　Location: B&TNH on the north side of the Severn River by
　　Homewood's Cove adjoining the Maggity River.
　　Persons mentioned: None.

　　Homewood's Parcel 8/24/1665 – 60/59 acres.
　　L8/105/SR7350
　　Location: B&TNH on the north side of the Severn River by
　　Fuller's Creek adjoining a tract called Pytherston.
　　Persons mentioned: William Fuller & William Pyther
　　(neighbors).

Homewood's Chance 8/2/1666 – 300 acres. L10/233
SR7352
Location: B&TNH at Young's Cove on the east side of Ferry
Creek near the head next adjoining tracts called Hammond's
Purchase and Young Richard.
Persons mentioned: **Richard Young** (neighbor). *Note: The
tract cannot be drawn and the actual acreage cannot be
determined due to incomplete boundary course information
in the patent document.*

Huckleberry Ally 7/10/1671 – 100/101 acres. L14/273
SR7356
Location: B&TNH in a neck of land called The Rich Neck
adjoining Scotcher's Creek.
Persons mentioned: **Major Richard Ewen, Robert Burle &
Richard Pettybone** (neighbors).

Homewood's Range 5/1/1672 – 300/332 acres. L14/452
SR7356
Location: B&TNH on the south side of the Patapsco River
next adjoining a tract called Radnidge.
Persons mentioned: **Thomas Homewood** (assignor of land
rights). **Davy Johnson & George Yate** (neighbors).

Homewood, Thomas
Unnamed Patent 9/20/1663 – 390/390 acres. L5/571
SR7347
Location: B&TNH at the mouth of the Maggity River.
Persons mentioned: **James Homewood, John Homewood,
John Covell, & Wadden Morrisson** (persons transported by
Homewood into this Province to inhabit). *Note: See
Unnamed Patent John Homewood (9/21/1663). In this
document John Homewood claims rights for transporting
Thomas Homewood.*

Homewood's Forrest 12/26/1668 – 100/103 acres.
L17/504 SR7358
Location: B&TNH on Bodkin Creek of the Patapsco River at
the mouth of a cove.
Persons mentioned: George Yate (Deputy Surveyor). **Baker
Brooke** (Surveyor Generall).

Homewood's Addition 3/10/1670 – 150/145 acres.
L14/177 SR7356
Location: B&TNH adjoining a tract called Homewood's
Parcel.
Persons mentioned: **Paul Dorrill** (neighbor).

The Complement 6/1/1672 – 100/80 acres. L16/519
SR7457
Location: B&TNH in the Mountaines adjoining Dorrell's
Creek.
Persons mentioned: None. *Note: The rights used for this tract
were "transferred" from an earlier patent called
Homewood, that was allowed to "lett fall".*

Homewood 6/1/1672 – 140 acres. L15/516 SR7357
Location: BNTNH on the east side at the mouth of the
Maggity River.
Persons mentioned: None. *Note 1: This tract was allowed to
"lett fall" by the owner and reverted to the LOP via the
Escheat Process (Marginal note. same reference) Note 2:
The tract cannot be drawn and the actual acreage cannot be
determined due to incomplete boundary course information
in the patent document.*

Homewood's Range 6/12/1676 – 150/153 acres. L18/285
SR7360
Location: B&TNH on the north side of the Maggity River at
the mouth of Homewood's Creek.
Persons mentioned: **George Yate** (Deputy Surveyor).

Homewood's Chance 8/23/1677 – **300 acres.** L10/609
SR7352
Location: B&TNH on the east side of Ferry Creek at the
mouth of Young's Cove.
Persons mentioned: **Jerome White, Esq.** (assignor of land
rights).

Homewood's Town 4/20/1678 – **635/657 acres.** L20/6678
SR7361
Location: B&TNH on the south side of Bodkin's Creek
adjoining a tract called Dorrell's Inheritance at the mouth of
the Patapsco River.
Persons mentioned: **John Homewood** (assignor of land
rights). **George Yate** (Deputy Surveyor). **Paul Dorrell**
(neighbor).

Homewood's Search 1/20/1698 – **78/78 acres.** LCC4i/163
SR7375
Location: B&TNH on the south side of Maggity Creek next
adjoining a tract called Homewood's Purchase.
Persons mentioned: **Charles Carroll** (assignor of land rights).
Richard Pettibone (neighbor).

Hooker, Thomas
> **Hooker's Purchase** 6/15/1663 – **300/300 acres.** L5/314
> SR7347
> Location: WRH about two miles from the head of Muddy
> Creek among the branches of the Patuxent River.
> Persons mentioned: **Robert Clarkson & Richard Preston**
> (assignors of land rights). **Thomas Taylor** (neighbor).
>
> **The Corant** 6/26/1683 – **31/30 acres.** LCB3i/320 SR7367
> Location: WRH among the branches of the West River.
> Persons mentioned: **William Richardson** (assignor of land
> rights).
>
> **Hooker's Neck** 10/11/1665 – **100/94 acres.** L9/181

SR7351
Location: HCH in Herring Creek Swamp on the north side of The South Creek.
Persons mentioned: **Matthew Selby** (neighbor).

Hooker's Addition 6/4/1677 – 210/206 acres. L19/596
SR736
Location: HCH in Herring Creek Swamp at the forke of The South Creek.
Persons mentioned: **John Doswell, Thomas Pratt, Ralph Boswell, & Thomas Crouchley** (neighbors).

Hooker's Chance 6/1683 – 154 acres. LSDA/93 SR7369
Location: WRH adjoining the main branch of the West River.
Persons mentioned: **George Yate** (assignor of land rights).
Note: The tract cannot be drawn and the actual acreage cannot be determined due to incomplete boundary course information in the patent document.

Hope, Edward
  Hog Neck 6/24/1663 – 250/233 acres. L5/353 SR7347
  Location: MNH on the north side of the South River.
  Persons mentioned: **Tobias Butler** (former owner). *Note: This tract was initially surveyed for Tobias Butler and named The Coombe.*

Hope, George
  The Plaine 2/10/1673 – 120/107 acres. L15/147 SR7347
  Location: B&TNH on the south side of the Patapsco River.
  Persons mentioned: **Robert Wilson & William Wheatly** of London, Mariner (assignor of land rights).

  Hope's Recovery 10/10/1685 – 31/31 acres. LWD105
  SR7372
  Location: B&TNH on the south side of Curtis Creek next adjoining a tract called Hope's Garden.
  Persons mentioned: **John Turner & Henry Constable**

(neighbors). *Note: The patent document places this tract in Baltimore County. I have included it here based on its location and proximity to Anne Arundel County tracts.*

Hope's Garden 6/5/1702 – 10/10 acres. LDD5i/60 SR7348
Location: B&TNH on the south side of Curtis Creek adjoining a tract called Tred Haven. Persons mentioned: **Charles Carroll** (assignor of land rights). **Joshua Mori_ _ _** (neighbor). *Note: The patent document places this tract in Baltimore County. I have included it here based on its location and proximity to Anne Arundel County tracts.*

Hopkins, William *(Planter)*
Hopkins Plantation 2/15/1659 – 215/152 acres. L4/454 SR7346
Location: B&TNH on the north side of the Severn River.
Persons mentioned: **Henry Catteline & Edward Lloyd, Esq.** (neighbors).

Strawberry Plaine 8/5/1664 – 100/130 acres. L7/283 SR7349
Location: B&TNH on the north side of the Severn River between tracts called Swan Neck & Little Piney Neck.
Persons mentioned: **Ann Butler & Jane Norman** (persons transported by **Hopkins** into this province here to inhabit). **Edward Lloyd, Esq.** (neighbor).

Deep Point 5/10/1671 – 60 acres. L14/254 SR7356
Location: B&TNH on the south side of the Maggity River and on the south side, at the mouth, of Deep Creek adjoining his own land.
Persons mentioned: **Abraham Dawson** (neighbor). *Note: The tract cannot be drawn and the actual acreage cannot be determined due to incomplete boundary course information in the patent document.*

Brushy Neck Bottom 8/8/1664 – 100/125 acres. L7347
SR7349
Location: B&TNH on the south side of the Maggity River at
Cedar Marsh.
Persons mentioned: None.

Hopkins Chance 8/5/1664 – 100/100 acres. L7/272
SR7349
Location: B&TNH on the south side of the Maggity River at
the head of Deep Creek.
Persons mentioned: **Susan Wright & Daniell _ _ _ _ _**
(persons transported by Hopkins to this Province here to
inhabit). **Richard Young** (neighbor).

Hopkins Fancy 8/5/1664 – 100/92 acres. L7/270 SR7349
Location: B&TNH on the north side of the Severn River at
Eagle's Nest Bay by Cypress Swamp.
Persons mentioned: **Thomas Mumford & John Hendrickson**
(persons transported by Hopkins to this Province here to
inhabit).

Little Piney Neck 8/5/1664 – 80/80 acres. L7/275 SR7349
Location: B&TNH on the south side of the Maggity River
between the westernmost branches of Forked Creek.
Persons mentioned: None.

Hopewell 9/28/1666 – 30/32 acres. L10/176 SR7352
Location: B&TNH on the north side of the Severn River.
Persons mentioned: **Peter Porter** (assignor of land rights).

Great Piney Neck 10/1/1666 – 100/97 acres. L10/181
SR7352
Location: B&TNH on the north side of the Maggity River
adjoining tracts called Strawberry Plaines and Piney Neck
Creek.
Persons mentioned: **Robert Franklin & John Shaw**
(assignors of land rights).

The Encrease 10/7/1671 – 100 acres. L13/128 SR7355
Location: B&TNH on the south of the Maggity River
adjoining Blay's Branch.
Persons mentioned: **Robert Wilson & Thomas Welborne**
(assignors of land rights). **Edward Wheelock, John Ray, &
Richard Moss** (neighbors). *Note: The tract cannot be drawn
and the actual acreage cannot be determined due to
incomplete boundary course information in the patent
document.*

Little Brushy Neck 5/1/1672 – 75 acres. L16/587 SR7357
Location: B&TNH on the south side of the Maggity River at
Hopkin's Creek.
Persons mentioned: None. *Note: The tract cannot be drawn
and the actual acreage cannot be determined due to
incomplete boundary course information in the patent
document.*

Smith's Range 5/20/1679 – 112/94 acres. L15/896 SR4327
Location: B&TNH on the north side of the Severn River on a
branch of the Maggity River.
Persons mentioned: **George Yate** (assignor of land rights).
John Askew (neighbor).

Little Brushy Neck Res. 7/30/1682 – 150/131 acres.
L21/461 SR7362
Location: B&TNH on the south side of the Magothy River
near Back Creek next adjoining Smith's Range.
Persons mentioned: **Henry Hanslap** (assignor of land rights).
George Yate (Deputy Surveyor). **Morris Baker** (neighbor).

The Contest 7/5/1684 – 100 acres. LCB2i/153 SR7366
Location: B&TNH lying near the Maggity River next
adjoining a tract called Luffman.
Persons mentioned: **George Yate & Nicholas Painter**
(assignors of land rights). **William Luffman** (neighbor).

Brown's Encrease 8/8/1670 – 250/200 acres. L13/31
SR7355
Location: MNH on the south side of the Ann Arundell River
(Severn) next adjoining a tract called Brown Stone.
Persons mentioned: None.

Hopkins Forebearance 8/10/1683 – 142/142 acres.
LSDA/413 SR7369
Location: B&TNH on the south side of the Magothy River
next adjoining a tract called Great Piney Neck.
Persons mentioned: Henry Hanslap & Coll. **Thomas Taylor**
(assignors of land rights). **Thomas Turner & Capt James**
Conaway (neighbors).

Hopkins His Addition 7/6/1687 – 100 acres. LCB3i/144
SR7366
Location: B&TNH between the Ann Arundell *(Severn)* &
Maggity Rivers at Cypress Swamp next adjoining tracts
called Hopkins His Fancy and Howard's Folly.
Persons mentioned: **George Yate & Nicholas Painter**
(assignors of land rights). **Nicholas Greenbury &**
Christopher Rolles (neighbors).

Horner, James

Locust Neck 11/22/1651 – 100/101 acres. LAB&H/254
SR7364
Location: MNH on the south side of the Severn River at
Locust Creek.
Persons mentioned: None.

Howard, Cornelius & Porter, Peter

Howard & Porter's Range 10/21/1666 - 500/1,230 acres.
L10/184 SR7352
Location: MNH on the north side of the South River
adjoining a tract called Howard's Hills.
Persons mentioned: **John Hammond** (neighbor). *Note: The*
discrepancy between certified and actual acreage is extreme,

even for this period. However, the boundary courses have been verified and the acreage is correct as shown above.

Howard & Porter's Fancy 6/20/1668 – 333/316 acres. L12/30 SR7354
Location: MNH on the north side of the South River adjoining a tract called Howard & Porter's Range.
Persons mentioned: None.

Howard, Cornelius

Howard's Heirship 8/8/1664 – 420/390 acres.
Location: MNH on the south side of the Severn River at Hockley Creek.
Persons mentioned: **Matthew, Samuel, & John Howard** (brothers and assignors of land rights).

The Chance 8/25/1664 –200/173 acres. L7/379 SR7349
Location: MNH on the south side of the Ann Arrundell *(Severn)* River.
Persons mentioned: **Cornelius Howard** transported himself, **Henry Kettlewell, & John Sherin** into this Province here to inhabit. **William Frizzell & James Warner** (neighbors).

The Encrease 8/8/1670 – 100 acres. L14/46 SR7356
Location: MNH on the south side of the Ann Arundell *(Severn)* River.
Persons mentioned: **George Yate** (assignor of land rights). **William Galloway** (neighbor).
Note: The tract cannot be drawn and the actual acreage cannot be determined due to incomplete boundary course information in the patent document.

Howard's Hill 9/10/1672 – 200/200 acres. L17/297 SR7358
Location: MNH on the south side of Severn River on the north side of Underwood's Cr.

Persons mentioned: **George Yate, Thomas Taylor, Charles Stevens, & Jerome White Esq.** (assignors of land rights). **William Luffman** (assignor of land rights obtained for transporting himself). **John Norwood** (assignor of land rights obtained for transporting **John Arrington**).

Howard, Elinor
The Good Mother's Endeavor 6/1/1698 – 285/285 acres. LBB3/539 SR7374
Location: MNH on the North Runn of the South River.
Persons mentioned: **John Howard** (deceased husband of Elinor Howard). **Ann Gremmell** (daughter of John Howard). **Coll Henry Darnall** (Surveyor Generall). **Edward Dorsey** (neighbor).

Howard, John & Stephens, Charles
The Woodyard 10/15/1663 – 150/139 acres. L6/109 SR7348
Location: MNH on the north side of the South River near the Round Bay.
Persons mentioned: **Nicholas Wyatt** (neighbor).

Howard, John
Howard's Interest 8/4/1664 – 150/209 acres. L7/252 SR7349
Location: MNH on the south side of the Severn River at Hockley Creek.
Persons mentioned: **Samuel, Cornelius, & Matthew Howard** (brothers and assignors of land rights).

Howard's Thickett 10/2/1666 – 50 acres. L10/186 SR7352
Location: MNH on the south side of the Severn River.
Persons mentioned: **Charles Stevens** (neighbor). *Note: The tract cannot be drawn and the actual acreage cannot be determined due to incomplete boundary course information in the patent document.*

Howard's Folly 10/2/1666 – 100/101 acres. L10/187
SR7352
Location: B&TNH on the south side of the Maggity River at
Cypress Swamp.
Persons mentioned: None.

Howard's Hills 9/22/1674 – 150 acres. L15/361/ SR4327
Location: MNH on the south side of the Severn River next
adjoining a tract called Howard & Porter's Fancy.
Persons mentioned: **Phillip Howard** (brother of **John** and
purchaser of this tract). *Note: The tract cannot be drawn and
the actual acreage cannot be determined due to incomplete
boundary course information in the patent document.*

Howard's Mount 4/12/1680 – 80/76 acres. L20/69
SR7361
Location: MNH on the south side of the Ann Arundell
(Severn) River near the Round Bay.
Persons mentioned: None.

Howard's Search 12/10/1690 – 121/119 acres. LCC4i/13
SR7375
Location: MNH at the Round Bay adjoining a tract called
Howard's Mount.
Persons mentioned: None.

Howard's Discovery 5/1/1697 – 50/50 acres. LCDi/18
SR7376
Location: MNH adjoining the south side of the Severn River
at Wyatt's Creek.
Persons mentioned: None.

Howard, John, Jr.
    Howard's Luck 11/10/1695 – 190/227 acres. L23/249
    SR7364
    Location: B&TNH on the north side of the Patuxent River in
    Huntington.

Persons mentioned: **Capt John Hammond** (neighbor). *Note: This tract lies in present day Howard County.*

Howard's Pointe 1/6/1702 – 40/37 acres. LDD5i/47
SR7378
Location: B&TNH on the south side of the Patapsco River next adjoining a tract called Marlborough.
Persons mentioned: None. *Note: The patent document places this tract in Baltimore County. I have included it here based on its location and proximity to Anne Arundel County tracts.*

Howard's Range 7/9/1702 – 240/188 acres. LDD5i/75
SR7378
Location: B&TNH on the south side of the Patapsco River
Persons mentioned: **Richard Painter** (neighbor). *Note: The patent document places this tract in Baltimore County. I have included it here based on its location and proximity to Anne Arundel County tracts.*

Howard, Mary
The Maiden 10/5/1683 – 40/38 acres. LSDA/417 SR7369
Location: MNH on the south side of the Severn River next adjoining a tract called Howard & Porter's Range.
Persons mentioned: **Henry Hanslap** (assignor of land rights). *Note: The tract was devised by Mary to her brother **Cornelius Howard, Jr.**, and subsequently sold by him to his uncle **Phillip Howard** in 1687. Ownership passed to **Richard Owen** (1685) and to **Jabez Pierpoint** in 1696 (MSA Land Index #73).*

Howard, Matthew *(Planter)*
Unnamed Pattent 7/3/1650 – 650 acres. LAB&H/254
SR7344
Location: MNH on the south side of the Severn River and on the south side of Marshes Creek.
Persons mentioned: None. *Note: The tract cannot be drawn and the actual acreage cannot be determined due to incomplete boundary course information in the patent*

document.

Howard's Inheritance 8/4/1664 – 130/100 acres. L7/247
SR7349
Location: B&TNH on the north side of the Severn River by
Crouches Cove.
Persons mentioned: Henry Cattlin (assignor of land rights).
William Hopkins & Thomas Browne (neighbors).

Howard's First Choice – 5/17/1668 – 160/194 acres.
L11/409 SR7353
Location: MNH on the south side of Severn River next
adjoining a tract called Salmon's Hill.
Persons mentioned: **Robert Salmon** (neighbor). *Note:*
Matthew Howard received five hundred acres for
transporting his wife and Sarah Darcy, John Pine, Thomas
Gleve, Thomas Stedloe, William Cook, Sarah Driver,
Elizabeth Warrenton, Samuel Dryer, and Joan Garnish
into this Province here to inhabit.

Howard's Addition 10/5/1683 – 22.5 acres. LCB3i/299
SR7367
Location: B&TNH on the north side of the Severn River
adjoining a tract called Flushing.
Persons mentioned: **Henry Hanslap** (assignor of land rights).
Samuell Underwood, Robert Tyler, & James Conaway
(neighbors). *Note: The tract cannot be drawn and the actual*
acreage cannot be determined due to incomplete boundary
course information in the patent document.

Howard's Range 9/10/1684 – 270/276 acres. LSDA/459
SR7369
Location: B&TNH on the south side of Bodkin Creek of the
Patapsco River next adjoining a tract called Pawson's Plaine.
Persons mentioned: None.

Howard's Pasture 5/10/1685 – 200/206 acres. LNS2i/112
SR7371

Location: B&TNH on the west side of the Maggity River.
Persons mentioned: George Saughier (neighbor).

Poplar Plaine 6/1/1695 – 500/515 acres. LNSBi/33
SR7370
Location: B&TNH on the north side of Bodkin Creek of the
Patapsco River.
Persons mentioned: Robert Proctor (neighbor).

Howard's Adventure 10/8/1683 – 500/502 acres.
LCB3i/374 SR7367
Location: MNH three miles from the head of the Severn River
next adjoining a tract called Cordwell.
Persons mentioned: Henry Ridgely (assignor of land rights).

Howard's Addition 2/11/1688 – 19/17 acres. LNSBi/619
SR7370
Location: B&TNH on the north side of the Ann Arundell
(Severn) River.
Persons mentioned: Thomas Richardson (assignor of land
rights). John Harris & John Howard, Jr. (neighbors).

Howard, Phillip

Howardston 2/15/1659 – 100 acres. L4/458 SR7346
Location: B&TNH on the north side of the Severn River.
Persons mentioned: Edward Lloyd, Esq. & Thomas
Browne (neighbors). *Note: The tract cannot be drawn and
the actual acreage cannot be determined due to incomplete
boundary course information in the patent document.*

Howard's Hills 12/10/1679 – 150/42 acres. L21/71
SR7362
Location: MNH on Severn Ridge next adjoining tracts called
Howard & Porter's Fancy and The March.
Persons mentioned: None. *Note: The discrepancy between
certified and actual acreage is extreme, even for this period.
However, the boundary courses have been verified and the*

acreage is correct as shown above.

Howard's Addition 8/10/1685 – 70/72 acres. LNS2i/113
SR7271
Location: MNH by the North Runn of the South River.
Persons mentioned: **Robert Jones & George Yate** (assignors
of land rights).

Howard, Samuel

Howard's Hope 8/4/1664 – 100/77 acres. L7/251 SR7349
Location: MNH on the south side of the Severn River.
Persons mentioned: **Cornelius, Matthew, & John Howard**
(brothers of Samuel and assignors of land rights.

Howard's Inheritance 5/1/1700 – 449/446 acres. LCDi/45
SR7346
Location: MNH on the south side of the Severn River.
Persons mentioned: **Coll Henry Darnall** (Surveyor Generall).
Cornelius Howard & James Warner (owners of tracts
"surveyed" into Howard's Inheritance).

Howell, Thomas

Unnamed Patent 8/27/1658 – 100/100 acres. LQ/92
SR7345
Location: MNH on the south side of the Severn River
adjoining the riverside and Howell's Creek.
Persons mentioned: **Elizabeth Howell** (wife, transported by
Howell to this Province here to inhabit). **Francis Beasley**
(neighbor).

Howerton, John

Howerton's Range 9/1/1670 – 400/370 acres. L14/87
SR7356
Location: HCH on the north side of a branch of the Patuxent
River.
Persons mentioned: **George Yate** (assignor of land rights).
Gabriel Parrott (neighbor). *Note: Note the patent document*

says that the tract is in Calvert County but adjoining an Anne Arundel tract (owned by Gabriel Parrot) on the <u>west side.</u> The rest of the location information is not decisive. The tract is included because it probably was located in Anne Arundel County.

Hudson, John

Lancaster Plaine 5/1/1676 – 180/151 acres. L19/357 SR7360

Location: MNH on the south side of the Severn River at Indian Branch.

Persons mentioned: Thomas Hedge (assignor of land rights).

Huggings, Richard & Wheeler, John

Timber Neck 8/20/1665 – 200/199 acres. L8/150 SR7370

Location: SRH on the south side of South River at Jacob's Creek.

Persons mentioned: George Puddington (assignor of land rights). Richard Beard. Richard Cheney, Marin Duvall, & William Young (neighbors).

Huggings, Richard

Huggings' Advantage 8/5/1664 – 50/50 acres. L7/294 SR7349

Location: SRH on the south side of South River adjoining a tract called Covell's Folly.

Persons mentioned: John Version (assignor of land rights and transporter of John Hutton to this Province here to inhabit in 1657). Ann Covell & Archer Arbuckle (neighbors).

Hunt, William

Hunt's Chance 9/25/1663 – 400/400 acres. L5/602 SR7347

Location: HCH in the woods about two miles west of Herring Creek.

Persons mentioned: Richard Wells and Joseph Morley

(neighbors).

Maid Stone 9/25/1663 – 350/350 acres. L5/600 SR7347
Location: HCH on the West side of the plantations of
Herring Creek Bay.
Persons mentioned: Francis Billingsly, Capt. Sampson
Warring (assignors of land rights). Sammuel & Thomas
Ford (neighbors).

Hunt, Wolfran
Hunt's Range 8/10/1684 – 200/199 acres. LSDA/449
SR7369
Location: B&TNH on a branch of Curtis Creek of the
Patapsco River.
Persons mentioned: William Ball (neighbor).

Illingsworth, Richard
Rattlesnake Point 2/6/1667 – 50/48 acres. L17/536
SR7358
Location: B&TNH at the head of a marsh adjoining a tract
called Burle's Marsh.
Persons mentioned: George Yate & Jerome White, Esq.
(assignors of land rights). Richard Ewen, Gent & Robert
Burle (neighbors). Matthew Clark (current owner of
Richard Ewen's neighboring tract).

Jackson, Isaac *(Cooper)*
Jackson's Venture 6/3/1686 – 350/350 acres. L22/182
SR7363
Location: B&TNH on the south side of the Patapsco River.
Persons mentioned: George Hope (neighbor). *Note: The
patent/survey document places this tract in Baltimore
County. MSA Land Index #55 places it in Anne Arundel
County. I have included it here based on its location.*

Jackson, James

Jackson's Chance 9/8/1687 – 150/150 acres. LNS2i/503
SR7311
Location: B&TNH on the west side of Curtis Creek at
Cabbin Branch.
Persons mentioned: **George Hope** (neighbor). *Note: The
patent/survey document places this tract in Baltimore
County. MSA Land Index #55 places it in Anne Arundel
County. I have included it here based on its location.*

James, John

Unnamed Patent 8/25/1658 – 300/300 acres. LQ/171
SR7345
Location: MNH next adjoining Tolley Point and The
Chesapeake Bay.
Persons mentioned: **William James**, father of John, who
transported himself, **Ann**, his wife and **James** his son into this
Province here to inhabit. **Thomas Tolley** (neighbor).

James' Hill 8/4/1664 – 100/69 acres. L7/225 SR7349
Location: MNH on the south side of the Severn River.
Persons mentioned: **Robert Babb & Edmond Thomas**
(persons transported by **James** into this Province here to
inhabit). **Samuel Withers** (neighbor).

James His Fancy 6/1/1685 – 55/59 acres. LNSBi/139
SR7370
Location: HCH on the east side of the Patuxent River in the
woods next adjoining a tract called Birkhead's Chance.
Persons mentioned: **Robert Jones** (assignor of land rights).

Treover 5/1/1701 – 100/72 acres. Ldd5i/43 SR7378
Location: B&TNH in Elk Ridge next adjoining a tract called
Heath's Choice.
Persons mentioned: **Edward Hunt** (assignor of land rights).
Ridgely (neighbor). *Note: This tract was located in
Baltimore County at the time of the patent/survey. I have
included it because the land had been, and would again be,
designated as Anne Arundel County before being absorbed*

into present day Howard County.

Jeffe, Thomas
> Jeffe's Encrease 5/10/1683 – 180/100 acres. LSDA/176
> SR7369
> Location: MNH on the north side of the South River next
> adjoining a tract called Wardrop Ridge.
> Persons mentioned: Henry Hanslap (assignor of land rights).

Jeffe, William
> Jeffe's Search 2/18/1688 – 39/39 acres. NSBi/676 SR7370
> Location: MNH on the north side of the South River.
> Persons mentioned: Thomas Richardson (assignor of land
> rights). Robert Parnaby, John Dorsey & William
> Fergueson (neighbors).

Johnson, Davy *(Planter)*
> The Dividing Point 10/7/1665 - 100/83 acres. L9/200
> SR7351
> Location: B&TNH on the south side of the Patapsco River
> and on the west side of Patapsco Creek.
> Persons mentioned: None.

Jones, Edward
> The Tryall 4/15/1685 – 164/164 acres. L22/252 SR7363
> Location: B&TNH on the south side of the Maggoty River at
> Short's Creek.
> Persons mentioned: Richard Beard (assignor of land rights).

Jones, John
> Push Pinn 10/1/1700 – 200/200 acres. LDD5i/15 SR7378
> Location: B&TNH on the Middle Runn of the Patuxent River
> next adjoining a tract called Dooughegan.
> Persons mentioned: Elizabeth Hunt (assignor of land rights).
> Charles Carroll (neighbor). *Note: This tract was located in
> Baltimore County at the time of the patent/survey. I have
> included it because the land had been, and would again be,*

*designated as Anne Arundel County before being absorbed
into present day Howard County.*

Unnamed Patent 8/25/1658 – 300/300 acres. KAB&H/290
SR7344
Location: MNH adjoining Tolley Point.
Persons mentioned: **Ann Jones** (wife), **John Jones** (son)
(persons transported by **William Jones**, late of Ann Arundall
County). **Thomas Tolley** (neighbor).

Jones, Robert

Unnamed Patent 8/20/1658 – 100/98 acres. LQ/167
SR7345
Location: SRH on the main branch of Herring Creek.
Persons mentioned: **William Stephenson** (transporter of
Dermott Mahalone into this Province here to inhabit).
Robert Jones (transporter of his wife **Annis** to this Province
here to inhabit). **Robert Cadger** (neighbor).

Jones, William

The Friend's Choice 8/8/1670 – 340/328 acres. L14/12
SR7356
Location: SRH on west side of South River.
Persons mentioned: **George Yate** (assignor of land rights).
Robert Franklin (neighbor).

Jones His Lott 8/8/1673 – 350/332 acres. L13/43 Sr7355
Location: SRH on the south side of the South River next
adjoining a tract called Hickory Hills.
Persons mentioned: **Robert Franklin & Richard Beard**
(neighbors).

Waterford 5/1/1674 – 800/813 acres. L19/347 SR7360
Location: SRH on the North Branch of the Patuxent River.
Persons mentioned: **Thomas Taylor & John Dearing**
(neighbors).

The Addition 10/10/1704 – 50/51 acres. LSDF/517
SR7373-2
Location: MNH on the south side of the Severn River
Persons mentioned: None.

Jordan, Thomas

Jordan's Adventure 7/29/1664 – 600/628 acres. L7/211
SR7349
Location: In Calvert or Anne Arundel County on the east side of the Patuxent River.
Persons mentioned: John Burrage and Walter Carr (assignors of land rights). Thomas Spriggs (neighbor).
Note: The patent document places this tract in Calvert County. Anne Arundel County Rent Rolls 1651-1774 (MSA SR7346) show it as being in the Herring Creek Hundred of Anne Arundel County. I have included it here based on its location (east side of Patuxent River).

Kendall, Daniel

Kendall's Delight 5/1/1701 – 500 acres. LWD/363
SR7372-2
Location: B&TNH on the north side of the North Branch of the Patuxent River.
Persons mentioned: Samuel Dryer & John Dodderidge (neighbors). *Note 1: This tract was located in Baltimore County at the time of the patent/survey. I have included it because the land had been, and would again be, designated as Anne Arundel County before being absorbed into present day Howard County. Note 2: The tract cannot be drawn and the actual acreage cannot be determined due to incomplete boundary course information in the patent document.*

Kendall's Enlargement *(date not shown)* – 400/409 acres. LCDi/177 SR7356
Location: BNTNH on the north side of the North Branch of the Patuxent River next adjoining a tract called Kendall's Delight.
Persons mentioned: None. *Note: This tract was located in*

Baltimore County at the time of the patent/survey. I have included it because the land had been, and would again be, designated as Anne Arundel County before being absorbed into present day Howard County.

Kendall, John

Kendall's Purchase 3/26/1696 – 100/102 acres. LWD/141 SR7372
Location: B&TNH on the north side of the Maggity River.
Persons mentioned: **Major Edward Dorsey** (assignor of land rights). **Josias Hall & George Burges** (neighbors).

Ketlin, Richard

Bold Venture 6/1/1700 – 200/167 acres. LDD5i/15 SR7378
Location: B&TNH on the main road to Elk Ridge.
Persons mentioned: **James Carroll** (Deputy Surveyor). *Note: This tract lies in present day Howard County.*

King, Joseph

King's Venture 10/10/1704 – 50/51 acres. LSDF/528 SR7373-2
Location: MNH on the forke of The Patuxent River.
Persons mentioned: None.

Kinsey, Paul *(Planter)*

Curtis Neck 6/29/1663 – 200/196 acres. L5/374 SR7347
Location: B&TNH on the south side of the Patapsco River by Broad Creek..
Persons mentioned: **John Collett**, Gent (assignor of land rights). *Note: The patent document places this tract in Baltimore County. I have included it here based on its location and proximity to Anne Arundel County tracts.*

White Oak Spring 6/29/1663 – 150/140 acres. L5/370 SR7347
Location: B&TNH on the south side of the Patapsco River.
Persons mentioned: **John Collett**, Gent (assignor of land

rights). *Note: The patent document places this tract in Baltimore County. I have included it here based on its location and proximity to Anne Arundel County tracts.*

Paul's Neck 6/30/1663 – 200/197 acres. L5/373 SR7347
Location: B&TNH on the south side of the Patapsco River by Broad Creek.
Persons mentioned: Alexander Mountnety, planter (assignor of land rights). *Note: The patent document places this tract in Baltimore County. I have included it here based on its location and proximity to Anne Arundel County tracts.*

Spring Point 6/30/1663 – 100/100 acres. L5/374 SR7347
Location: B&RNH on the South Branch of the Patapsco River.
Persons mentioned: **Margarett Kinsey** (**Paul's** mother and the assignor of land rights).
Note: The patent document places this tract in Baltimore County. I have included it here based on its location and proximity to Anne Arundel County tracts.

Brendon 8/17/1663 – 250/160 acres. L6/104 SR7348
Location: B&TNH on the south side of the Patapsco River and on the south side, at the mouth, of Deep Creek.
Persons mentioned: None.

Harborrow 8/6/1664 – 350/365 acres. L7/320 SR7349
Location: B&TNH on the south side of the South Branch of the Patapsco River.
Persons mentioned: **Joseph Wicks** (assignor of land rights). **John Thomas, John Davis, Abraham Messenger, Catherine Kinsey, & Elizabeth Beane** (persons transported by Kinsey into this Province to inhabit). **Nicholas Davis & Roger Rice** (persons transported by Joseph Wicks into this Province to inhabit).

Paul Kinsey, Jr.

Duke's Cove Res. 6/10/1671 – 350/335 acres. L14/244
SR7356
Location: B&TNH on the west side of the Patapsco River.
Persons mentioned: Paul Kinsey (deceased father of Paul,
Jr.). Richard Ewan (former owner). *Note: This tract may
have been known as Dake's Cove.*

Kirkland, Robert
The Girles Porcon 6/4/1672 – 100/100 acres. LCDi/310
SR7376
Location: B&TNH in Elk Ridge between the branches of the
Patuxent River next adjoining a tract called Doughoregan.
Persons mentioned: Charles Carroll (neighbor). *Note: This
tract was located in Baltimore County at the time of the
patent/survey. I have included it because the land had been,
and would again be, designated as Anne Arundel County
before being absorbed into present day Howard County.*

Knighton, Thomas
Knighton's Fancy 5/1/1672 –100/109 acres. L16/581
SR7357
Location: B&TNH on the south side of the Patapsco River
next adjoining a tract called White Oak Spring.
Persons mentioned: Robert Wilson (assignor of land rights).
Paule Kinsey & Richard Mascall (neighbors).

Knighton's Purchase 7/20/1680 – 197/187 acres.
LCB2i/37 SR7366
Location: HCH three miles west of Herring Creek in the
woods.
Persons mentioned: George Holland (assignor of land
rights). Humphrey Emmerton (neighbor).

Ladd, Richard
Charles His Gift 5/16/1676 – 1,000/1133 acres. L19/273
SR7360
Location: Three Holes area near the Bayside.

<u>Persons mentioned:</u> **Joseph Horsely & Richard Preston** (former owners). **Thomas Cole** (neighbor). *Note 1: The tract was originally patented by Richard Preston as Preston's Clifts, on 4/26/1650. Subsequently, it was sold to Joseph Horsely who died without heirs and the tract escheated to the LOP and was granted to Ladd. Note 2: The 3-holes area is not a hundred. This designation identifies a small number of tracts adjoining a cliff with three holes that served as a landmark. Other than being in Ann Arundell Manor, there is nothing in the patent documents to indicate where this cliff or these tracts were located.*

Lambert/Covell/Covill/Mott, Ann *(widow)*

Covell's Cove 1661 – 430/425 acres. L5/292 SR7347
<u>Location:</u> MNH on the north side of South River adjoining the west side of Broad Creek.
<u>Persons mentioned:</u> **Neale Clarke,** planter (neighbor). *Note: Although patented as Covell's Cove, in 1681, Ann Lambert sold separate pieces of this tract to **Samuel White & John Robinson** listing the tract name as Covell's Troubles in later years. Following her death, the administrators of her estate restored the legally correct name (Covell's Cove) to the remaining portion of the tract.*

Covell's Folly 5/29/1663 – 500/386 acres. L5/293 SR7347
<u>Location:</u> SRH on the south side of the South River and on west side of The Flatt Creek next adjoining a tract called Elk Thickett.
<u>Persons mentioned:</u> **John Covill/Covell,** deceased (former husband of **Ann Covell**). **Archer Arbuckle** (neighbor).

Rocky Point 7/8/1680 – 50/12 acres. LCB2i/13 SR7366
<u>Location:</u> MNH on the north side of South River at Forked Branch.
<u>Persons mentioned:</u> **George Holland** (assignor of land rights). *Note: The discrepancy between certified and actual acreage is extreme, even for this period. However, the boundary courses have been verified and the acreage is*

correct as shown above.

Larkin, John

Lark's Hill 6/26/1663 – 450/296 acres. L5/359 SR7347
Location: SRH westward of a creek of the Rode River called
Muddy Creek.
Persons mentioned: Thomas Taylor (assignor of land rights).

Larkin's Choice 8/12/1670 – 311/311 acres. L14/44
SR7356
Location: SRH adjoining a tract named Champe's Adventure.
Persons mentioned: George Yate (assignor of land rights).
John Champe (neighbor).

Mill Haven 2/26/1682 – 201/210 acres. LCB3i/145
SR7367
Location: WRH on Beaver Dam Branch.
Persons mentioned: Dominic Marimon, Andrew Roberts,
Robert Lloyd, & Thomas Winant (neighbors).

Lawe, William

Lawe's Chance 5/27/1675 – 46/44 acres. L19/16 SR7360
Location: SRH on the western branch of Back Creek of the
Road River.
Persons mentioned: George Yate (assignor of land rights).
Richard Snowden (neighbor).

Lawrence. Benjamin

Benjamin's Fortune 12/10/1679 – 115 acres. L20/348
SR7361
Location: WRH next adjoining a tract called Ewen Upon
Ewenton.
Persons mentioned: William Richardson (assignor of land
rights). Richard Ewen & Fernando Batten (neighbors).
*Note: The tract cannot be drawn and the actual acreage
cannot be determined due to incomplete boundary course
information in the patent document.*

Lazenby, Charles Calvert

Portland Manor Part Of 7/10/1701 – 1,000 acres.
LCDi/111 SR7376
Location: HCH adjoining the **Widow Dalb's** plantation.
Persons mentioned: None. *Note: The tract cannot be drawn and the actual acreage cannot be determined due to incomplete boundary course information in the patent document.*

Leafe, Francis

The Narrow 9/9/1679 – 100/103 acres. L21/76 SR7362
Location: B&TNH on the south side of the Patapsco River and on the north side of Stoney Creek.
Persons mentioned: None. *Note: The patent document places this tract in Baltimore County. I have included it here based on its location and proximity to Anne Arundel County tracts.*

Lewis, Henry

Lewis His Addition 9/20/1680 – 325/325 acres. LCBi/702
SR7366
Location: B&TNH between the Maggity & Severn Rivers.
Persons mentioned: **James Crouch, Jr. & George Yate** (assignors of land rights). **Christopher Rowles** (neighbor).

Linham, John

Linham's Search 6/12/1688 – 38/41 acres. LNSB2i/718
SR7371
Location: SRH on the south side of the South River on the north side of Selby's Creek.
Persons mentioned: **Thomas Richardson** (assignor of land rights). **Edward Selby, John Brewer, & Edward Loarson** (neighbors).

Linnescomb, Thomas

Linnescomb's Stopp 7/4/1677 – 50/50 acres. L15/695
SR4327
Location: SRH on the south side of the South River next adjoining a tract called Margaret's Fields.

Persons mentioned: Adam DeLapp (neighbor).

Linnescomb's Lott 5/22/1679 – 70 acres. L20/256 SR7361
Location: SRH on the north side of Three Island Bay at the head of the Great Pond.
Persons mentioned: **George Yate** (assignor of land rights).
Adam DeLapp (neighbor).
Note: The tract cannot be drawn and the actual acreage cannot be determined due to incomplete boundary course information in the patent document.

Linthicum, Thomas
Linthicum Walks 10/10/1704 – 631/624 acres. LRYi /368 SR7468
Location: SRH on the west side of the South River adjoining a tract called Coape's Hill.
Persons mentioned: **Coll. Henry Darnall** (Surveyor Generall).

Lloyd, Edward, Esq. *(Councillman)*
Unnamed Cert 12/2/1650 – 570 acres. LAB&H/255 SR7344
Location: B&TNH on the north side of Severn River.
Persons mentioned: None. *Note: The tract cannot be drawn and the actual acreage cannot be determined due to incomplete boundary course information in the patent document.*

Pendenny 2/15/1659 – 200/178 acres. L4/466 SR 7346
Location: B&TNH on the north side of the Severn River by the riverside.
Persons mentioned: None.

Swan Neck 2/16/1659 – 600 acres. L4/475 SR7346
Location: B&TNH on the north side of the Severn River by the riverside.
Persons mentioned: None. *Note: The tract cannot be drawn and the actual acreage cannot be determined due to*

incomplete boundary course information in the patent document.

Landisell 9/15/1659 – 425/406 acres. L4/109 SR7316
Location: B&TNH on the north side of the Patapsco River near the Broad Creek.
Persons mentioned: **Richard Owens & Nicholas Gassaway** (persons transported by Lloyd in 1649, here to inhabit).
Note: The patent document places this tract in Baltimore County. I have included it here based on its location and proximity to Anne Arundel County tracts.

Lloyd, John

Lloyd's Chance 6/17/1686 – 60/61 acres. L22/249 SR7363
Location: B&TNH on the south side of the Maggity River next adjoining a tract called Floyd's Chance.
Persons mentioned: **Lawrence Draper** (assignor of land rights). **John Gray & William Luffman** (neighbors).

Lloyd, Robert, Esq.

Triangle Neck 8/5/1666 – 100/101 acres. L7/284 SR7349
Location: SRH on the south side of the Rode River on the north side of Beaver Dam Neck.
Persons mentioned: **Thomas Games** (assignor of land rights). **Denis McConough** (neighbor).

Lockwood, Robert

The Triangle 4/12/1670 – 100 acres. L14/184 SR735
Location: WRH northward of Ann Arundell Manor adjoining a tract called The Hole.
Persons mentioned: **Thomas Taylor & Jerome White** (assignors of land rights). **Thomas Harwood** (neighbor).
Note: The tract cannot be drawn and the actual acreage cannot be determined due to incomplete boundary course information in the patent document.

Lockwood's Addition 5/10/1673 – 100/80 acres. L19/299 SR7360

Location: WRH in Herring Cr. Swamp on the north side of the North Branch of Deep Cr.

Persons mentioned: **William Shepherd** (transported by **Lockwood** to this Province to inhabit). **Edward Parrish** (neighbor).

Lockwood's Lott 7/20/1674 – 100/100 acres. L18/257 SR7359

Location: WRH next adjoining a tract called Water Town.

Persons mentioned: **Robert Wilson** (assignor of land rights). **Nicholas Waterman** (neighbor).

Lockwood's Range 5/10/1676 – 235/234 acres. L19/341 SR7360

Location: WRH in Herring Creek Swamp.

Persons mentioned: **Edward Parrish & Thomas Harwood** (assignors of land rights). **Richard Talbott** (neighbor).

Lockwood's Adventure 5/5/1679 – 400/400 acres. L20/261 SR7361

Location: B&TNH on the south side of the Patapsco River and on the east side of Galloway's Branch.

Persons mentioned: **Anthony Holland** (neighbor*). Note: The patent/survey document places this tract in Baltimore County. MSA Land Index #55 places it in Anne Arundel County. I have included it here based on its location.*

Lockwood's Security 10/5/1683 – 170/269 acres. LSDA/64 SR7369

Location: WRH in Herring Creek Swamp.

Persons mentioned: **Henry Hanslap** (assignor of land rights). **Nicholas Waterman** (neighbor). *Note: The discrepancy between certified and actual acreage is extreme, even for this period. However, the boundary courses have been verified and the acreage is correct as shown above.*

Lockwood's Park 10/5/1685 - 50/41 acres. LCB3/351
SR7367
Location: WRH in Herring Creek Swamp adjoining The
Chesapeake Bay & Island Creek.
Persons mentioned: **Henry Hanslap** (assignor of land rights)
Edw. Parrish (neighbor).

Little Buxton 6/5/1687 – 29/29 acres. LIB&IL/269
SR7368-2
Location: WRH in Herring Creek Swamp.
Persons mentioned: **John Gray** (assignor of land rights).
John Cumber (neighbor).

Tearecoat Thickett 6/5/1687 – 108/105 acres.
LIB&ILC/209 SR7368
Location: WRH in Herring Creek Swamp by Cattaile
Swamp.
Persons mentioned: **John Gray** (assignor of land rights).
John Cumber & Robert Franklin (neighbors).

Lockwood's Luck 7/6/1698 – 50/83 acres. LCC4/2
SR7375
Location: WRH at Herring Creek adjoining Beaver Dam
Branch.
Persons mentioned: **James Ford** (neighbor).

Lockwood, Thomas
Lockwood's Great Park 6/12/1688 – 33 acres. LNS2/733
SR7371
Location: WRH on the north side of Island Creek.
Persons mentioned: **Thomas Richardson** (assignor of land
rights). *Note: The tract cannot be drawn and the actual
acreage cannot be determined due to incomplete boundary
course information in the patent document.*

Lorbitt, John

    Chinkopinn Forrest 6/22/1694 – 61/59 acres. LBB3B/10
    SR7374
    Location: B&TNH on the north side of Deep Creek next
    adjoining a tract called Brandon.
    Persons mentioned: **Richard Beard** (assignor of land rights).
    Note: The patent/survey document places this tract in
    Baltimore County. MSA Land Index #55 places it in Anne
    Arundel County. I have included it here based on its
    location.

Love, Robert

    Love's Neck 8/12/1664 – 50/45 acres. L7/246 SR7349
    Location: SRH on the north side of the Road River between
    Shaw's & Woolman's Creeks.
    Persons mentioned: **Robert Lloyd** (assignor of land rights).

Luffman, William

    Luffman's Due 9/5/1685 – 131/131 acres. L22/250
    SR7363.
    Location: B&TNH on the south side of the Maggity River.
    Persons mentioned: **Richard Jones & Richard Beard**
    (assignors of land rights). **Joseph Green** (neighbor).

Lunn, Edward

    Lunn's Addition 8/10/1683 - 55/55 acres. LCBi/279
    SR7367
    Location: B&TNH between the Ann Arundell *(Severn)* &
    Maggity Rivers adjoining tracts called Asketon and Little
    Netlam.
    Persons mentioned: **Henry Hanslap** (assignor of land rights).
    John Smith, Edward Bates & Edward Bowsley
    (neighbors).

Lusby. Robert

    Lusby 8/5/1664 – 50 acres. L7/286 SR7349
    <u>Location:</u> B&TNH on the north side of the Severn River on
    the west side of Ferry Creek.
    <u>Persons mentioned:</u> **Thomas Mears, Phillip Howard, &**
    Thomas Brown (neighbors). *Note: The tract cannot be*
    drawn and the actual acreage cannot be determined due to
    incomplete boundary course information in the patent
    document.

Lynthicum, Hezikiah

    Duvall's Range Res. 11/25/1703 – 1,527/1,493 acres.
    LDD5i/469 SR7378
    <u>Location:</u> MNH between the South and Severn Rivers next
    adjoining a tract called Owen Woods Thickett.
    <u>Persons mentioned:</u> None.

Lytfoote, Thomas

    The Health 7/4/1684 – 236/221 acres. L22/98 SR7363
    <u>Location:</u> B&TNH between the Maggity & Patapsco Rivers
    next adjoining a tract called Pawson's Plains.
    <u>Persons mentioned:</u> **Thomas Richardson** (assignor of land
    rights). *Note 1: Rights were certified for 284 acres but only*
    236 were granted. No explanation found. Note 2: A
    marginal note states that Lytefoote assigned this tract to
    George Yate (same reference). Yate's patent for this tract
    was not found.

    The Addition 7/8/1684 – 48/50 acres. L22/94 SR7363
    <u>Location:</u> MNH in the woods between the South & Severn
    Rivers next adjoining a tract called The March.
    <u>Persons mentioned:</u> **Thomas Richardson** (assignor of land
    rights). **George Yate** (Deputy Surveyor and neighbor).
    George Talbott, Esq. (Surveyor Generall).

    The Range 8/10/1684 – 384/430 acres. LDSA/484 SR7369

Location: MNH about one mile from the head of the Ann Arundell River next adjoining a tract called The March.
Persons mentioned: Capt. Richard Hill (assignor of land rights).

The Pleasant Hills 11/17/1686 – 350/ 343 acres. L22/290 SR7363
Location: B&TNH on the south side of the Patapsco River by a draught of Cabbin Branch of Curtis Creek next adjoining tracts called Body's Adventure and Knighton's Fancy.
Persons mentioned: None. *Note: The patent/survey document places this tract in Baltimore County. MSA Land Index #55 places it in Anne Arundel County. I have included it here based on its location.*

MacDowell, William

Unnamed Patent 2/11/1651 – 200/184 acres. L5/237 SR7347
Location: MNH on the Chesapeake Bay.
Persons mentioned: **Thomas Cole & Robert Howard** (assignors of land rights). **Pricilla Cole** (wife of Thomas Cole who was transported by him to this Province to inhabit). **Thomas Todd** (neighbor).

Maddox/Maddock, Thomas

Maddox Adventure 6/4/1683 – 148/147 acres. LSDA/422 SR7369
Location: SRH on the south side of the South River next adjoining a tract called Roper's Range.
Persons mentioned: **George Yate** (assignor of land rights).

Rachell's Hope 6/4/1683 – 72/89 acres. LCB3i/514 SR7367
Location: SRH on the south side of the South River on the south side of the Flatt Creek.
Persons mentioned: **George Yate** (assignor of land rights). **Richard Beard** (neighbor).

Marsh, John

Marshe's Forrest 11/10/1696 – 60/63 acres. LCC4i/11
SR7375
Location: MNH near to the branches of the Severn River.
Persons mentioned: Charles Stevens & Nicholas Shepherd
(neighbors.)

Marsh, Sarah

The Heir's Purchase 5/20/1664 – 90/90 acres.
L44/SR7349
Location: B&TNH on the north side of the Severn River
adjoining Woolchurch Cove.
Persons mentioned: Thomas Marsh, Jr. (son of Sarah
Marsh).

Marsh, Thomas *(merchant)*

Unnamed Certification 10/21/1651 – 150/147 acres.
LAB&H/260 SR7344
Location: HCH on the west side of Herring Creek near the
head of a branch of The West Creek called Parker's Branch.
Persons mentioned: None. *Note: A marginal note states that
the tract was patented by* **John Hall,** *as Marshes Seate, in
1661.*

Unnamed Certification 10/25/1651 – 1,000/996 acres.
LAB&H/261 SR7344
Location: HCH adjoining the Chesapeake Bay.
Persons mentioned: Richard Bennett (neighbor).

Unnamed Certification 10/27/1651 – 600/499 acres.
LAB&H/461 SR7344
Location: MNH on the north side of the South River.
Persons mentioned: John Norwood (neighbor). *Note 1: a
marginal note indicates that this tract was named The
Manning. No patent found under this name. Note 2: The
discrepancy between certified and actual acreage is extreme,
even for this period. However, the boundary courses have*

147

been verified and the acreage is correct as shown above.

Poplar Neck 8/20/1652 - 300 acres. LAB&H/298 SR7344
Location: Isle of Kent on the east side of the island near the
head of Smith's Creek.
Persons mentioned: **Robert Clark** (Surveyor). *Note 1:
Although located on Kent Island, a cert for this tract is
shown in AA County listings in the MSA Land Index #54.
Also, a marginal note says, "Patt AA fol" which I have
interpreted to mean that it was patented and in Anne
Arundel Mannor although, a patent was not found. Note 2:
The tract cannot be drawn and the actual acreage cannot be
determined due to incomplete boundary course information
in the patent document.*

Mascall/Maschall, Richard *(Planter)*
Mascall's Rest 10/10/1670 – 230/232 acres. L16/158
SR7357
Location: B&TNH on the west side of the Patapsco River
next adjoining a tract called White Oak Spring.
Persons mentioned: **John Boring** (carpenter), **Robert
Wilson, & John Pawson** (assignors of land rights). **Paul
Kinsey** and the **Orphans Kinsey** (neighbors). *Note: The
tract was patented on 7/1/1671 and escheated to his LOPs.
Granted to* **George Yate** *in 1678.*

Mascall's Adventure 7/10/1671 – 140/138 acres. L14/286
SR7356
Location: B&TNH on the South side of Patapsco Creek of
the Patapsco River.
Persons mentioned: **John Boring** (assignor of land rights).
Richard Dorrill (neighbor).

Mascall's Hope 6/30/1699 – 100 acres. L12/311 SR7354
Location: B&TNH on the south side of Curtis Creek
adjoining a tract named The Range.
Persons mentioned: **George Yate** (assignor of land rights).
Henry Goodrick (neighbor).

Note: The tract cannot be drawn and the actual acreage cannot be determined due to incomplete boundary course information in the patent document.

MacClannin, James *(Planter)*

Little Beginning 8/22/1709 – 19/23 acres. LDD5i/523 SR7378

Location: HCH next adjoining tracts called Wells and Holland's Addition.

Persons mentioned: **George Wells** (neighbor). *Note: This patent is included because the Cert and/or Survey date was within the targeted period.*

McConnough, Dennis

Beaver Dam Neck 12/7/1662 – 100/100 acres. L5/624 SR7347

Location: SRH on the west side at the head of the Rode River on the south side of Muddy Creek.

Persons mentioned: None.

McCubbin, John

Timber Neck 9/15/1665 – 40/24 acres. L8/294 SR7350

Location: MNH on the north side of the South River near the mouth of Broad Creek.

Persons mentioned: None.

Meade, Francis

Beare Neck 7/7/1687 – 225/239 acres. LCB2i/152 SR7366

Location: B&TNH on the north side of Cattail Cr. on the south side of the Maggity River.

Persons mentioned: **George Holland** (assignor of land rights).

Meares/Meers, Thomas

Meares 10/27/1651 – 400/370 acres. LAB&H/262 SR7344

Location: Three Holes area adjoining the Chesapeake Bay.

Persons mentioned: **Leonard Strong** (neighbor). *Note 1: The patent conveys two adjoining tracts. The larger was* *patented as Meares. The smaller tract is unnamed. Note 2: The 3-hole area is not a hundred. This designation identifies a small number of tracts adjoining a cliff with three holes that served as a landmark. Other than being in Ann Arundell Manor, there is nothing in the patent documents to indicate where this cliff or these tracts were located.*

Unnamed Cert 10/27/1651 – 100/92 acres. LAB&H/262 SR 7344

Location: Three holes area adjoining the Chesapeake Bay and a tract called Meares.

Persons mentioned: **Leonard Strong,** (neighbor). *Note 1: This tract was conveyed in the same patent document as Meares, above. Note 2: The 3-holes area is not a hundred. This designation identifies a small number of tracts adjoining a cliff with three holes that served as a landmark. Other than being in Ann Arundell Manor, there is nothing in the patent documents to indicate where this cliff or these tracts were located.*

The Expectation 8/20/1665 – 300 acres. L8/141 SR7350

Location: Three holes area on the north side of the Severn River on a cliff over the riverside.

Persons mentioned: None. *Note 1: The 3-holes area is not a hundred. This designation identifies a small number of tracts adjoining a cliff with three holes that served as a landmark. Other than being in Ann Arundell Manor, there is nothing in the patent documents to indicate where this cliff or these tracts were located. Note 2: The tract cannot be drawn and the actual acreage cannot be determined due to incomplete boundary course information in the patent document.*

Medcalfe/Metcalfe, John

Medcalfe's Chance 8/10/1685 – 80/71 acres. LSDA/104 SR7369

Location: MNH among the branches of the South River next adjoining a tract called Howard & Porter's Range.

Persons mentioned: Coll Wm. Burges & Henry Hanslip
(assignors of land rights).

Medcalfe's Mount 5/10/1685 – 70/70 acres. LNSBi/174
SR7370
Location: MNH between the branches of the North Runn of
South River next adjoining tracts called Medcalfe's Chance
and Howard & Porter's Range.
Persons mentioned: Robert Jones & George Yate (assignors
of land rights).

Batchellor's Hall 3/26/1695 – 180 acres. LC3i/298
SR7377
Location: B&TNH at Elk Ridge adjoining a tract called
Timber Neck.
Persons mentioned: John Dorsey (assignor of land rights).
Elinor Harbitt & William Budd (neighbors). *Note 1: This
tract lies in present day Howard County. Note 2: The tract
cannot be drawn and the actual acreage cannot be
determined due to incomplete boundary course information
in the patent document.*

Range 12/6/1703 – 75/44 acres. LDD5i/193 SR7378
Location: WRH adjoining Cattaile Slash and a tract called
Crouchley's Choice
Persons mentioned: None.

Range Res. 4/2/1706 – 75/45 acres. LWD/551 SR7372-1
Location: MNH on the north side of the South River.
Persons mentioned: John Baldwin (former owner). *Note:
This tract was patented by John Baldwin in 1666, as
Baldwin's Addition.*

Meeke, Guy
Guy's Rest 8/1670 – 100/98 acres. L13/32 SR7355
Location: MNH on the south side of the Severn River next
adjoining a tract called Guy's Will.

Persons mentioned: George Yate (assignor of land rights).

Guy's Will 5/1/1672 –100/92 acres. L14/464 SR7356
Location: MNH at the head of the South River next adjoining
a tract called Guy's Rest.
Persons mentioned: **George Yate & Richard Ewen**
(assignors of land rights).
Francis Watkins & Mary Davis (persons transported by
Meeke into this Province here to inhabit).

Rosse 5/18/1679 – 136/139 acres. L20/203 SR7361
Location: MNH on the south side of the Severn River next
adjoining a tract called Howard's First Choice.
Persons mentioned: **George Yate** (assignor of land rights).
Matthew Howard (neighbor).

Meeke's Rest 10/1/1681 – 350/356 acres. L21/353 SR7362
Location: MNH on the south side of the Ann Arundell River.
Persons mentioned: **Henry Hanslap & Wm. Burges**
(assignors of land rights). *Note: According to the
certification (LWC2/273 SR7340), this is a resurvey and
consolidation of Guy's Rest, Guy's Will, and Rosse into one
tract as the result of a Special Warrant of Resurvey granted
to Meeke on 11/2/1680.*

Weston 8/4/1683 130/129 acres. LSDA/101 SR7369
Location: MNH on the south side of the Ann Arundell River
among the branches of Plum Creek.
Persons mentioned: **Henry Hanslap & Coll William Burges**
(assignors of land rights).

Merriken, Christian *(Widow)*

Merriken 8/25/1666 – 50 acres L8/131 SR7350
Location: B&TNH on the north side of the Severn River and
on the west side of Scotcher's Creek.
Persons mentioned: **Thomas Bradley** (assignor of land
rights). *Note 1: Related information from L10/217 dated*

*6/1/1666: "Laid out for Christin Merriken a parcell of land lying in Ann Arundell County on the north side of Severn River and on the west side of Scotchers Creek....". The following is written on the back of this document: "I the within mentioned Christian Merriken doe afsigne all my rights, title, and interest in and of the land specified unto my son **Hugh Merriken,** son of my late husband **John Merriken,** deceased. Witness my hand 6/25/1666." No explanation found as to why she assigned the tract to her son in June and, then, patented the tract herself in August. Note 2: The tract cannot be drawn and the actual acreage cannot be determined due to incomplete boundary course information in the patent document.*

Merriken, Hugh

Point Lookout 11/10/1695 – 40/43 acres. LC3i/117 SR7377

<u>Location:</u> B&TNH on the north side of Curtis Creek next adjoining a tract called Rockholds Purchase.

<u>Persons mentioned:</u> None. *Note: After mistakenly occupying this 40-acre area, thinking it was within the bounds of his own tract, Merriken purchased it from the LOP for five lbs sterling.*

Merriott, John

Cordwell 10/15/1682 – 300/296 acres. LCB3i/511 SR7367
<u>Location:</u> MNH in the woods about three miles from the head of the Severn River.

<u>Persons mentioned:</u> **Henry Hanslap** (assignor of land rights). **Thomas Brown & Matthew Howard** (neighbors).

Merriton, John

Merriton's Fancy 6/5/1687 500/439 acres. LIB&ILC/268 SR7368-1
<u>Location:</u> SRH on the North Great Branch of the Patuxent River.

<u>Persons mentioned:</u> **John Stinson** (neighbor). *Note: This tract lies in present day Howard County.*

Miller, Christopher

    Soldier's Fortune 10/10/1704 – 100/80 acres. LDSF/539
    SR7373-2
    Location: SRH at the Forke on the North Branch of the
    Patuxent River north of Ivy Hill.
    Persons mentioned: **Richard Snowden, Jr. & James Carroll**
    (assignors of land rights).

Minter, John

    The Encrease 5/15/1668 – 50/33 acres. L11/407 SR7353
    Location: MNH on the south side of the Severn River.
    Persons mentioned: **Henry Sewell** (neighbor).

Mitchell, William *(Planter)*

    Mitchell's Chance 5/10/1682 – 205/185 acres. LNSBi/209
    SR7370
    Location: SRH on the south side of the South River on the
    west side of Puddington's Cr.
    Persons mentioned: **Robert Jones & George Yate** (assignors
    of land rights). **George Puddington & George Westhill**
    (neighbors).

    Mitchell's Addicion 12/17/1704 – 18.5/18 acres.
    LDD5i/211 SR7348
    Location: SRH on the south side of the South River next
    adjoining s tract called Puddington.
    Persons mentioned: **Thomas Larkin** (assignor of land
    rights).

Mitley, Christopher and Elizabeth

    Mitley's Purchase 10/20/1698 - 121/121 acres. LCDi/17
    SR7356
    Location: HCH
    Persons mentioned: **Theodorus Young** (former owner).
    Mordecai Price & John Cumber (neighbors).

Moore, Mordecai, *(Dr).*
>   Moore's Morning Choice 11/10/1685 – 1,358/1,374 **acres.**
>   LC3i/1880 SR7377
>   Location: B&TNH at Elk Ridge on the main branch of the
>   Patapsco River.
>   Persons mentioned: **Edward Talbott** (neighbor). *Note: This*
>   *tract lies in present day Howard County.*

Morley, Joseph & Gray, John
>   Trent 9/17/1666 – 450/450 acres. L10/135 SR7352
>   Location: HCH on the west side of Herring Creek.
>   Persons mentioned: **William Hunt, Nathan Smith,** &
>   **Samuel Chew** (neighbors).

Morley, Joseph *(Planter)*
>   Morley 7/17/1663 – 300/300 acres. L6/102 SR7348
>   Location: HCH about two miles from Herring Creek.
>   Persons mentioned: **Francis Holland,** & **William Hunt**
>   (neighbors).

>   Morley's Choyce 7/4/1671 – 300/300 acres. L16/256
>   SR7357
>   Location: B&TNH on the south side of the Patapsco River on
>   Curtis Creek.
>   Persons mentioned: **Murrene Duvall** (co-owner of land rights
>   and assignor of his share to **Morley**).

>   Morley's Lott 1/20/1667 – 300/300 acres. L11/253 SR7353
>   Location: HCH about three miles from Herring Creek Bay
>   next adjoining tracts called Trent and Gowery Banks.
>   Persons mentioned: None.

>   Morley's Lott 7/10/1671 – 450/471 acres. L16/260
>   SR7357
>   Location: SRH on the southwest side of the South River.
>   Persons mentioned: **Marin Duvall** (assignor of land rights).

Morley's Grove 7/10/1674 – 320 acres. L14/270 SR7356
Location: SRH on a branch of the Patuxent River.
Persons mentioned: **Marin Duvall** (assignor of land rights).
*Note: The tract cannot be drawn and the actual acreage
cannot be determined due to incomplete boundary course
information in the patent document.*

Moss, Ralph

Mosses Discovery 1702 – 100/102 acres. LDD5i/135
SR7378
Location: B&TNH between the Severn & Maggity Rivers on
the north side of Blay's Br.
Persons mentioned: **Robert Eagle** (neighbor).

Moss, Richard *(Planter)*

The Addition 6/20/1688 – 100 acres. L12/29 SR7354
Location: B&TNH at the head of Deep Creek.
Persons mentioned: **Thomas Turner, William Slade,
Richard Young, & Ralph Hawkins** (neighbors). *Note: The
tract cannot be drawn and the actual acreage cannot be
determined due to incomplete boundary course information
in the patent document.*

The Advantage 8/24/1665 – 40/23 acres. L8/110 SR7350
Location: MNH on the south side of the Severn River.
Persons mentioned: **Thomas Turner & Richard Young**
(neighbors).

Mosses Purchase 9/8/1666 – 100/102 acres. L10/147
SR7352
Location: B&TNH in the mountains by the Maggity River
adjoining Indian Swamp.
Persons mentioned: **James Orrouck** (ward of **Richard
Moss**). **John Orrouck** (brother of James and neighbor).

Moss His Purchase 6/1/1667 – 32/32 acres. LNS2i/535
SR7371

Location: B&TNH on the north side of the Maggity River
and on the south side of Deep Creek.
Persons mentioned: George Burges (assignor of land rights).
John Worrell & James Conaway (neighbors).

Murphy, Patrick
    Murphy's Choice 7/19/1684 – 125/124 acres. L22/143
SR7363
Location: B&TNH on the north side of the Maggity River
and on the north side of Gray's Creek.
Persons mentioned: **Richard Beard** (assignor of land rights).
Thomas Turner (neighbor).

    Lucke 10/10/1695 – 15/16 acres. LC3i/511 SR7377
Location: B&TNH on the north side of the Magothy River by
a cove.
Persons mentioned: **George Hope** (assignor of land rights).
*Note: The patent/survey document places this tract in
Baltimore County. MSA Land Index #55 places it in Anne
Arundel County. I have included it here based on its
location.*

Myles/Miles, Thomas
    Watkins 9/21/1652 – 300 acres. LAB&H/276 SR7344
Location: WRH
Persons mentioned: **Roger Grosse** (neighbor). *Note: The
tract cannot be drawn and the actual acreage cannot be
determined due to incomplete boundary course information
in the patent document.*

    Unnamed Certification 9/21/1652 – 300 acres.
LAB&H/276 SR7344
Location: SRH
Persons mentioned: **Roger Grosse** (neighbor). *Note: The
tract cannot be drawn and the actual acreage cannot be
determined due to incomplete boundary course information
in the patent document.*

Mary's Mount 12/10/1664 – 600/610 acres. L4/485
SR7349
Location: WRH on the south side of the Rode River adjoining
the beaver dams.
Persons mentioned: **William Grinnell, Susan Streith,
Nathaniel Heathcoate, Mary Smidrick, George Bell,
Thomas Morgan, Rachell Mitchell, John Daly, Francis
Brown, & Mary Minenock** (persons transported by **Myles**
to this province here to inhabit). **Bartholemew Herring**
(assignor of land rights). **John Watson & John Buzard**
(neighbors). *Note: The grant was for 600 acres although the
certification was for 500 acres. No explanation found.*

Neale, Johnathan

Neale's Purchase 10/10/1695 – 198/193 acres. LB23i/325
SR7365
Location: B&TNH on the north side of the Maggity River
next adjoining a tract called Homewood's Outlett.
Persons mentioned: **Richard Beard** (assignor of land rights).
George Burges (neighbor).

Nettlefold, George

Foldland 2/26/1661 – 200/212 acres. L5/290 SR7347
Location: SRH on the west side of the South River adjoining
a tract called Elk Thickett.
Persons mentioned: **Archibald Arbuckle** (neighbor). *Note: In
8/1663,* **Ruth Nettlefold** *assigned the tract to Richard
Tydings who sold it to* **Elizabeth Burns**, *widow (no date
shown).*

Nettleland 9/17/1666 – 200/200 acres. L5/289 SR7349
Location: SRH on the west side of the South River near the head.
Persons mentioned: None. *Note: The grant conveys two adjoining 100-acre tracts.*

Nicholson, John

Nicholson's Adventure 6/1/1685 – 32/38 acres. LNS2i/167 SR7371
Location: B&TNH on the north side of the Maggity River and on the south side, at the head, of Cornfield Creek next adjoining a tract called Pawson's Plaine.
Persons mentioned: Richard Beard (assignor of land rights). Thomas Turner (neighbor).

Nicholson's Addition 10/19/1695 – 35/35 acres. LB23i/334 SR7365
Location: B&TNH on the north side of the Maggity River adjoining Pawson's Plain.
Persons mentioned: Davis Ellet (assignor of land rights). George Burges & Zacariah Gray (neighbors).

Norman, George

Graves End 8/8/1670 – 30/31 acres. L13/25 SR7355
Location: B&TNH on the north side of the Severn River adjoining a bayside.
Persons mentioned: George Yate (assignor of land rights). John Askew (neighbor).

Norman's Fancy 8/8/1670 – 25/25 acres. L14/37 SR7356
Location: B&TNH on the north side of the Severn River.
Persons mentioned: William Hopkins (assignor of land rights).

Norman. John

Norman's Dams 6/13/1668 – 100/103 acres. L11/483 SR7353

Location: WRH adjoining Muddy Creek.
Persons mentioned: George Yate (Deputy Surveyor). **Jerome White, Esq.** (Surveyor Generall). **Andrew Roberts & Thomas Mills** (neighbors).

Norwood, Andrew

Norwood's Angles 8/10/1684 – 103/109 acres. LSDA/446 SR7369
Location: MNH on the south side of the Ann Arundell River at Todd's Creek.
Persons mentioned: **Robert Jones & George Yate** (assignors of land rights). **Daniel Edge & Richard Petticoate** (neighbors).

Norwood's Recovery 6/10/1686 – 104/103 acres. LIB&ILC/229 SR7368-1
Location: MNH on the south side of the Ann Arundell River to the north of Norwood's Cove.
Persons mentioned: **John Norwood** (neighbor).

Norwood, John, Capt. *(Boatwright)*

Norwood 10/27/1651 - 200/196 acres. LAB&H/264 SR7344
Location: MNH adjoining The Chesapeake Bay.
Persons mentioned: **Thomas Meares** (neighbor). *Note 1: This could be the same tract as Norwood's Unnamed Patent (8/27/1658), included below.*

Norwood 2/8/1658 – 230/333 acres. LQ/396 SR7345
Location: MNH on the south side of the Severn River adjoining a tract called Wayfield.
Persons mentioned: **Joan & Arthur Norwood (Norwood's** children), **Elizabeth Fletcher** (Norwood's servant). All transported by Norwood to this Province to inhabit). **Nicholas Wyatt** (neighbor). *Note: In the same year, John Norwood also claimed, and received, fifty acres of land for transporting **John Harrington** (L5/485 SR7347)*

Unnamed Patent 8/27/1658 – 200 acres. LQ/18 SR7345
Location: MNH adjoining the Chesapeake Bay.
Persons mentioned: Thomas Meares (neighbor). *Note 1:*
Norwood's rights were due him for transporting himself and
his wife to this Province to inhabit. Note 2: The tract cannot
be drawn and the actual acreage cannot be determined due
to incomplete boundary course information in the patent
document.

Norwood's Fancy 2/161659 – 420/381 acres. L4/426
SR7246
Location: SRH on the south side of the Severn River at The
Round Bay.
Persons mentioned: Norwood transported his wife
(unnamed), children Andrew & John, & servants John Hage
& Elizabeth Hills into this Province here to inhabit in 1658.
Also, Thomas Hall & George Barrett in 1657, & Lucy
Child (no date given). *Note: Norwood willed "moiety"in this*
tract to children Andrew, Hannah, Ann, and Elizabeth
Beall. Andrew sold the tract to William Yieldhall and
following his death ownership passed to his brother Charles
Yieldhall who sold the tract to William Griffith.

The Intacke 10/3/1659 – 100 acres L4/425 SR7346
Location: MNH on the south side of the Severn River and the
west side of Dorsey's Creek.
Persons mentioned: Richard Yate, John Field, & Joann
Burrington (persons transported by Norwood into this
Province to inhabit). John Freeman (neighbor). *Note: The*
tract cannot be drawn and the actual acreage cannot be
determined due to incomplete boundary course information
in the patent document.

Oatley, Christopher
Oatley 9/14/1659 – 400 acres. L4/101 SR7346

Location: MNH on the north side of the South River at Oatley's Point.

Persons mentioned: Oatley & **Sampson Warring** transported themselves and two unnamed persons into this Province here to inhabit. *Note 1: Although not mentioned in the patent document,Warring must have assigned his rights to Oatley. Note 2: The tract cannot be drawn and the actual acreage cannot be determined due to incomplete boundary course information in the patent document.*

Orwick/Orruck/Orrourck, James

Orrourck 9/18/1666 – 190/195 acres. L10/146 SR7352
Location: B&TNH in the mountains by the bayside.
Persons mentioned: Thomas Hammond (neighbor).

Orwick's Fancy 8/10/1684 – 150 acres. LSDA/424 SR7369
Location: B&TNH on the north side of Severn River on the east side of Eagle's Nest Bay.
Persons mentioned: **Henry Hanslap** (assignor of land rights). **Christopher Rowles** (neighbor). *Note: The tract cannot be drawn and the actual acreage cannot be determined due to incomplete boundary course information in the patent document.*

Owen, Ann

Smith's Neck Res. 5/8/1684 – 338 acres. L22/69 SR7363
Location: MNH on the north side of the South River at Smith's Creek.
Persons mentioned: **Coll. Thomas Taylor** (Obtained a Special Warrant to Resurvey a tract called Smith's Neck on behalf of Ann Owen, relict of **Richard Owen). GeorgeYate** (Deputy Surveyor). **George Talbott** (Surveyor Generall). *Note 1: This resurvey included Smith's Neck and another adjoining tract for a total of 328 acres. Note 2: The tract cannot be drawn and the actual acreage cannot be determined due to incomplete boundary course information in the patent document.*

Owen/Owings, Richard (*Merchant/Planter*)

Smith's Neck 2/12/1650 – 685 acres. LQ/408 SR7345
Location: MNH on the north side of the South River at Smith's Branch.
Persons mentioned: Zephaniah Smith (assignor of land rights). Himself, **Robert Thompson, Robert Knight, Richard Vaughn, James Copes, Grace Wells, & Phillip Baggley** (persons transported to this Province by Zephaniah Smith in 1651, here to inhabit). *Note: The tract cannot be drawn and the actual acreage cannot be determined due to incomplete boundary course information in the patent document.*

Landisell 11/25/1652 – 425/410 acres. LAB&H/292 SR7346
Location: B&TNH on the north side of the Patapsco River near Broad Creek.
Persons mentioned: None. *Note 1: MSA Land Index #54 places this tract in Anne Arundel County. The patent document places the tract in Baltimore County. I have included it here based on its location and proximity to Anne Arundel County tracts. Note 2: This tract was patented under the same name by* **Edward Lloyd** *in 1659.*

Locust Thickett 2/18/1688 – 384/442 acres. LNSBi/631 SR7370
Location: B&TNH at Elk Ridge at the head of a branch of the Patapsco River.
Persons mentioned: **William Little** (assignor of land rights). **Adam Shipley & Edward Dorsey** (neighbors). *Note: This tract lies in present day Howard County.*

Owens Range 3/26/1696 – 162/162 acres. LC3i/360 SR7277
Location: MNH.
Persons mentioned: **Jabez Pierpoint** (neighbor).

The Valley of Owen 5/20/1705 – 360/473 acres.
LDD5i/174 SR7379
Location: B&TNH on the south side of the Patapsco River
next adjoining a tract called Chew's Resolution Mannor.
Persons mentioned: **Samuel Chew** (neighbor). *Note 1: This
tract was located in Baltimore County at the time of the
patent/survey. I have included it because the land had been,
and would again be, designated as Anne Arundel County
before being absorbed into present day Howard County.
Note 2: The discrepancy between certified and actual
acreage is extreme, even for this period. However, the
boundary courses have been verified and the acreage is
correct as shown above.*

Paca/Peca, Robert

Dann 7/8/1663 – 490/489 acres. L5/479 SR7347
Location: HCH adjoining Burkitt's Branch.
Persons mentioned: **Steven Burson & Nathan Smith**
(neighbors). *Note: a patent for this tract was not found
although it is referenced in several other patent documents.*

Peca His Chance 5/25/1679 – 45/45 acres. L15/875
SR4327
Location: HCH on the south side of Herring Creek Bay.
Persons mentioned: None.

Padgett, William

Padgett 2/22/16159 – 250/231 acres. L4/521 SR7346
Location: HCH on west side of Herring Creek Branch
running north out of Herring Creek Bay.
Persons mentioned: **Edward Selby, James & George
Pascall** (neighbors).

Painter, Richard

Andover 2/15/1677 – 1,640/1,640 acres. L19/570 SR7360
Location: B&TNH on the south side of the Patapsco River in
the woods.

Persons mentioned: Anthony Holland & Robert Lockwood (neighbors). *Note: The patent document places this tract in Baltimore County. I have included it here based on its location and proximity to Anne Arundel County tracts.*

Greeniston Res. 5/22/1683 – 700/722 acres. LSDA/353 SR7369
Location: B&TNH about three miles from the head of the Ann Arundell *(Severn)* River next adjoining a tract called The Diamond.
Persons mentioned: James Greeniston (former owner). Thomas Browne (neighbor).

Parker, George
Godwell Res. 10/13/1679 – 805/774 acres. L21/21 SR7362
Location: SRH near the head of the South River at Walker's Branch.
Persons mentioned: **George Nettlefold, Marin Duvall, John Chilcotte** (owners of tracts that were "surveyed" into Godwell). **John Gray, Richard Snowden, John Welch, Leonard Wayman & William Frizzell** (neighbors).

Parker. Quinton
Parker's Increase 6/26/1669 – 200/207 acres. L12/310 SR7354
Location: B&TNH on the south side of the Patapsco River next adjoining a tract called Curtis Neck.
Persons mentioned: **George Yate** (Deputy Surveyor). *Note: This is a Cert. Patent not found. The tract was not found in the Rent Rolls although a marginal note on the Cert document states that it was "charged" to the Rent Rolls.*

Parker, William
Unnamed Certification 10/24/1651 – 600 acres. LAB&H/287 SR7344
Location: HCH
Persons mentioned: **Sampson Warring & Thomas Davis**

(neighbors). *Note: The tract cannot be drawn and the actual acreage cannot be determined due to incomplete boundary course information in the patent document.*

St. Edmund's 1/9/1661 – 500/500 acres. L4621/ SR7346
Location: HCH adjoining the land of **Richard Bennett, Esq.**
Persons mentioned: **Thomas Sparrow** (assignor of land rights due him for transporting **Robert Humphrey, John Ball, & Katherine Judion** into this Province to inhabit).

Unnamed Patent 9/4/1666 – 200 acres. L10/35 SR7352
Location: HCH on the south side of Herring Creek near the mouth of Parker's Branch.
Persons mentioned: **William Ayres & Thomas Marsh** (neighbors). *Note: The tract cannot be drawn and the actual acreage cannot be determined due to incomplete boundary course information in the patent document.*

Parrish, Edward

Clarye's Hope 7/20/1664 – 150/135 acres. L7/192 SR7349
Location: WRH in the Great Swamp near the Three Islands.
Persons mentioned: **George Pascall** (assignor of land rights). **William Spencer, Thomas Watkins, & Rowland Morgan** (persons transported by Pascall into this Province here to inhabit).

Parrishes Park 7/29/1664 – 100 acres. L7/194 SR7356
Location: WRH on the south side of the West River at the head of Cutfos *(probably Curtis)* Creek.
Persons mentioned: **George Pascall** on behalf of his wife **Magdalena** for performing her time of service (assignors of land rights). **Matthew Selby** (neighbor). *Note: The tract cannot be drawn and the actual acreage cannot be determined due to incomplete boundary course information in the patent document.*

Parrishes Choice 9/6/1670 – 150 acres
Location: WRH in Herring Creek Swamp standing over against the Three Islands.
Persons mentioned: **Jerome White, Esq.** (assignor of land rights). **Matthew Selby** (neighbor). *Note: The tract cannot be drawn and the actual acreage cannot be determined due to incomplete boundary course information in the patent document.*

Locust Neck 7/10/1671 – 50/43 acres. L16/200 SR7357
Location: WRH in Herring Creek Swamp on the west side of the West Branch of Deep Creek.
Persons mentioned: **James White, Esq.** (assignor of land rights). **John Cumber, Jr.** (neighbor).

Parrishes Delay 7/10/1671 – 100 acres. L14/299 SR7356
Location: WRH in Herring Creek Swamp at the head of the South Creek.
Persons mentioned: **George Pascall & John Gale** (assignors of land rights). **John Shaw** (neighbor). *Note: The tract cannot be drawn and the actual acreage cannot be determined due to incomplete boundary course information in the patent document.*

Papa Ridge 7/20/1674 – 155/113 acres. L18/212 SR7359
Location: HCH in Herring Creek Swamp.
Persons mentioned: **George Yate & William Burges** (assignors of land rights), **John Cumber** (neighbor).

Parrish, John
> **Parrishes Purchase 6/1/1700 – 50/52 acres.** LIB&ILC/402 SR7368-3
> Location: SRH
> Persons mentioned: **Soloman Sparrow** (neighbor).

Parry, John

Parry's Purchase 6/1/1700 – 50/50 acres. LIB&ILC/402 SR7368
Location: WRH next adjoining a tract called Sparrow's Purchase
Persons mentioned: Soloman Sparrow (neighbor).

Parsons, Thomas & Shaw, John

Bipartite 2/16/1659 – 100/100 acres. L4/511 SR7346
Location: WRH on the east side of the West River at Shaw's Cove.
Persons mentioned: None.

Parsons, Thomas

St. Thomas Neck 8/5/1664 – 50/42 acres. L7/393 AR 7349
Location: WRH in the swamp between Herring Creek and the Three Islands.
Persons mentioned: None.

The Friendship 2/13/1677 – 50/64 acres. L20/21 SR7361
Location: HCH at the mouth of Broad Creek next adjoining a tract called Greenwood.
Persons mentioned: William Andrews, Robert Wilson & William Wheatley (assignors of land rights). Armigill Greenwood (neighbor).

Parson's Hill 2/6/1666 150/146 acres. L10/383 SR7352
Location: WRH on the west side of the West River.
Persons mentioned: John Gray Taylor & Humphrey Belt (assignors of land rights). James Bonnor & John Cumber (neighbors).

Pascall, George

Pascall's Chance 8/4/1664 – 300/300 acres. L7/233 SR7349
Location: HCH at the head of the West River near to the mouth of the Rode River.

Persons mentioned: George Pascall, **Mandley** (his wife), **James Pascall, Elizabeth** (his wife), **William Neal,** & **Elaine Dobbins** (persons transported by Pascall into this Province to inhabit in 1651).

Barren Point 3/22/1665 – 40/48 acres. L9/286 SR7351
Location: HCH adjoining Beaver Dam Branch and his own land.
Persons mentioned: **George Yate** & **Thomas Marsh** (assignors of land rights).

The Idle Combe 11/19/1665 – 300/296 acres. L9/140 SR7451
Location: HCH on Herring Creek.
Persons mentioned: **William Padgett** (neighbor).

Pawley, Lionel

Bush Bay 9/6/1670 – 80/96 acres. L14/131 SR7356
Location: HCH next adjoining a tract called Jerrico.
Persons mentioned: **Robert Wilson** & **Capt. William Burges** (assignors of land rights). **Nathan Smith** & **Robert Peca** (neighbors).

Soldier's Delight 7/10/1671 – 100/100 acres. L14/262 SR7356
Location: HCH in the woods adjoining tracts called Gowery Banks and Trent.
Persons mentioned: **Charles Bevin, Thomas Ford, John Gray, Joseph Morley,** & **Benjamin Wells** (neighbors).

Pawson, John

Pawson's Plaine 10/9/1670 – 400/300 acres. L16/159 SR7357
Location: B&TNH between the branches of the Maggity & Patapsco Rivers at the head of Beaver Dam Creek.
Persons mentioned: **George Yate** & **Jerome White Esq.** (assignors of land rights). *Note: The discrepancy between certified and actual acreage is extreme, even for this period.*

However, the boundary courses have been verified and the acreage is correct as shown above.

The Plaine 5/10/1671 – 400/337 acres. L14/260 SR7356
Location: B&TNH between the bounds of the Maggity & Patapsco Rivers at the head of Beaverdam Creek.
Persons mentioned: **John Booth, William Hat, W. Wilson, John Pawson, & Rosamond** (persons transported by Pawson into this Province here to inhabit).

Peasley, Francis

Peasley's Neck 1/1/1666 250 acres. L9/463 SR7351
Location: MNH on the south side of the Severn River at Besson's Creek.
Persons mentioned: **Thomas Howell** (neighbor). *Note: The tract cannot be drawn and the actual acreage cannot be determined due to incomplete boundary course information in the patent document.*

Peasley, John

Peasley's Inheritance 7/5/1688 – 100 acres. LCB2i/39 SR7366
Location: B&TNH on the north side of the Maggity River.
Persons mentioned: None. *Note: The tract cannot be drawn and the actual acreage cannot be determined due to incomplete boundary course information in the patent document.*

Peasley's Lott 5/10/1685 – 109/109 acres. NSBi/152 SR7370
Location: B&TNH on the north side of the Maggity River at the mouth of the West Branch next adjoining a tract called Murphy's Choice.
Persons mentioned: **Patrick Murphy & Thomas Turner** (neighbors).

Pell, William

>Unnamed Patent 8/27/1658 – 280/264 acres. LQ/116
>SR7345
>Location: SRH on the south side of the South River at the mouth next adjoining Pennington's Pond.
>Persons mentioned: William Pennington (assignor of land rights and transporter of his wife, Elizabeth, to this Province here to inhabit).

Penn, Edward

>Planter's Pleasure 10/1/1699 – 100/100 acres. LDD5i/18
>SR7378
>Location: B&TNH on the north side of the Patuxent River next adjoining a tract called The Contrivance.
>Persons mentioned. None. *Note: This tract was located in Baltimore County at the time of the patent/survey. I have included it because the land had been, and would again be, designated as Anne Arundel County before being absorbed into present day Howard County.*

Pennington, Thomas

>Foothold 10/15/1685 – 135/134 acres. LSDA/105 SR7369
>Location: B&TNH on the south side of the Maggity River next adjoining a tract called Luffman's Due
>Persons mentioned: Henry Hanslap (assignor of land rights). William Luffman, Abraham Dawson, Dariell Hilliard, Robert Tyler, & James Connaway (neighbors).

Pennington, William

>Pennington's Search 1696 – 100/98 acres. LC39/3676
>SR7377
>Location: B&TNH
>Persons mentioned: Robert Taylor (neighbor). *Note: The patent document does not indicate where this tract was located. However, the Rent Rolls confirm that it was in the Broad & Town Neck Hundred.*

Petticoate, William

Petticoate's Rest 9/9/1679 – 100/52 acres. L21/99 SR7362
Location: MNH in the woods next adjoining a tract called Edge's Addition.
Persons mentioned: **Daniel Edge** (neighbor). *Note: The discrepancy between certified and actual acreage is extreme, even for this period. However, the boundary courses have been verified and the acreage is correct as shown above.*

Pettybone/Pettibone, Richard

Pettybone's Rest 10/25/1673 – 280 acres. L17/225 SR7358
Location: B&TNH adjoining the Chesapeake Bay, Burle's Ponds, and Maggity Creek.
Persons mentioned: None. *Note: The tract cannot be drawn and the actual acreage cannot be determined due to incomplete boundary course information in the patent document.*

Phelps, Thomas

Piney Point 1/30/1668 – 50 acres. L12/423 SR7354
Location: MNH on the south side of Clarkston's Creek adjoining Horne Neck.
Persons mentioned: **Robert Clarkston** (neighbor). *Note: The tract cannot be drawn and the actual acreage cannot be determined due to incomplete boundary course information in the patent document.*

Phelps, Walter & Green, Nicholas

The Batchellor's Hope 10/20/1665 – 240 acres. L10/253 SR7352
Location: MNH on the north side of the South River on the east side of Broad Creek.
Persons mentioned: **Robert Franklin, John Shale, & James Chilcott** (assignors of land rights). *Note: The tract cannot be drawn and the actual acreage cannot be determined due to incomplete boundary course information in the patent document.*

Phelps, Walter

Phelps Increase 77/11/1681 – 300/299 acres. LCB2i/214
SR7366
Location: B&TNH on the north side of the Severn River and
on the west side of Cypress Swamp.
Persons mentioned: Elizabeth, his wife, Rebecca, his mother,
& Johnathan Compton, Merke Clint, & Marke Bauston
(persons transported to this Province by Phelps here to
inhabit). Bernard Eagleston (neighbor).

Phelps His Choice 6/1/1685 – 200/197 acres. LNS2i/97
SR7371
Location: SRH on the west side of the northmost Great
Branch of the Patuxent River.
Persons mentioned: None.

Phelps His Luck 9/1/1687 – 83/56 acres. LNS2i397
SR7371
Location: SRH on the south side of South River adjoining a
branch of Flatt Creek.
Persons mentioned: John Dorsey (assignor of land rights).
Richard Cheney & Archer Arbuckle (neighbors).

Phelps His Luck 12/10/1695 – 238/186 acres. LC3i/327
SR7377
Location: B&TNH in Elk Ridge.
Persons mentioned: Mordecai Moore (assignor of land
rights). Edward Talbott, Richard Owens, & Edward
Dorsey (neighbors). *Note: This tract lies in present day
Howard County.*

Elk Thickett Res. 4/13/1701 – 35/35 acres. LDD5i/16
SR7378
Location: SRH near the head of the South River on Huggin's
Path.
Persons mentioned: Robert Davis (assignor of land rights).

Philke, Edward

Philke's Rest 9/20/1680 – 316/316 acres. LCB2i/63
SR7366
Location: B&TNH on the north side of the Severn River.
Persons mentioned: **George Yate & Coll. William Burges**
(assignors of land rights).

Pierpoint, Amos

Pierpoint's Chance 2/11/1688 – 418/453 acres. LNSBi/630
SR73770
Location: B&TNH on the north side of the Maggity River by
the riverside.
Persons mentioned: **Henry Pierpoint & Thomas Richardson**
(assignors of land rights). **Steven Burle** (neighbor). *Note: a
marginal note states that Amos Pierpoint "let fall" this
patent and his rights to the land therein mentioned are
reserved for future warrants.*

What is Left 6/4/1702 – 105/110 acres. LSDF/403
SR7373-2
Location: MNH on Taylor's Branch of the Patuxent River
next adjoining a tract called Cordwell.
Persons mentioned: **Henry Hanslap** (assignor of land rights).
Thomas Brown & Matthew Howard (neighbors).

Pierpoint, Henry

Pierpoint's Lott 9/15/1666 – 150/207 acres. L10/106
SR7352
Location: MNH in the woods about two miles from the Ann
Arundell *(Severn)* River.
Persons mentioned: None. *Note: Henry Pierpoint was issued
a warrant for 350 acres on 1/1/1666, for transporting
himself, wife Elizabeth, children Arnis, Jabes, & Elizabeth ,
and Hannah Pierpoint Mopes (L9/34 SR7351). The acreage
certified was 200 acres but the amount granted was only
150. A note on the patent document states that the patent
was "lett fall" and a Warrant Of Resurvey was issued to the*

s'd Pierpoint. Results of the resurvey were not found. However, when the tract was sold in 1685, by Jabes Pierpoint (C3i/311 SR7377), it measured 200 acres. Note: The discrepancy between certified and actual acreage is extreme, even for this period. However, the boundary courses have been verified and the acreage is correct as shown above.

Pierpoint's Rocks 4/1/1672 – 85/57 acres. L14/487 SR7356
Location: MNH on the north side of the South River on the northwest side of Broad Creek.
Persons mentioned: **John Covill** (neighbor)

Pierpoint's Branch 6/1/1673 – 40/38 acres. L17/198 SR7358
Location: SRH
Persons mentioned: **Robert Wilson & William Burges** (assignors of land rights). **Mrs. Brewer, Christopher Hall, & David Steward** (neighbors).

Pierpoint, Jabes

Pierpoint's Range 11/19/1695 – 200/200 acres. LWDi/136 SR7372-2
Location: MNH in the woods.
Persons mentioned: **Henry Pierpoint** (assignor of land rights).

Pinkstone/Pinkston/Pinxton, Peter

Pinkstone's Delight 3/26/1696 – 200/199 acres. LC3i/348 SR7377
Location: B&TNH at Elk Ridge by a branch of the Patuxent River.
Persons mentioned: **Thomas Freeborne** (neighbor). *Note: The tract lies in present day Howard County.*

Pinkston's Folly 10/1/1700 – 180/174 acres. LDD5i/4
SR7378
Location: SRH on a branch of the Patuxent River called
Rogue's Harbor Branch *(aka Snowden's River)* adjoining the
north side of Hatton's Branch.
Persons mentioned: James **Carroll** (Deputy Surveyor).
William Ridgely (neighbor). *Note: This tract lies in present
day Howard County.*

Marlborough Plaine 4/2/1707 – 150/140 acres. LDD5i/654
SR7378
Location: B&TNH on the north side of the Great Branch of
Patuxent River next adjoining Stoney Runn.
Persons mentioned: None. *Note 1: This patent is included
because the Certification and/or Survey date is within the
targeted period. Note 2: This tract lies in present day
Howard County.*

Pinxton's Randan 4/2/1707 – 100/100 acres. LDD5I 647
SR7378
Location: B&TNH on Ridgely's Runn of the Patuxent River.
Persons mentioned: James **Boyde** (assignor of land rights).
John Harrisson (neighbor). *Note 1: The certification is for
300 acres and only 100 acres was granted. No explanation
found. Note 2: This patent is included because the
Certification and/or Survey date is within the targeted
period. Note 3: This tract lies in present day Howard
County.*

Porter, Peter
Unnamed Cert. 11/20/1651 – 200 acres. LAB&H/266
SR7344
Location: MNH on the north side of the South River.
Persons mentioned: James **Warner** (neighbor). *Note: The
tract cannot be drawn and the actual acreage cannot be
determined due to incomplete boundary course information
in the patent document.*

Hare Hill 9/11/1674 – 100/102 acres. L18/254 SR7359
Location: MNH in the woods about three miles from the head
of the Ann Arundell *(Severn)* River.
Persons mentioned: **Richard Wilson** (assignor of land rights).

Porter, Peter, Jr.

Porter's Hill 9/19/1659 – 200/130 acres. L14/129 SR7346
Location: MNH on the south side of Severn River at
Bustion's Point.
Persons mentioned: **Peter Porter** (the elder) who transported
himself and his wife, **Frances**, to this Province here to
inhabit. *Note: The discrepancy between certified and actual
acreage is extreme, even for this period. However, the
boundary courses have been verified and the acreage is
correct as shown above.*

Powell, James & John

Powell's Inheritance 4/1/1685 – 125/107 acres.
LIB&ILC/236 SR7368-2
Location: SRH on the south side of the South River next
adjoining a tract called Elk Neck.
Persons mentioned: **Richard Huggings & John Grange**
(assignors of land rights). **Archer Arbuckle** (neighbor).

Pratt, Thomas

Turkey Hill 8/5/1664 100/103 acres. L7/312 SR7349
Location: HCH
Persons mentioned: **John Cumber** (assignor of land rights.)
Edward Foster &Thomas Prior (persons transported by
Cumber to this Province here to inhabit). **John Burrage &
George Pascall** (neighbors).

Hogg's Harbor 8/5/1664 – 50/50 acres. L7/315 SR7349
Location: WRH in the great swamp near the Three Islands at
the head of Island Creek.
Persons mentioned: **Robert Comins** (transported by **Pratt**
into this Province here to inhabit).

Pratt's Choice 7/10/1671 – 100/102 acres. L16/229
SR7357
Location: WRH in Herring Creek Swamp at the head of a
pond called the Cattaile Slash.
Persons mentioned: **Richard Pascall** (assignor of land rights).

Pratt's Neck 9/10/1672 100/92 acres. L17/295 SR7358
Location: WRH in Herring Creek Swamp at the head of the
Cattaile Slash Pond.
Persons mentioned: **George Yate, Thomas Taylor, &
Jerome White Esq.** (assignors of land rights).

Pratt's Choice Res. 1/10/1673 - 166/165 acres. L17/527
SR7358
Location: WRH in Herring Creek Swamp at the head of
Cattaile Pond.
Persons mentioned: **George Yate & Capt. William Burges**
(assignors of land rights).

Pratt's Security 10/5/1683 – 150 acres. LSDA/415
SR7369
Location: WRH in Herring Creek Swamp at the mouth of
Island Creek.
Persons mentioned: **Henry Hanslap** (assignor of land rights).
Theodorus Young & Anthony Holland (neighbors). *Note 1:
The grant conveys two non-adjoining tracts. Note 2: The
tract cannot be drawn and the actual acreage cannot be
determined due to incomplete boundary course information
in the patent document.*

Preston, Richard
 Preston's Cliffs 4/26/1658 – 1.000/1,177 acres. LQ/1
 SR7345
 Location: Three holes area.
 Persons mentioned: **Thomas Cole** (neighbor). *Note: The 3-
 hole area is not a hundred. This designation identifies a*

*small number of tracts adjoining a cliff with three holes that
served as a landmark. Other than being in Ann Arundell
Manor, there is nothing in the patent documents to indicate
where this cliff or these tracts were located.*

Price, Edward & Elizabeth

Holloway or Oliver's Preservation 2/7/1670 – 147/147
acres. LWDi/183 SR7372
<u>Location:</u> HCH by Gott's Creek..
<u>Persons mentioned:</u> **Thomas Lunn** (former owner of tract and
father of Elizabeth Price). *Note: (from the patent document.)
Originally patented by Oliver Holloway, the tract escheated
for lack of heirs. Purchased next by Luna however, his
patent was not issued until after his death when his daughter
and her husband successfully petitioned for the patent to be
issued but only after paying a fee of 1,840 lbs of tobacco.*

Elinor's Neck 5/17/1700 – 147/144 **acres.** LCC4/151
SR7375
<u>Location:</u> HCH near the head of Gott's Creek.
<u>Persons mentioned:</u> **Thomas Lunn** (former owner through
escheat and regrant). *Note: This was a Special Warrant of
Resurvey to identify surplus land within the bounds of the
tract. Although confusing, it appears that the Prices were
either to be charged four thousand pounds of tobacco per
one hundred acres of surplus land found, or the cost of the
surplus was included in the base price. Apparently no
surplus was found. In fact, the acreage was actually less
than the amount certified.*

Price, Edward

Bright Seate 4/10/1673 – 400/443 **acres.** L17/111 SR7358
<u>Location:</u> SRH on the south side of the South River adjoining
a tract called White's Hall.
<u>Persons mentioned:</u> **George Yate** (assignor of land rights).
Evan Davis (neighbor).

Proctor, Robert *(Inn Keeper)*

The Landing 9/8/1668 – 70/57 acres. L11/484 SR7354
Location: SRH on the east side of the North Runn of the
South River.
Persons mentioned: **William Bateman** (assignor of land
rights). **Charles Calvert, Esq.** (witness).

Greenspring 2/20/1673 – 200/198 acres. L15/148 SR4327
Location: MNH next adjoining a tract called White's Hall.
Persons mentioned: **Jerome White, Esq.** (neighbor). **Phillip
Howard** (purchaser of a portion of Greenspring within weeks
of the patent date).

Proctor's Forrest 7/20//1673 – 100/100 acres. L15/87
SR4327
Location: MNH on the north side of the South River.
Persons mentioned: **Robert Wilson** (assignor of land rights).
Robert Clarkson (neighbor).

Slatbourne 5/10/1676 – 380/340 acres. L19/329 SR7360
Location: MNH among the branches of South River in the
woods next adjoining a tract called Freemans Fancy.
Persons mentioned: **George Yate** (assignor of land rights).
*Note: This patent was eventually voided when it was found
to be within the bounds of an older tract (Abingdon).*

Proctor's Chance 6/29/1680 – 30/14 acres. LCB2i/13
SR7366
Location: MNH on the south side of Severn River adjoining a
tract called The Intacke.
Persons mentioned: **George Holland** (assignor of land
rights). *Note: The discrepancy between certified and actual
acreage is extreme, even for this period. However, the
boundary courses have been verified and the acreage is
correct as shown above*

Mill Land 5/10/1683 – 100/102 acres. NS2i/111 SR7371

Location: MNH on the north side of the South River adjoining the east side of Broad Creek.
Persons mentioned: None.

Proctors Park 10/1/1683 – 518/512 acres. LCB3i/309 SR7367
Location: B&TNH on the north side of the Maggity River at Cuckold's Creek next adjoining a tract called Sturton's Rest.
Persons mentioned: **George Sturton** (neighbor).

Green Spring 8/10/1684 – 250/250 acres. LSDA/445 SR7369
Location: B&TNH at the head of a creek called Bodkin's Creek.
Persons mentioned: None.

Bare Neck 8/10/1684 – 146/141 acres. LSDA/456 SR7369
Location: B&TNH on the south side of Bodkin Creek.
Persons mentioned: None.

Poplar Ridge 8/10/1684 – 500/383 acres. LSDA/454 SR7369
Location: B&TNH on Bodkin Creek next adjoining a tract called Homewood's Range.
Persons mentioned: None. *Note: The discrepancy between certified and actual acreage is extreme, even for this period. However, the boundary courses have been verified and the acreage is correct as shown above*

Timber Neck 8/10/1684 – 463/463 acres. LSDA/439 SR7369
Location: B&TNH on the south side of Rock Creek by a cove.
Persons mentioned: None.

Milford 6/1/1685 – 717/768 acres. LNSBi/82 SR7370
Location: B&TNH on the north side of the Maggity River.

Persons mentioned: Robert Taylor, John P____, &
William Corkley (neighbors).

Puddington, George

Puddington 2/7/1650 – 160/165 acres. LQ/393 SR7345
Location: SRH on the south side of the South River
Persons mentioned: Jane Puddington (wife of George.
Transported by him to this Province to inhabit). Richard
Huggings & William Burges (neighbors).

West Puddington 2/8/1650 – 340/340 acres. LQ/395
SR7345
Location: SRH on the south side of the South River on the
north side of Burges' Branch.
Persons mentioned: Mary & Comfort Puddington &
Elizabeth Robins (persons transported by Puddington to this
Province in 1649, here to inhabit.).

Puddington's Enlargement 6/30/1662 – 300/300 acres.
L5/348 SR7347
Location: SRH on the west side of the South River adjoining
a tract called Nettleland.
Persons mentioned: Thomas Hipsley, John Burrage, &
Margaret Joy (transported to this Province by Puddington
in 1649, here to inhabit), George Nettlefold (neighbor). *Note:
The grant conveys 2 unadjoining (but neighboring) tracts.*

Puddington's Harbor 9/29/1663 – 700 acres. L5/618
SR7347
Location: SRH on the south side of the South River at
Jacob's Creek.
Persons mentioned: Richard Huggings (assignor of land
rights). *Note: The tract cannot be drawn and the actual
acreage cannot be determined due to incomplete boundary
course information in the patent document.*

Purnell, Richard

Purnell's Angle 5/30/1683 – 149/80 acres. LSDA/102
SR7369
Location: HCH on the Main Branch of Lyon's Cr.
Persons mentioned: George Holland (assignor of land
rights). William Moore & John Grammar (neighbors).
*Note: The discrepancy between certified and actual acreage
is extreme, even for this period. However, the boundary
courses have been verified and the acreage is correct as
shown above.*

Pyther, Will

Unnamed Certification 6/20/1650 – 250 acres.
LAB&H/296 SR7344
Location: SRH on the south side of the South River at
Pyther's Creek.
Persons mentioned: Patrick Gossum (neighbor). *Note 1: The
certification document does not identify this tract by name.
However, MSA Land Records #54 indicates that it was
patented by John Brewer and called Pytherston. A "Brewer"
patent for this tract was not found. Note 2: The tract cannot
be drawn and the actual acreage cannot be determined due
to incomplete boundary course information in the patent
document.*

Pytherston 2/28/1659 – 60/55 acres. L4/491 SR7346
Location: B&TNH on the north side of the Severn River and
on the east side of Broad Creek in a neck of land called The
Broad Neck next adjoining a tract called Maidenstone.
Persons mentioned: Elizabeth Strong (neighbor).

Randall, Christopher

Randall's Fancy 5/14/1680 – 5.6/7 acres. L20/344 SR7361
Location: B&TNH on the north side of the Severn River next
adjoining a tract called Hopkins His Fancy.
Persons mentioned: George Yate, Francis Leafe, Nicholas
Paxton, & David Frye (assignors of land rights).

Randall's Purchase 1680 – 102/102 acres. LCB2i/65
SR7365
Location: B&TNH on the north side of Severn River next adjoining tracts named Hopkins His Fancy and Norman's Fancy.
Persons mentioned: **Coll William Burges & George Yate** (assignors of land rights). **George Norman & William Hopkins** (neighbors).

Randall's Range 7/7/1681 – 100/121 acres. LCB2i/150
SR7376
Location: B&TNH on the south side of the Maggity River at Cattaile Creek next adjoining tracts called Hopkins His Fancy and Greenbury's Forrest.
Persons mentioned: **George Yate & Nicholas Painter** (assignors of land rights). **Nicholas Greenbury** (neighbor).

Rawlings, Richard

Rawlings 8/14/1680 – 50 acres. L21/256 SR7362
Location: MNH on the North Runn of the South River next adjoining a tract called Wyatt's Ridge.
Persons mentioned: **Nicholas Wyatt, John Stinson, Amos Pierpoint** (neighbors). *Note 1: This is a resurvey of a portion of a tract called Vennell's Inheritance formerly laid out for* **John Vennell**. *Note 2: The tract cannot be drawn and the actual acreage cannot be determined due to incomplete boundary course information in the patent document.*

Rawling's Purchase 8/30/1682 – 50/48 acres. LCB3i/146
SR7367
Location: MNH on the north side of the South River at Hogg Neck Runn.
Persons mentioned: **John Vennell** (former owner of a portion of this tract).

Ray, John

Ray's Chance 10//1/1667 – 115/115 acres. LNS2i/412
SR7371
Location: B&TNH on the south side of the Maggity River.
Persons mentioned: Richard Beard (assignor of land rights).
Richard Moss & Henry Woolchurch (neighbors).

Read, Elizabeth

Widow's Addition 5/18/1679 – 130/134 acres. L20/199
SR7361
Location: MNH on the south side of the Ann Arundell
(Severn) River next adjoining a tract called Read's Lott.
Persons mentioned: George Yate (assignor of land rights).
William Read (neighbor).

Read, William *(Planter)*

Read's Lott 9/15/1665 – 40/20 acres. L8/290 SR7350
Location: MNH on the south side of the Severn River at
Beasley's Creek.
Persons mentioned: Robert Clarkson (neighbor).

Read's Lott 11/15/1665 – 100/100 acres. L8/150 SR7351
Location: MNH on the south side of the Severn River.
Persons mentioned: None.

Reade, Thomas

Thomastown 9/5/1659 – 100/97 acres. L4/100 SR7346
Location: Three holes area.
Persons mentioned: Joseph Halifield (former owner).
Thomas Batmason (transported by Thomas Reade to this
Province here to inhabit in 1650). **William Fuller** (asssignor
of land rights earned by transporting **John Chanells** in 1650).
Thomas Emerson (neighbor). *Note: The 3-hole area is not a
hundred. This designation identifies a small number of
tracts adjoining a cliff with three holes that served as a
landmark. Other than being in Ann Arundell Manor, there is
nothing in the patent documents to indicate where this cliff
or these tracts were located.*

Lower Fuller Res. 9/5/1659 – 100/98 acres. L4/100
SR7346
Location: Three holes area.
Persons mentioned: **William Fuller** (former owner and
assignor of land rights due him for transporting **Thomas Burl**
to this Province to inhabit). **Phillip Thomas** (neighbor).
*Note: The 3-holes area is not a hundred. This designation
identifies a small number of tracts adjoining a cliff with
three holes that served as a landmark. Other than being in
Ann Arundell Manor, there is nothing in the patent
documents to indicate where this cliff or these tracts were
located.*

Richardson, Lawrence
Richardson's Joy 6/23/1663 – 200/195 acres. L5/344
SR7347
Location: MNH on the south Side of the Severn River at the
south end of The Round Bay.
Persons mentioned: **Sarah**, wife, & children **Thomas &
Sarah** (persons transported by Richardson into this Province
here to inhabit).

Upper Toynton 8/15/1666 – 280/280 acres. L10/20
SR7352
Location: MNH on the south side of the Severn River
adjoining his own land.
Persons mentioned: **Richardson** transported himself, wife
Sarah and an unnamed daughter to this Province in 1649.
*Note 1: The certification was for 200 and the grant was 280
acres. No explanation found. Note 2: Richardson also
claimed rights for transporting wife Sarah for the preceding
tract (Richardson's Joy). Note 3: The tract was willed to
sons **Larrance, Jr.** & **John Richardson**. Note 4: On
8/9/1666, Larrance Richardson also received fifty acres of
land for transporting **Gilbert Thurston** to this Province to
inhabit in 1662.*

Richardson, Thomas *(Planter)*

    Tredhaven Point 7/10/1671 – 150/140 acres. L16/246
    SR7357
    Location: B&TNH on the south side of the Patapsco River to
    the south of a small creek.
    Persons mentioned: **George Yate** (assignor of land rights).

Richardson, William

    Talbott's Hope 7/31/1677 – 96/95 acres. L19/1578
    SR7360
    Location: WRH adjoining Talbott's Angles.
    Persons mentioned: **George Yate** (Deputy Surveyor), **Baker**
    Brooke, Esq. (Surveyor Generall). **Richard Talbott**
    (neighbor).

    The Diligent Search 10/1/1678 – 75/69 acres. L20/94
    SR7361
    Location: SRH in the branches of the Rode River.
    Persons mentioned: **George Yate** (Deputy Surveyor). **Baker**
    Brooke (Surveyor Generall). **Ferdinand Batten & Richard**
    Talbott (neighbors). *This tract is located in an area close to*
    the line between the West River the Herring Creek
    Hundreds. The tract is completely surrounded by tracts of
    these hundreds. However, the Rent Rolls place it in the
    South River Hundred.

    First Patt for Prevention 6/1/1700 – 200/240 acres.
    LDD5i/3 SR7378
    Location: WRH adjoining Ann Arundell Manor and a tract
    called Anthony's Purchase.
    Persons mentioned: **Coll Henry Darnall** (Surveyor Generall),
    Anthony Smith & Samuel Thomas (neighbors).

Ridgely, Henry & Ridgely, Henry, Jr.

    Huntington Quarter 5/1/1698 – 259/290 acres. LC3i/382
    SR7377

Location: B&TNH in Huntington on the North West Great Branch of the Patuxent River.

Persons mentioned: None. *Note 1: From a note written in the margin of the Survey. "Upon this tract of land before survey was built one fifteen square foot dwelling house, one thirty foot house, one cornfield cleared and tended, sixteen or seventeen thousand corn hills besides the beginning of a bridge over a branch then three or four years seated." Note 2: This tract lies in present day Howard County.*

Ridgely, Henry *(Planter)*

Broome Res. 11/12/1670 – 220/153 acres. L16/23 SR7357
Location: MNH on the north side of the South River and on the west side of Broad Cr.

Persons mentioned: **Richard Beard** (former owner).

Ridgely's Beginning 11/10/1695 – 282/217 acres. LB23i/299 SR7365
Location: B&TNH on the North Branch of the Patuxent River at Huntington.

Persons mentioned: None. *Note: This tract is located in present day Howard County.*

Ridgely's Forrest 4/2/1696 – 264/259 acres. LC3i/340 SR7377
Location: B&TNH on the east side of the North Great Branch at Huntington.

Persons mentioned: **John Howard** (assignor of land rights). *Note: This tract lies in present day Howard County.*

Ridgely, Henry, Jr.

Ridgely's Lott 11/10/1695 – 273/177 acres. L23/251 SR7364
Location: B&TNH on the northeast side of Ridgely's Great Branch between Huntington and Elk Ridge.

Persons mentioned: **Richard Beard** (neighbor). *Note: This tract lies in present day Howard County.*

Ridgely, William

Ridgely's Beginning 5/18/1679 – 40/60 acres. L20/205
SR7361
Location: MNH on the north side of the South River next
adjoining a tract called Clark's Enlargement.
Persons mentioned: George Yate (assignor of land rights)

Ridgely's Chance 10/2/1694 – 305/302 acres. LC3i/412
SR7377
Location: MNH on the forke of Rogue's Harbor Branch of
the Patuxent River.
Persons mentioned: Henry Ridgely, Jr. (assignor of land
rights).

Rigby, James

Rigby 2/16/1659 – 125 acres. L4/484 SR7346
Location: B&TNH on the north side of the Severn River and
on the east side of Broad Creek.
Persons mentioned: Richard Deaver (neighbor). *Note: The
tract cannot be drawn and the actual acreage cannot be
determined due to incomplete boundary course information
in the patent document.*

Roberts, Andrew, *(Tailor)*

Sharp Pointe 11/30/1666 – 30/23 acres. L10/205 SR7352
Location: SRH at the head of the Road River near the head of
Muddy Creek.
Persons mentioned: None. *Note: From the Rent Rolls, 1651-
1774 Ann Arundell County, pg 44, "I do not find that
Roberts ever paid rent for this nor did I find any new claim.
Supposed (it) to be mistaken Survey."*

The Triangle Res. 9/5/1681 – 100/132 acres. LCB2i/224
SR7366
Location: WRH on the south side of the South River next
adjoining Beaver Dam Branch.

Persons mentioned: Robert Lloyd (former owner). **John Norman, John Larkin, Richard Tydings, & Donnie** *(or Dennis)* **Maccumus** (neighbors).

Robinson, Henry *(Planter)*

Robinston 2/10/1659 – 300/283 acres. L4/526 SR7346
Location: Three holes area.
Persons mentioned: **William Parker** (former owner). *Note: Six hundred acres were certified but the tract was laid out for three hundred acres. No explanation found. Note 2: The 3-hole area is not a hundred. This designation identifies a small number of tracts adjoining a cliff with three holes that served as a landmark. Other than being in Ann Arundell Manor, there is nothing in the patent documents to indicate where this cliff or these tracts were located.*

Rockhold, John

The Rich Neck 7/30/1666 – 90 acres. L10/235 SR7362
Location: B&TNH on the north side of the Severn River by Scotcher's Creek next adjoining a tract called Wadlingon.
Persons mentioned: None. *Note: The tract cannot be drawn and the actual acreage cannot be determined due to incomplete boundary course information in the patent document.*

Rockhold's Range 8/10/1684 – 200/169 acres. LSDA/458 SR7369
Location: B&TNH on the south side of the Patapsco River at the head of Rock Creek next adjoining a tract called Rattlesnake Neck.
Persons mentioned: **Henry Hanslap** (assignor of land rights). **John Deaver** (neighbor).

Rockhold's Purchase 4/10/1696 – 243/227 acres. LC3i/398 SR7377
Location: B&TNH on the north side of Curtico *(probably Curtis)* Creek.

Persons mentioned: George Hope (neighbor).

Rockhold's Search 10/19/1686 – 180/164 acres. LC3i/394
SR7377
Location: B&TNH on the south side of the Patapsco River.
Persons mentioned: John Boddy (neighbor).

Rockhold, Robert *(Gunsmith)* **& John**
   Rockwould 9/7/1659 – 400/300 acres. L4/94 SR7346
   Location: MNH adjoining Chesapeake Bay.
   Persons mentioned: **Robert Rockhold** (the elder) transported
   Sarah, his wife, and sons **Robert & Thomas** into this
   Province here to inhabit. **John Scotcher** (former owner).
   William Parker (neighbor). *Note: The discrepancy between
   certified and actual acreage is extreme, even for this period.
   However, the boundary courses have been verified and the
   acreage is correct as shown above.*

Rolls/Rooles, Christopher *(Cooper)*
   The Addition 3/21/1666 – 150/139 acres. L17/536 SR7378
   Location: B&TNH on the north side of the Severn River near
   the head of Eagles Nest Bay.
   Persons mentioned: **William Hopkins** (neighbor).

   Roole's His Chance 8/9/1681 - 11 acres. L21/352 SR7362
   Location: B&TNH on the south side of the Maggity River at
   Little Piny Neck Point.
   Persons mentioned: **Coll. Thomas Taylor & Henry Hanslap**
   (assignors of land rights). **George Yate** (Deputy Surveyor).
   Vincent Lowe (Surveyor Generall). *Note: The tract cannot
   be drawn and the actual acreage cannot be determined due
   to incomplete boundary course information in the patent
   document.*

Rooker, Thomas
   Rooker's Range 4/1/1702 – 500/460 acres. LDD5i/62
   SR7378

Location: B&TNH lying between the Middle & North Runns of the Patuxent River at the head of Cattaile Branch.
Persons mentioned: **Robert Kirkland** (neighbor). *Note: This tract was located in Baltimore County at the time of the patent/survey. I have included it because the land had been, and would again be, designated as Anne Arundel County before being absorbed into present day Howard County.*

Roper, Thomas
The Roper's Yard 9/13/1664 – 200/234 acres. L7/342 SR7349
Location: MNH on the north side of the South River adjoining the riverside.
Persons mentioned: **John Edwards, Quentin Camell, & Erasmus Yeatman** (assignors of land rights). *Note: The rights assigned by Yeatman and Edwards were due them for their own transportation into this Province here to inhabit.*

The Chance 9/10/1665 15/10 acres. L8/408 SRSR7350
Location: MNH on the south side of the Ann Arundell *(Severn)* River.
Persons mentioned: **William Frizzell** (neighbor). *Note: a marginal note on the Cert (same liber & folio) indicates that 150 acres was certified. However, the patent document and another marginal note clearly indicate that the grant was for 15 acres.*

Roper's Neck Res. 3/1/1673 – 300/348 acres. L15/153 SR7347
Location: MNH on the north side of the South River and on the east side of Green Gingerville Creek.
Persons mentioned: **Daniel Edge** (assignor of land rights). **John Baldwin** (neighbor).

Roper, William & Gray, John
Roper Gray 8/2/1683 – 480/487 acres. LSDA/410 SR7369
Location: SRH in the woods by the North Branch of the Patuxent River.

Persons mentioned: David Frye, Henry Hanslap, & Thomas Taillor (assignors of land rights).

Roper, William

Roper's Range 9/6/1670 – 420/419 acres. L14/54 SR7356
Location: SRH next adjoining a tract called Roper Gray.
Persons mentioned: Robert Wilson, William Burges, & Jerome White, Esq. (assignors of land rights).

Rowles, Thomas

The Stones 11/20/1705 – 400/370 acres. LCDi/268 SR7376
Location: B&TNH on the south side of the Patapsco River at the head of Curtis Creek on a draught of Marley Runn.
Persons mentioned: None. *Note 1: This patent is included because the Certification and/or Survey date is within the targeted period. Note 2: The patent/survey document places this tract in Baltimore County. MSA Land Index #55 places it in Anne Arundel County. I have included it here based on its location.*

Ruly, Anthony

Ruly's Search 8/26/1696 – 74/109 acres. LBB3/486 SR7374
Location: MNH on the north side of South River next adjoining a tract called Edward His Neck.
Persons mentioned: None. *Note: The discrepancy between certified and actual acreage is extreme, even for this period. However, the boundary courses have been verified and the acreage is correct as shown above.*

Rutland, Thomas

Rutland's Purchase Inlarged 4/19/1700 – 260/300 acres. LDD5i/788 SR7378
Location: SRH on a branch of the Patuxent River called Snowden's River.

Persons mentioned: **Clement Hill** (Surveyor Generall). *Note: The tract lies partially in Prince George's County and, in the words of the surveyor; he received "Epistolarry Power" from Mr. Clement Hill to survey the part in PG County.*

Salloway, Anthony

Silverston (Anthony Salloway) 2/22/1659 – 80/89 acres. L4/525 SR7347
Location: HCH adjoining Fishing and Barret's Creeks and the "Bay."
Persons mentioned: **Samuel Chew** (neighbor). *Note1: The grant is divided into two adjoining tracts. Note 2: It is not known if the "Bay" reference is to Herring Creek Bay or to The Chesapeake Bay.*

Salmon, Ralph

Salmon's Hill 9/22/1665 – 100/100 acres. L8/414 SR7350
Location: MNH on the south side of the Severn River at the head of Plum Creek.
Persons mentioned: None.

Saughier, George

Georgeston 2/16/1659 – 190/139 acres. L4/593 SR7346
Location: B&TNH near Durand's Creek next adjoining The Chesapeake Bay.
Persons mentioned: None.

Margaret's Fields Res. 6/4/1670 – 280 acres. L12/590 SR7356
Location: SRH at the mouth of the South River next adjoining Pennington's Ponds.
Persons mentioned: **William Pennington & William Pell** (assignors of land rights). **Jerome White Esq.** (Surveyor Generall). **George Yate** (Deputy Surveyor). **M. Blomfield** (Chief Clerk of the Land Office). **Richard Mascole** (messenger from the land office). *Note: The tract cannot be drawn and the actual acreage cannot be determined due to incomplete boundary course information in the patent*

document.

Content 9/10/1683 – 150/156 acres. LDSA/470 SR7369
Location: B&TNH on the south side of the Maggity River
next adjoining a tract called Alderidge's Beginning.
Persons mentioned: **Nicholas Gassaway** (assignor of land
rights). **Nicholas Alderidge** (neighbor).

Saunders, James

Batchellor's Hope 8/8/1670 – 200 acres. L13/49 SR7355
Location: MNH on the north side of the South River.
Persons mentioned: **George Yate & David Poole** (assignors
of land rights). **Robert Franklin, Neale Clarke, & John
Dearing** (neighbors). *Note: The tract cannot be drawn and
the actual acreage cannot be determined due to incomplete
boundary course information in the patent document.*

The Equality 5/10/1685 – 140/137 acres. LNS2i/138
SR7371
Location: SRH at John's Cabbin Branch next adjoining the
Flatt Creek.
Persons mentioned: **Richard Cheney** (neighbor).

Saundry, Francis

Knockers Hale 5/1/1672 – 50/50 acres. L14/547 SR7356
Location: WRH in the swamp between the West River and
The Chesapeake Bay.
Persons mentioned: **John Cumber** (neighbor).

Scott, Edward

Scott's Folly 3/20/1695 – 200/195 acres. LC3i/509 SR7377
Location: B&TNH on the Middle Runn on the south side of
the Patapsco River.
Persons mentioned: None.

Selby, Edward *(Planter)*

Selby's Marsh 4/28/1658 – 490/262 acres. LAB&H/225
SR7344
Location: SRH on the south side at the mouth of the South
River on the west side of the Rode River at Selby's Marsh.
Persons mentioned: **John Watkins, John Franklin &**
Jeremy Haxling (neighbors). *Note: The discrepancy between*
certified and actual acreage is extreme, even for this period.
However, the boundary courses have been verified and the
acreage is correct as shown above.

Pascall's Purchase 6/21/1667 – 300/292 acres. L10/555
SR7353
Location: HCH on west side of Herring Creek near the West
Creek.
Persons mentioned: **Thomas Marsh** (neighbor).

Selby, Edward, Jr.

Selby's Stopp 6/12/1688 – 201/202 acres. LNS2i//730
SR7371
Location: SRH on the north side of the Road River at the
mouth of Woolman's Creek.
Persons mentioned: **Richard Beard, John Hall, Madame**
Ursala Burges, & Coll. William Burges (assignors of land
rights). **Edward Selby** *(the elder)* **& William Rumsay**
(neighbors).

Selby, John

Knavery Prevented 4/10/1702 – 400/399 acres. LDSF/300
SR7373
Location: B&TNH in the forke of Curtis Creek.
Persons mentioned: None. *Note: The patent/survey document*
places this tract in Baltimore County. MSA Land Index #55
places it in Anne Arundel County. I have included it here
based on its location.

Selby, Matthew

Selby's Enlargement 9/1/1670 – 50/42 acres. L14/62
SR7356
Location: WRH on the east side of the West River
Persons mentioned: Richard Smith (assignor of land rights).
John Shaw & Francis Parsons (neighbors).

Selby, Thomas & Edward

Poplar Hill 9/15/1655 – 100/100 acres. L8/296 SR7350
Location: SRH on the north side of the Road River adjoining
Woolman's Creek.
Persons mentioned: George Puddington (assignor of land
rights).

Sewell/Sewall, Henry

Hope 8/8/1664 – 100/107 acres. L7/343 SR7349
Location: MNH on the south side of the Severn River about
one mile from Plum Creek.
Persons mentioned: Himself & William Rinthell (transported
by Sewell to this Province to inhabit). *Note 1: The
boundaries of the tract begin at a marked Oak by an
"Indian Path" which is a portion of present day General's
Highway (MD Rt. 178). Note 2: The tract was sold to John
Minter (12/16/1675) and, following his death, it was devised
to Elizabeth Williston.*

Henry's Addition 4/14/1673 – 30/30 acres. L13/504
SR7355
Location: MNH on the south side of the Severn River at The
Round Bay.
Persons mentioned: William Wheatly of London, Marriner &
Robert Wilson (assignors of land rights). George Yate
(Deputy Surveyor). William Galloway (neighbor).

Henry's Encrease 7/1/1680 – 43/43 acres. LCB2i/41
SR7366

Location: on the south side of the Severn River next adjoining a tract called Brown's Increase.
Persons mentioned: George Holland (assignor of land rights). Thomas Brown (neighbor).

Sewell's Increase 9/20/1680 – 500/512 acres. LCB2i/75 SR7366
Location: MNH on the north side of the Severn River at Sewell's Cove & Bear Point.
Persons mentioned: Henry Ridgely & Abraham Child (assignors of land rights).). *Note 1: Although the patent document places this tract on the north side of the Severn River in the B&TNH, it also identifies a tract called Mill Meadow as an adjoining tract. Mill Meadow is on the south side of the Severn in the MNH. Note 2: Sewell's Last Will & Testament (dated 9/29/1699) devised 150 (of 500) acres to son Henry Jr. Anticipating that the will might be questionable, elder brother James gave up all claim to an equal amount and, in 1702, James conveyed 100 acres each to brothers Joshua & Phillip in accordance with their father's wishes as expressed in his LWT (WT2/75 & 105).*

Sewall's Fancy 7/16/1706 – 300/259 acres. LDD5i/443 SR7378
Location: MNH lying above the head of the Severn River next adjoining tracts called Littleworth & Sewall's Increase.
Persons mentioned: Stephen Gill (assignor of land rights).
Note: This patent is included because the certification and/or survey date is within the targeted period.

Shaw, John

Shaw's Folly 9/15/1666 – 260/275 acres. L10/108 SR7352
Location: SRH on the west side of the Road River.
Persons mentioned: None.

Shaw's Folly Res. 4/1/1672 – 360/ 394 acres. L16/554 SR7357

Location: SRH on the west side of the Road River at Shaw's Creek.
Persons mentioned: **George Yate & Capt James Connaway** (assignors of land rights).

Shepheard/Shepherd/Sheppard, Nicholas Maj.
Shepheard's Right 10/1/1674 – 100/93 acres. L18/260 .
SR7359
Location: MNH on the south side of the Ann Arundell *(Severn)* River next adjoining a tract called The Friend's Choice.
Persons mentioned: **Robert Wilson** (assignor of land rights). **William Grimes** (neighbor).

Shepheard's Grove 8/10/1684 – 120/117 acres. LSDA/461
SR7369
Location: MNH about three miles from the head of the Ann Arundell *(Severn)* River.
Persons mentioned: **Henry Hanslap** (assignor of land rights).

Shepheard's Choice 6/1/1687 – 240/240 acres. LNS2i/482
SR7371
Location: MNH on the south side of the Severn River.
Persons mentioned: **John Gray** (assignor of land rights). **John Warfield** (neighbor).

Sheppard's Forrest 7/7/1702 – 292/297 acres. LCDi/78
SR7376
Location: B&TNH on the southwest side of the Patuxent River.
Persons mentioned: **Dryer** (neighbor). *Note: The patent/survey document places this tract in Baltimore County. MSA Land Index #55 places it in Anne Arundel County. I have included it here based on its location.*

Shipley/Shepley, Adam

Shepley's Choice 1/20/1681 –200/205 acres. LCBi/463
SR7366
Location: MNH on the south side of the Ann Arundell
(Severn) River near the head.
Persons mentioned: George Yate (assignor of land rights).
*Note: The patent document uses two spellings for the
owner's name, i.e., Shepley and Shipley. Note: Tract
ownership subsequently passed to Shepley's son John who
gave it to his sisters Lois Shepley & Keturah Barnes in
1698(IH#2 1/82).*

Adam The First 1/1/1689 – 500/503 acres. LNS2i/572
SR7371
Location: B&TNH about sixteen miles from the head of the
Severn River on the side of a branch of the Patapsco River.
Persons mentioned: Richard Beard (assignor of land rights).
Note: The tract lies in present day Howard County.

Sisson, Elizabeth

The Orphant's Inheritance 5/21/1666 - 200/210 acres.
L9/465 SR7351
Location: MNH on the south side of the Severn River at The
Round Bay.
Persons mentioned: John Sisson, deceased (father of
Elizabeth & her sister Jane Sisson). William Crouch &
John Howard (assignors of land rights). William Galloway
& John Norwood (neighbors). *Note: The spelling of the
word "orphans" as orphants was not uncommon.*

Sisson, Jane

Jane's Inheritance 6/20/1668 – 50/51 acres. L12/28
SR7454
Location: MNH on the south side of the Severn River at
Sunken Ground Creek.
Persons mentioned: John Sisson, deceased (father of Jane &
Elizabeth Sisson and a former owner). John Herman

(person transported by John Sisson to this Province to inhabit).

Skidmore, Edward
Hamilton (aka Hambleton) 8/4/1664 – 350/350 acres. L7/238 SSR7379
Location: MNH on the north side of the South River on the east side of Broad Creek at the mouth of McCubbin's Cove. Persons mentioned: **Ellenor & Abraham Ursulead & Elias Goddfrey** (persons transported by Skidmore into this Province here to inhabit). **Oliver Sprye** (assignor of land rights). *Note: Skidmore sold the tract to **John Struther** who was convicted of murder (4/30/1669). Through the escheat process the tract was returned to Skidmore. At some point later the patent was vested in **Joseph Finder** who eventually forfeited the land.*

Skidmore 8/5/1664 – 200/195 acres. L7/266 SR7349
Location: B&TNH at the mouth of Fishing Creek.
Persons mentioned: **Robert Park** (assignor of land rights). **Rize Bozill, Henry Lloyd, & Sanders Scrivner** (persons transported into this Province by **Skidmore** here to inhabit).

Skipworth, George
The Addition 6/4/1680 - 21 acres. L20/373 SR7361
Location: WRH among the branches of the West River.
Persons mentioned: **George Yate** (assignor of land rights). **Richard Talbott & Richard Ewen** (neighbors). *Note 1: The tract cannot be drawn and actual acreage determined because of incomplete boundary course information. Note 2: The number of acres certified is unclear. It is assumed that Skipworth's warrant was for at least eighteen acres and that Yate assigned an additional three acres.*

Slade/Slaid, William
Slade's Hope 8/5/1664 – 50/50 acres. L7/278 SR7349
Location: B&TNH on the north side of the Severn River.

Persons mentioned: Hendrick Cornelius (assignor of land rights). Edward Lloyd, Esq. (neighbor).

Wolf's Neck 8/4/1664 – 100/96 acres. L7/223 SR7349
Location: B&TNH on the north side of the Severn River and on the west side of Ferry Creek.
Persons mentioned: Richard Preston (assignor of land rights). Emmanuel Drue & Edward Blay (neighbors).

Slade's Addition 11/20/1671 – 50/56 acres. L14.375 SR7356
Location: B&TNH on the east side of the Severn River in a valley at Slade's Branch.
Persons mentioned: Stephen Thurgood & Robert Ridgely (assignors of land rights).
William Blea *(probably Blay)* & William Fuller (neighbors).

Slade's Addition 11/10/1695 – 112 acres. LC3i/74 SR7377
Location: B&TNH by Curtis Creek next adjoining a tract called Curtis Neck.
Persons mentioned: None. *Note: The tract cannot be drawn and actual acreage cannot be determined due to inaccurate boundary course information.*

Smith, Anthony

Anthony's Purchase 6/16/1699 – 325/325 acres. LCC4/132 SR7325
Location: SRH next adjoining a tract called Ann Arundell Mannor.
Persons mentioned: Coll. Henry Darnall (Surveyor Generall). Soloman Sparrow (neighbor).

Smith, Edward

Smith's Desire 4/13/1686 - 250/249 acres. LIB&ILC/161 SR7368-2
Location: B&TNH on the south side of Curtis Creek.

Persons mentioned: George Burges, Gent. (assignor of land rights).

Smith, James

Swan Neck Res. 10/8/1674 – 250/270 acres. L15/298 SR4327
Location: B&TNH on the north side of the Severn River at the mouth of Timber Neck Creek.
Persons mentioned: **Edward Lloyd** (former owner). **Robert Ridgely** (assignor of land rights). *Note: Smith purchased Swan Neck from Lloyd as a 600-acre tract for 1,340 lbs of tobacco. A resurvey discovered an additional 250 acres surplus (within the bounds) and Robert Ridgely assigned sufficient rights to Smith to cover the surplus, which was then granted to Smith.*

Jacob's Point 1676 – 21/19 acres. L21/280 SR7362
Location: SRH on the south side of South River at the head of Jacob's Creek.
Persons mentioned: **George Holland & George Yate** (assignors of land rights). **Edward Towning & George Puddington** (neighbors).

Smith, Nathan

Smithfield 7/8/1664 – 100/100 acres. L7/183 SR7349
Location: HCH on Herring Creek next adjoining tracts called Smith's Delight and Trent.
Persons mentioned: **Jacob Dukettaway** *(probably Duhaddaway)* assignor of land rights, **Samuel Chew, Robert Morley, John Gray, & Thomas Ford** (neighbors).

Smith's Delight 9/20/1665 – 300/300 acres. L8/407 SR7350
Location: HCH about 1.5 miles from the river next adjoining a tract called Chew's Right.
Persons mentioned: **Samuel Chew** (neighbor).

Lord's Bounty 2/5/1685 – 210/213 acres. LCB3i/95
SR7367
Location: HCH on the North Branch of Herring Creek.
Persons Mentioned: John Burrage (initial owner). Margaret
Burrage Smith (daughter of John Burrage and wife of
Nathan Smith). Major John Welch, Dalton James, John
Wilson, Margaret Evans, Grace Burrage (assignors of land
rights assigned to them by Nathan Smith)

Smith, Philemon

Smith's Forrest 10/10/1695 – 200/200 acres. LWD/113
SR7372-1
Location: B&TNH on the south side of Curtis Creek.
Persons mentioned: William Gosnell (assignor of land
rights). Morris Baker (neighbor).

Smith, Walter

Smith's Rest 8/15/1664 - 150/188 acres. L7/282 SR7379
Location: MNH on the north side of the South River.
Persons mentioned: None. *Note: Smith devised the tract to
his son **Manuell** who sold it to **Lawrence Draper**.*

Smith, Zephaniah

Smith 6/21/1650 – 585 acres. L3/1 SR7343
Location: MNH on the north side of the South River
adjoining Smith's & Inlargement Creeks.
Persons mentioned: None. *Note 1: Another patent can be
found in LAB&H/41 SR7344. Note 2: The tract cannot be
drawn and the actual acreage cannot be determined due to
incomplete boundary course information in the patent
document.*

Town Neck On the Severne 6/21/1650 – 15 acres. L3/1
SR7343
Location: B&TNH on the north side of the Severn River
adjoining Town Branch and The Chesapeake Bay.

Persons mentioned: Samuel Wills & George Saughier (neighbors). *Note: The patent for this tract was conveyed in the same document as the preceding tract (Smith). This tract cannot be drawn or measured due to incomplete boundary course information.*

Unnamed Cert 11/27/1651 100/94 acres. LAB&H/265 SR7344
Location: MNH on the north side of the South River at Smith's Branch next adjoining a tract called Smith.
Persons mentioned: None.

Snowden, Richard

Robin Hood's Forrest 8/1/1686 – 1,976/1,684 acres. LIB&ILC/230 SR7368-1
Location: MNH on the Great Forke of the Patuxent River
Persons mentioned: None. *Note 1: The tract lies in present day Prince George's County in the general area of the intersection of MD. Route 197 and the Baltimore Washington Parkway. Note 2: The discrepancy between certified and actual acreage is extreme, even for this period. However, the boundary courses have been verified and the acreage is correct as shown above.*

Turkey Neck 9/10/1698 – 200/188 acres. LCC4i/122 SR7375
Location: SRH on the north side of the Great Forke of Patuxent River next adjoining a tract called Phelps His Choice.
Persons mentioned: **John Gaither** (neighbor).

Snowden, Richard Jr.

Walter's His Lott 10/10/1704 – 611/594 acres. LDSF/514 SR 7373-2
Location: SRH on the Great Forke of the Patuxent River north of a tract called Robin Hood's Forrest.
Persons mentioned: **James Carroll** (assignor of land rights).

Solling, Harman

    Smith's Range 3/22/1666 – 100/94 acres. L9/364 SR7351
Location: B&TNH on the north side of the Severn River at Great Piney Creek.
Persons mentioned: Thomas Waddy (assignor of land rights). John Askew (neighbor).

Sparrow, Soloman

    Soloman's Purchase 1/15/1699 – 150/150 acres. LWD/274 SR7372-2
Location: SRH at the head of the Road River.
Persons mentioned: None.

    The Addition 8/18/1699 – 100/100 acres. LDD5i/3 SR7378
Location: WRH near the head of the Rode River next adjoining a tract called Anthony's Purchase.
Persons mentioned: Coll Henry Darnall (Surveyor Generall), Anthony Smith (neighbor).

Sparrow, Thomas, Jr. *(Planter)*

    Sparrow's Rest 9/7/1659 – 590/590 acres. L4/97 SR7346
Location: WRH on the west side of the Rode River at the mouth of Herring Branch.
Persons mentioned: Elizabeth Sparrow (wife), Thomas *(III)* & Elizabeth (children), of
Thomas Sparrow, Jr., who transported them, along with John Dennis, to this Province to inhabit in 1649.

    Sparrow's Addition 5/28/1675 – 100/48 acres. L19/8 SR7360
Location: SRH by the Road River at Nettlefolds Branch.
Persons mentioned: None.

Spencer, John

    Spencer's Search 5/29/1683 – 17.2/21 acres. LSDA/91 SR7369

Location: HCH in Herring Creek Bay next adjoining a tract called Kequestan Choice.
Persons mentioned: **George Holland & Thomas Miles** (assignors of land rights). **Mr. Aires** (neighbor).

Spriggs, Thomas
Friendship 9/3/1663 – 1,650/1,688 acres. L5/444 SR7347
Location: HCH on the east side of the Patuxent River near the branches of Lyon's Creek.
Persons mentioned: **Thomas Stone**, Gent, & **Thomas Jordan**, Merchant (assignors of land rights. **Christopher Burkitt** (neighbor).

Stear, Richard
Stear's Park 10/10/1695 – 100/78 acres. LWD/120 SR7372-2
Location: B&TNH at the head of Stony Creek.
Persons mentioned: **Richard Beard** (assignor of land rights). **Morris Baker, Amos Pierpoint, & Peter Bond** (neighbors).

Stephens, Charles & Howard, John
Charles' Hill 2/9/1662 – 200/200 acres. L5/632 SR7347
Location: MNH on the south side of the Severn River on the south side of Underwood's Creek in a neck of land called The Mountain Neck.
Persons mentioned: **Henry Sewell & John Norwood** (neighbors).

Stephens/Stevens, Charles
Charles' Hills 7/23/1679 – 271/271 acres. L20/255 SR7361
Location: MNH on the west side of the Ann Arundell *(Severn)* River.
Persons mentioned: **George Yate** (assignor of land rights).

Hicory Ridge 11/10/1695 – 262/265 acres. L23/255 SR7264

Location: MNH lying among the branches of the Severn River.
Persons mentioned: **Capt John Hammond** (neighbor). *Note: Stevens willed this tract to his son & heir **William Stevens** (MSA Land Index #73).*

Timber Neck 11/10/1695 – 303/298 acres. LDW/143
SR7372 –2
Location: MNH adjoining a tract called Pierpoint's Range.
Persons mentioned: **Thomas Richardson** (assignor of land rights). **Jabez Pierpoint** (neighbor).

What You Please 11/10/1695 – 72/68 acres. Lc3i/303
SR7377
Location: MNH in the woods next adjoining a tract called Brandy.
Persons mentioned: **Thomas Richardson & Michael Taylor** (assignors of land rights). **Matthew Howard** (neighbor).

Stephen's Forrest 5/10/1709 – 702/571 acres. LDD5i/572
SR7378
Location: B&TNH on the east side of the Patuxent River in Elk Ridge next adjoining a tract called Long Reach.
Persons mentioned: **Edward Dorsey** (neighbor). *Note: The discrepancy between certified and actual acreage is extreme, even for this period. However, the boundary courses have been verified and the acreage is correct as shown above. Note 2: This patent is included because the cert and/or survey date is within the targeted period. Note 3: This tract was located in Baltimore County at the time of the patent/survey. I have included it because the land had been, and would again be, designated as Anne Arundel County before being absorbed into present day Howard County.*

Stimson/Stinson, John
Long Venture 7/20/1673 – 250/278 acres. L17/170
SR7358

Location: MNH between the Severn and South Rivers next adjoining a tract called Wyatt's Ridge.
Persons mentioned: **Robert Wilson** (assignor of land rights).
Henry Pierpoint & Nicholas Wyatt (neighbors).

Stinson's Choice 2/20/1684 – 618/695 acres. LWD126
SR7368-1
Location: SRH at the Forke of the North Great Branch of the Patuxent River next adjoining a tract called Merriton's Fancy.
Persons mentioned: None. *Note 1: This tract lies in present day Howard County. Note 2: The discrepancy between certified and actual acreage is extreme, even for this period. However, the boundary courses have been verified and the acreage is correct as shown above.*

Stinchcomb, Nathaniel

Stinchcombe's Addition 5/1/1672 – 36/40 acres. L16/590
SR7357
Location: B&TNH in a neck of land called The Broad Neck.
Persons mentioned: **Robert Wilson** (assignor of land rights).
D. Lewis & Strong, _ _ _ _ _ (neighbors).

Stockett, Francis

Dodon 7/20/1671 – 664 acres. L14/329 SR7376
Location: SRH on the south side of the South River adjoining Stockett's Runn.
Persons mentioned: **Henry & Thomas Stockett** (brothers). *Note: The tract cannot be drawn and the actual acreage cannot be determined due to incomplete boundary course information in the patent document.*

Stockett, Henry

Bridge Hill 7/9/1671 – 663 acres. L16/287 SR7357
Location: SRH on the north side of a tract called Ann Arundell Manor next adjoining a tract called Taylor's Choice.
Persons mentioned: **Francis & Thomas Stockett** (brothers). *Note: The tract cannot be drawn and the actual acreage*

cannot be determined due to incomplete boundary course
information in the patent document.

Stockett, Thomas

Obligation 1/20/1670 – 663 acres. L16/483 SR7357
Location: SRH at the northmost corner oak of a tract called
Taylor's Choice.
Persons mentioned: Francis & Henry Stockett (brothers).
Note: The tract cannot be drawn and the actual acreage
cannot be determined due to incomplete boundary course
information in the patent document.

Strong, Elizabeth

Maidenstone 2/18/1659 – 250 acres. L4/489 SR7346
Location: B&TNH on the north side of the Severn River and
on the east side of Broad Creek.
Persons mentioned: Leonard Strong, deceased (father of
Elizabeth Strong and bequeathor of land rights). *Note: The*
tract cannot be drawn and the actual acreage cannot be
determined due to incomplete boundary course information
in the patent document.

Angellica 10/1/1670 – 651 acres. L14/40 SR7456
Location: MNH adjoining the land of William Fuller.
Persons mentioned: Robert Clarke (Surveyor Generall).
Charles James (husband of Elizabeth Strong, the sole heir
of Leonard Strong, deceased). *Note: The tract cannot be*
drawn and the actual acreage cannot be determined due to
incomplete boundary course information in the patent
document.

Elizabetha 10/1/1670 – 200 acres. L14/41 SR7376
Location: MNH adjoining the land of William Fuller.
Persons mentioned: Robert Clarke (Surveyor Generall).
Charles James (husband of Elizabeth Strong, the sole heir
of Leonard Strong, deceased). *Note: The tract cannot be*
drawn and the actual acreage cannot be determined due to

incomplete boundary course information in the patent document.

Strong, Leonard

Unnamed Cert 10/7/1651 – 200/170 acres. LAB&H/260
SR7344
Location: MNH on the north side of the South River adjoining The Chesapeake Bay.
Persons mentioned: **William Fuller** (neighbor).

Sturton, George

Sturton's Rest 7/10/1671 – 100/111 acres. L14/291
SR7356
Location: B&TNH on the north side of the Maggity River at Cedar Point opposite Cattaile Neck.
Persons mentioned: **Robert Wilson & Thomas Welborn** (assignors of land rights).

Summerland, John

Summerland's Lott 8/10/1683 – 60 acres. LSDA/429
SR7369
Location: B&TNH on the south side of the Maggity River near the head of Bate's Branch.
Persons mentioned: **Henry Hanslap & Thomas Taillor** (assignors of land rights). *Note: The tract cannot be drawn and the actual acreage cannot be determined due to incomplete boundary course information in the patent document.*

Sumers, John

Little Town 10/10/1704 – 280/269 acres. LSDF/518
SR7372-2
Location: MNH at the forke of the North Branch of the Patuxent River.
Persons mentioned: None.

Sutton, Thomas

Sutton's Choice 7/11/1681 – 307/315 acres. LCB2i/216
SR7366
Location: B&TNH on the south side of the Maggity River.
Persons mentioned: **George Yate & Nicholas Painter**
(assignors of land rights).

Sutton's Addition 2/11/1688 – 20/19 acres. LNSBi/621
SR7370
Location: SRH on the south side of the South River at
Burges' Creek.
Persons mentioned: **Thomas Richardson** (assignor of land
rights). **William Burges, Edward Cox, & Thomas Besson**
(neighbors).

Symmons, George & Hall, Richard

Kickalan's Choice 5/30/1711 – 482/477 acres. LDD5/713
SR7378
Location: HCH near the branches of Herring Creek.
Persons mentioned: **Faith Wilson** (wife of Richard Hall),
Thomas Larkin (Deputy Surveyor), **Clement Hill** (Surveyor
Generall), **Sammuel Chew** and **John Burrage** (neighbors).
*Note: Although the tract was not patented until 5/30/1711,
this resurvey was undertaken on 3/14/1703*

Talbott, Edward & John

Talbott's Ridge Res. 5/25/1676 144/149 acres. L19/274
SR7360
Location: WRH next adjoining a tract called Ann Arundell
Mannor.
Persons mentioned: None: **Richard Talbott** (father and
former owner). *Note: "Whereas Edward & John Talbott,
orphans of the s'd Richard have informed us that part of the
s'd land lies within the lines of the Mannor of Ann Arundell
and requested a resurvey. Doe hereby grant the Letters
Pattent."*

Talbott, Edward

> Talbott's Angles 11/5/1686 – 157/157 acres. LCDi/231
> SR7346
> Location: WRH on the west side of Beaver Dam Branch.
> Persons mentioned: Nathaniel Heathcote, John Welch &
> Abel Hill (neighbors).

Talbott, Richard

> **Poplar Knowle 9/14/1659 – 200 acres.** LAB&H/103
> SR7346
> Location: WRH on the north side of the West River at the
> mouth of Brown's Branch
> Persons mentioned: **Susan Talbott** (transported by her father
> Richard Talbott to this Province to inhabit). **Christopher
> Bowles** (transported himself to this Province and assigned
> rights to Richard Talbott). **Richard Moseby & Edward
> Lloyd, Esq.** (assignors of land rights). *Note1: The tract was
> also known by the name of Northwest River. Note 2: The
> tract cannot be drawn and the actual acreage cannot be
> determined due to incomplete boundary course information
> in the patent document.*

> **Talbott's Timber Neck 5/8/1664 – 82/63 acres.** L7/293
> SR7349
> Location: WRH on the south side of the West River by the
> South Creek.
> Persons mentioned: **Richard Ewen** (assignor of land rights).

> **Talbott's Ridge 8/5/1684 – 300/163 acres.** L7/229 SR7349
> Location: WRH on the north side of the West River
> Persons mentioned: **Nicholas Winfly, Ann Pickson, John
> Fresh, & Thomas Maddock** (persons transported by **Talbott**
> into this Province here to inhabit). **John Bonner** (neighbor).
> *Note: The discrepancy between certified and actual acreage
> is extreme, even for this period. However, the boundary
> courses have been verified and the acreage is correct as*

shown above.

Taylor, Michael
>What You Please 2/14/1689 – 72/68 acres. LC3/302
>SR7377
>Location: MNH near the head of the Ann Arundell (Severn)
>River next adjoining a tract called Brandy.
>Persons mentioned: Thomas Richardson (assignor of land
>rights). Matthew Howard & Richard Warfield
>(neighbors). *Note: This tract was eventually patented by*
>*Charles Stephens on 11/10/1695.*

Taylor, Robert
>Chance 5/10/1685 – 32/32 acres. LNS2i/114 SR7371
>Location: B&TNH on the south side of the Maggity River
>next adjoining a tract called Brushy Neck.
>Persons mentioned: Richard Beard (assignor of land rights).
>Thomas Turner (neighbor).

Taylor, Thomas & Elizabeth
>South Canton 1659 – 200 acres. L4/107 SR7346
>Location: B&TNH on the south side of the Patapsco River.
>Persons mentioned: Thomas Sparrow (former owner and
>assignor of land rights). Elizabeth Sparrow, William Hyde
>& Edward Johnson (persons transported by Sparrow into
>this Province here to inhabit). *Note: The tract cannot be*
>*drawn and the actual acreage cannot be determined due to*
>*incomplete boundary course information in the patent*
>*document.*

Taylor, Thomas
>Taylor's Chance & Hale 5/23/1663 – 500/300 acres,
>L5/349 SR7347
>Taylor's Chance (tract 1) 300/150 acres. Hale (tract 2)
>150/150 acres.
>Location: WRH westward of Muddy Creek among the
>branches of the Patuxent River.

Persons mentioned: **William Burges** (assignor of land rights). *Note 1: The Grant conveys two adjoining tracts. Note 2: A later patent is found in L10/373 SR7352. The details of each are the same except the latter patent refers to the first tract as Taylor's Choice and the second tract as the The Hale or possibly The Hole.*

Rowdown 12/12/1670 – 800/775 acres. L6/34 SR7377
Location: SRH on the north side of Stockett's Runn next adjoining a tract called The Friend's Choice.
Persons mentioned: **George Yate** (assignor of land rights). **William Jones & John Gray** (neighbors).

The Tryangle 9/10/1672 – 36/36 acres. L17/300 SR7357
Location: WRH adjoining Beaver Pond Branch.
Persons mentioned: **George Yate & Jerome White, Esq.** (assignors of land rights). **John Larkin** (neighbor).

Taylor's Addition 9/10/1672 – 100/107 acres. L17/299 SR7352
Location: SRH adjoining tracts called Taylor's Choice & Hale.
Persons mentioned: **George Yate & Jerome White, Esq.** (assignors of land rights). Thomas Mills (neighbor).

Roedown Security 6/20/1675 – 477/369 acres. L19/28 SR7360
Location: SRH on the east side of the North Branch of the Patuxent River.
Persons mentioned: None. *Note: The discrepancy between certified and actual acreage is extreme, even for this period. However, the boundary courses have been verified and the acreage is correct as shown above.*

Taylor's Search 2/1/1688 – 18.5/18.6 acres. LAB#B/620 SR7370

Location: WRH between the line of Ann Arundell Mannor and a bounded tree of a tract called Hale.
Persons mentioned: Thomas Richardson (assignor of land rights). Thomas Miles (neighbor).

Taylor, William

Wrighton 9/7/1650 – 100 acres. LAB&H/96 SR7346
Location: SRH on the west side of the Road River near Three Island Bay on Harwood's Branch.
Persons mentioned: Walter Mansfield (transporter of himself into this Province to inhabit and assignor of land rights).
Note: The tract cannot be drawn and the actual acreage cannot be determined due to incomplete boundary course information in the patent document.

Taylord, William

Taylord's Enlargement 7/10/1702 – 36/37 acres.
LDD5i/137 SR7378
Location: B&TNH on the south side of the Maggity River adjoining tracts called Bate's Chance & Rowle's Addition.
Persons mentioned: Thomas Woods (neighbor).

Hampton's Enlargement 11/5/1702 36/39 acres.
LSDF/530 SR7373
Location: B&TNH on the south side of the Maggity River adjoining tracts called Rolls *(probably Rowles)* Addition and Bate's Chance.
Persons mentioned: Thomas Woods (neighbor).

Tench, Thomas

The Fish Pond (Thomas Tench) 12/4/1704 – 58/56 acres.
L14/516 SR7356
Location: HCH in the woods about one mile from Herring Creek next adjoining Beaver Dam Runn.
Persons mentioned: Thomas Larkin (Deputy Surveyor), William Padgett (neighbor).

Terrat, Nicholas, Jr.

Wrighten 11/10/1697 – 715/703 acres. LCDi/6 SR7376
Location: SRH adjoining a tract called Ann Arundell Manor and the Patuxent River.
Persons mentioned: Nicholas Terrat (father of Nicholas Terrat, Jr.)

Thomas, Phillip

Beckley 2/9/1650 - 500/500 acres. LQ/325 SR7345
Location: WRH next adjoining a tract called Carter Bennett
Persons mentioned: Sarah Thomas (wife), Phillip, Sarah, & Elizabeth (children of Phillip Thomas. All transported by him into this Province here to inhabit). Capt. Edward Carter & Tristram Bennett (neighbors). *Note: Fourteen years later Thomas would again claim land rights for transporting the same persons named above. (See Fuller's Point.)*

Fuller's Point 1664 – 70/73 acres. L9/292 /SR7351.
Location: MNH at the junction of Fishing Creek and the South River.
Persons mentioned: Sarah Thomas (wife), Caleb & Phillip (sons), Sarah & Elizabeth (daughters) of Phillip Thomas. Arnold Jackson (all transported to this Province by Phillip Thomas LQ/425 SR7345). *Note: The grant conveys two adjoining tracts.*

Thomas, Samuel

Samuel's Purchase 1/16/1699 – 200/196 acres. LCC4/132 SR7375
Location: HCH beginning at a bound Hickory in the line of a tract called Ann Arundell Manor.
Persons mentioned: Coll Henry Darnall (Surveyor Generall), Smith (apparently the original owner although this is well out of the area known to be settled by the Smiths).

Thurston, Thomas

The Tanyard 2/20/1665 – 120/119 acres. L9/301 SR7371

Location: B&TNH on the north side of the Severn River in a neck of land called The Broad Neck, by Fuller's Creek.
Persons mentioned: **George Yate** (assignor of land rights). **Andrew Skinner** (former owner). **John Homewood, Ema Dreives, & Ralph Hawkins** (neighbors).

Tideings, Richard

Hazlenut Ridge Res. **7/13/1688 – 166/164 acres.** LCB2i/14 SR7366
Location: WRH near the head of the Rode River.
Persons mentioned: **George Yate** (assignor of land rights). **Nicholas Gassaway, Thomas Smithrick, Thomas Taylor, & Thomas Sparrow** (neighbors).

Todd, Thomas *(Shipwright)*

Todd **6/8/1651 – 100/117 acres.** LAB&H/288 SR7344
Location: MNH on the south side of Severn River on Oyster Sell Point.
Persons mentioned: **Thomas Hall** (neighbor).

Todd's Range 5/4/1664 – 120/136 acres. L7/244 SR7349
Location: MNH on the north side of the South River adjoining land he now liveth on.
Persons mentioned: **Joyce Bayne, John Barker, & Matthew Burin** (persons transported by Todd into this Province here to inhabit).

Todd's Harbor 4/10/1671 120/113 acres. L14/191 SR7356
Location: MNH on the west side of the Ann Arundell *(Severn)* River at Todd's Creek.
Persons mentioned: **Robert Wilson** (assignor of land rights). **Richard Acton & Thomas Hall** (neighbors). *Note: This grant includes land formerly certified to* **Todd***, called Todd that was surveyed on 7/8/1661, and adjoined Richard Acton's land in Annapolis Town.*

Todd's Pasture 6/29/1675 – 29/24 acres. L19/122 SR7360
Location: MNH adjoining Todd's Neck.
Persons mentioned: George Yate (assignor of land rights).

Tolley, Thomas
Unnamed Cert 10/27/1651 – 300 acres. LAB&H/290
SR7344
Location: MNH on the south side of the Severn River
adjoining The Chesapeake Bay.
Persons mentioned: Phillip Thomas (neighbor). *Note: The
tract cannot be drawn and the actual acreage cannot be
determined due to incomplete boundary course information
in the patent document.*

New Worster 10/1/1679- 103 acres. L21/154
Location: MNH adjoining the Chesapeake Bay at a point of
land called Tolley's Point.
Persons mentioned: Nicholas Greenbury (assignor of land
rights). *Note 1: No patent found. Note 2: The tract is
occasionally referenced as New Worster at Tolley Point.
Note 3: The tract cannot be drawn and the actual acreage
cannot be determined due to incomplete boundary course
information.*

Tolley's Point 9/9/1683 - 140 acres. L22/69 SR7363
Location: MNH on the north side of the South River
adjoining Howell's Creek and The Chesapeake Bay at a point
of land called Tolley's Point.
Persons mentioned: George Yate (Deputy Surveyor). George
Talbott, Esq. (Surveyor Generall). *Note: The tract cannot be
drawn and the actual acreage cannot be determined due to
incomplete boundary course information in the patent
document.*

Towgood, Josias
The Lott 1704 – 50/37 acres. LSDF/512 SR7372-2
Location: HCH on the north side of Lyon's Creek next
adjoining a tract called Grammar's Choice

Persons mentioned: None

Townhill, Edward *(Planter)*

Townhill 2/16/1659 – 400/393 acres. L4/503 SR7346
Location: WRH on the west side of the Rode River and on the
north side of Muddy Creek.
Persons mentioned: **William Burges & John Brewer**
(neighbors). *Note: In his Last Will & Testament (dated
4/9/1684) Townhill devised the tract in 100-acre portions to*
**Leonard Wayman, Nicholas Gassaway, Richard Snowden,
Jr.***, and his wife* **Kathryn Townhill** *for the rest of her
natural life. Upon her death, her share would revert to*
Deborah Wayman*. The Lord Proprietor determined that,
because it was intended that the entire tract would be owned
by the legators following the death of Kathryn Townhill, the
land should escheat to him, "for want of heirs of the s'd
Townhill." The Conditions of Plantation provide that
although land can be sold to anyone, land owned by a
person without heirs escheats to the LOP upon his/her
death.* **Coll Thomas Taylor,** *however, convinced the LOP to
agree to implement the wishes of the deceased. A 3-man
panel consisting of* **Coll Henry Darnall, William Diggs,** *&*
Maj. Nicholas Shepheard *was appointed to oversee the
issuance of patents in accordance with Townhill's will.
Leonard Wayman and Kathryn Townhill died and their
shares were patented to* **Edmund Waymam** *(brother of
Leonard) and* **Deborah Wayman Linescomb** *(the wife of*
Thomas Linescomb *at that time). Their patent documents,
which do not include boundary courses, are found in
LCDi/43. No patents of this land were found for Richard
Snowden, Jr. and Nicholas Gassaway, although a 1705,
certification number (415) for 400 acres called Townhill
was found for Gassway in MSA Land Records #54.*

Unnamed Patent 8/9/1658 – 270 acres. LQ/111 SR7345
Location: SRH on the west side of the West River next
adjoining a tract called Townhill's Branch.
Persons mentioned: **Patrick Gossum** and his wife **Elizabeth**

(transported themselves into this Province to inhabit and assigned their land rights to **Townhill**). *Note: The tract cannot be drawn and the actual acreage cannot be determined due to incomplete boundary course information in the patent document.*

Troster, John

Troster's Purchase 10/30/1661 – 300/310 acres. L4/604 SR7346
Location: Three holes area.
Persons mentioned: **Thomas Tolley** (former owner and assignor of land rights). **Margaret Tolley** & **Thomas Tolley, Jr.** (wife & son transported by Tolley into this Province). **Phillip Thomas** (neighbor). *Note: The 3-hole area is not a hundred. This designation identifies a small number of tracts adjoining a cliff with three holes that served as a landmark. Other than being in Ann Arundell Manor, there is nothing in the patent documents to indicate where this cliff or these tracts were located.*

Truman, Thomas

Upton 4/1/1664 – 300/305 acres. L6/270 SR7348
Location: HCH on the east side of the Patuxent River by Lyon's Creek at Burkitt's Branch.
Persons mentioned: None.

Tucksberry, William

Mavorne Hill 7/24/1679 – 50/54 acres. L15/901 SR7347
Location: HCH in the woods.
Person's mentioned: **George Yate** (assignor of land rights). **Richard Hall** (neighbor).

Turner, Thomas

Truroe 8/5/1664 – 50/50 acres. L7/278 SR7349
Location: B&TNH on the north side of the Severn River.
Persons mentioned: **Richard Preston** (assignor of land rights). **Richard Young** (neighbor).

Gray Lands 8/20/1665 – 150/150 acres. L8/109 SR7350
Location: B&TNH on the north side of the Magothy River at the mouth of Little Island Creek.
Persons mentioned: None.

Deep Creek Point 8/24/1665 – 50/39 acres. L8/106 SR7350
Location: B&TNH on the south side of the Maggity River next adjoining a tract called Swan Neck.
Persons mentioned: **Edward Lloyd & Richard Moss** (neighbors).

Flushing 5/1/1672 – 100/108 acres. L14/469 SR7356
Location: B&TNH between the Ann Arundell *(Severn)* and Maggity Rivers.
Persons mentioned: **Robert Ridgely & Lawrence Highman** (assignors of land rights). **Richard Moss** (neighbor).

Cornfield Creek Plaine 3/10/1670 – 100/100 acres. L14/173 SR7356
Location: B&TNH on the east side of the Maggity River,
Persons mentioned: **Thomas Harwood & Paul Dorrill** (neighbors).

Tyler, Robert & Dawson, Abraham
The Plaine 8/5/1664 – 100/97 acres. L7/27 SR7349
Location: B&TNH on the north side of the Severn River and on the west side of a branch of Ferry Creek.
Persons mentioned: **Edward Lloyd, Esq. & Thomas Underwood** (assignors of land rights).

Tyler, Robert
Deep Creek Neck 8/11/1664 – 50 acres. L7/350 SR7349
Location: B&TNH on the west side of Deep Creek on the north side of a small runn.
Persons mentioned: **Thomas Bradley** (assignor of land

rights). **William Hopkins & William Dawson** (neighbors).
Note: The tract cannot be drawn and the actual acreage cannot be determined due to incomplete boundary course information in the patent document.

Forked Creek Point 8/11/1664 – 100/108 acres. L7352 SR7349
<u>Location:</u> B&TNH on the south side of the Maggity River.
<u>Persons mentioned:</u> Thomas Bradley (assignor of land rights).

Brushy Neck 9/20/1665 – 100/108 acres. L8/395 SR7350
<u>Location:</u> B&TNH on the north side of the Severn River.
<u>Persons mentioned:</u> Abraham Dawson (assignor of land rights). **Thomas Turner & William Hopkins** (neighbors).

Tyler's Lott 10/20/1666 – 100/100 acres. L10/275 SR7352
<u>Location:</u> B&TNH on the north side of the Severn River.
<u>Persons mentioned:</u> George _ _ _ _ & Henry Pierpoint (assignor of land rights). **Matthew Howard, Thomas Browne, & Thomas Underwood** (neighbors).

Tyler's Lott 7/1/1680 – 100/100 acres. LCB2i/14 SR7366
<u>Location:</u> B&TNH on the south side of the Maggity River.
<u>Persons mentioned:</u> John Peasley (neighbor).

Underwood, Samuel & Cokley, William
The Mutual Consent 5/10/1685 – 50/50 acres. LNSBi/181 SR7370
<u>Location:</u> B&TNH in the woods between the Maggity and Ann Arundell *(Severn)* Rivers near Ferry Creek Branch.
<u>Persons mentioned:</u> None.

Underwood, Samuel
The Addition 10/5/1683 – 22/21 acres. LSDA/170 SR7369
<u>Location:</u> B&TNH on the north side of Severn River adjoining a tract called Flushing.
<u>Persons mentioned:</u> **Henry Hanslap** (assignor of land rights).

Thomas Turner & Capt. James Connaway (neighbors).

Underwood, Thomas *(Planter)*
>**The Landing 8/8/1664 – 100/62.5 acres.** L7/348 SR7349
>Location: B&TNH on the north side of Severn River at the head of Ferry Creek.
>Persons mentioned: Richard Young (neighbor). *Note: The discrepancy between certified and actual acreage is extreme, even for this period. However, the boundary courses have been verified and the acreage is correct as shown above.*
>
>**Middle Neck 8/6/1665 – 50/50 acres.** L7/254 SR7349
>Location: B&TNH on the north side of the Severn River by Ferry Creek.
>Persons mentioned: John Meares & Richard Preston (assignors of land rights).

Utie, Nathaniel *(Carpenter/Councillor)*
>**Town Neck 1650 – 150/140 acres.** LQ/386 SR7345
>Location: B&TNH on the east side of the Ann Arundell *(Severn)* River adjoining Town Creek & Ferry Creek.
>Persons mentioned: Richard Bennet, Esq. (former owner and assignor of the tract to Utie). *Note: From the patent document: " Whereas **William Pell, George Sophir, Robert Rockhold, William Penny, Christopher Oatley, Oliver Sprye, John Lordking, & Richard Bennet, Esq.**, did in the year 1649, transport themselves into our Province here to inhabit and for their mutual security take up severall small parcells in Town Neck to the intent that they might seat close together. And whereas the severall parcells did since become the sole Property of the s'd Richard Bennett, Esq., who, for a valuable consideration sold and assigned same to Nathaniel Utie, wee doe hereby grant unto the s'd Utie the aforesaid tracts combined into one called Town Neck. "*

Vennell, John
>**Batchellor's Hope 8/8/1669 – 100 acres.** L12/400 SR7354
>Location: B&TNH on the south of the Patapsco River on

Jeffe's Island adjoining White Oak Spring.
Persons mentioned: **George Yate** (assignor of land rights).
Paul Kinsey (neighbor). *Note 1: Location & boundary
course information was found in the Certification
(L12/313 SR7354). Note 2: The tract cannot be drawn and
the actual acreage cannot be determined due to incomplete
boundary course information in the patent document.*

Vennell's Inheritance 10/10/1671 – 100 acres. L14/363
SR7356
Location: MNH on the east side of the North Runn of South
River next adjoining a tract called Pierpoint's Lott.
Persons mentioned: **Robert Wilson** (assignor of land rights).
Tobias Butler (neighbor). *Note 1:A 50-acre portion was
sold by Vennell to John Barber who sold it to William
Ridgely and wife Elizabeth in 1710. Note 2: The tract
cannot be drawn and the actual acreage cannot be
determined due to incomplete boundary course information
in the patent document.*

Vines, William

Vines His Fancy 3/20/1697 – 60/57 acres. LWDi/317
SR7372-1
Location: B&TNH in Elk Ridge.
Persons mentioned: **Cornelius Howard** (assignor of land
rights). **Samuel Chew & Adam Shepley** (neighbors). *Note:
This tract lies in present day Howard County.*

Wade, Robert

Wade's Encrease 5/18/1679 – 75/73 acres. L20/257 SR
7361
Location: SRH on the south side of the South River at Johns
Cabbin Branch of Flatt Creek.
Persons mentioned: **Richard Cheney & William Burges**
(neighbors).

Walker, George

Plumpton 6/22/1663 – 282/281 acres. L5/357 SR7347
Location: SRH on the west side of the South River by a great swamp.
Persons mentioned: **Robert Clarkson & George Puddington** (assignors of land rights). **Marin Duvall** (neighbor). *Note 1: The grant conveys two adjoining tracts. Note 2: The tract was originally surveyed for George Walker as Walker in 1661.*

Walters, John

Walters Adventure 2/27/1667 – 90/86 acres. L20/82 SR7361
Location: WRH at the head of the West River near Herring Creek Swamp.
Persons mentioned: **Robert Lockwood**, attorney for **Thomas Harwood** (assignor of land rights). **John Cumber, James White, William Harney, Robert Franklin, & Richard Arusto** (neighbors).

The Forke 7/2/1677 – 90/86 acres. L20/65 SR7361
Location: WRH near the head of the West River near to Herring Creek Swamp.
Persons mentioned: **Robert Franklin, John Cumber, James White, William Horner, & Richard Arrusto** (neighbors).

Wardner/Warner, James & Ridgely, Henry

Wardridge 6/26/1663 – 600/524 acres. L5/535 SR7347
Location: MNH on the north side of the South River next adjoining a tract called Broome.
Persons mentioned: **Richard Beard** (neighbor).

Wardner/Warner, James *(Planter)*

Wardner's Neck 1/5/1658 – 320 acres. LQ/237 SR7345
Location: MNH on the south side of the Severn River near Warner's Creek.
Persons mentioned: James Wardner transported himself, wife

Joan, one unnamed child, and servant **John Matthews** to this Province to inhabit in 1650. *Note 1:Following Wardner's death, one hundred twenty acres of this tract were devised to his wife Elizabeth (apparently a later wife) who willed her* portion to their daughter **Johana Sewell,** the wife of **John Sewell.** *Note 2: The tract cannot be drawn and the actual acreage cannot be determined due to incomplete boundary course information in the patent document.*

Wardner's Neck Res. 6/20/1668 – 320/293 acres. L12/23 SR7354
Location: MNH on the south side of the Severn River near Warner's Creek.
Persons mentioned: None.

Wardrop 2/26/1664 – 200/150 acres. L5/354 SR7347
Location: MNH on the north side of the South River east of Broad Creek.
Persons mentioned: None. *Note: Wardner sold this tract to Patrick Dunken in 1671 (WH4/142). Dunken sold to Mary Gibbs for 4,500 lbs of tobacco in 1671 (WH4/145), and Gibbs sold to John Maccubbin in 1675* (WH4/146).

Warfield, Benjamin

Ben's Discovery 1/2/1704 – 380/386 acres.
Location: MNH on the westernmost side of Towser's Branch next adjoining a tract called Grenniston.
Persons mentioned: **Matthew Howard** (neighbor).

Warfield, John & Alexander

Benson Park 12/28/1701 – 800/1,062 acres. LDD5i/62 SR7378
Location: B&TNH the Patuxent River and a branch called Hammond's Branch next adjoining a tract called Warfield's Range.
Persons mentioned: None. *Note 1: This tract lies in present day Howard County. Note 2: The discrepancy between certified and actual acreage is extreme, even for this period.*

However, the boundary courses have been verified and the acreage is correct as shown above.

Vinson Park 7/2/1702 – 800/800 acres. LCDi/73 SR7376
Location: B&TNH between the Patuxent River and a branch called Hammond's Branch next adjoining a tract called Warfield's Range.
Persons mentioned: None. *Note 1: Although not indicated in the patent document, this has to be some sort of resurvey resulting in a "reduced" version of Benson Park. Note 2: This tract lies in present day Howard County.*

Warfield, John & Richard

Warfield's Range 3/26/1696 – 1,080/1,183 acres. LC3i/356 SR7377
Location: B&TNH on the west side of the Middle Runn of the Patuxent River at Hammond's Great Branch.
Persons mentioned: **John Howard, Jr.** (assignor of land rights). *Note: This tract lies in present day Howard County.*

Warfield, Richard

Warfield's Right 7/14/1675 – 50/37 acres. L19/45 SR7360
Location: MNH on the south side of the Severn River at The Round Bay.
Persons mentioned: **John Rockhold** (neighbor).

Warfield's Forrest 4/11/1678 – 184/141 acres. L20/59 SR7361
Location: MNH in the woods next adjoining his own tract called The Addition.
Persons mentioned: **George Yate & William Burges** (assignors of land rights).

Warfield's Plaines 1/6/1680 – 300/315 acres. LCB2i/295 SR7366
Location: MNH on the south side of The Severn River at the head of Indian Cabbin Branch.
Persons mentioned: **George Yate** (assignor of land rights).

Brandy 8/10/1683 – 300/274 acres. LCB3i/496 SR7367
Location: MNH about five miles from the head of the Ann Arundell *(Severn)* River.
Persons mentioned: William Burges & Henry Hanslap (assignors of land rights). Phillip Howard, Robert Proctor, John Gaither (neighbors).

The Addition 10/8/1683 – 50/50 acres. CB3i/411 SR7367
Location: MNH in the woods about four miles from head of Severn River next adjoining a tract called Haire Hill.
Persons mentioned: Henry Hanslap (assignor of land rights). Peter Porter (neighbor).

Wincopin Neck 7/9/1702 – 883/826 acres. LDD5i/61 SR7378
Location: B&TNH in the forke of the Middle & North Branches of the Patuxent River.
Persons mentioned: None. *Note: This tract was located in Baltimore County at the time of the patent/survey. I have included it because the land had been, and would again be, designated as Anne Arundel County before being absorbed into present day Howard County.*

Warring, Sampson & Davis, Thomas
Unnamed Cert 10/27/1651 – 300/277 acres. LAB&H/371 SR7344
Location: MNH adjoining the Chesapeake Bay.
Persons mentioned: John Covill (neighbor).

Warrring, Sampson *(Carpenter)*
Warrinston 9/2/1663 - 200/200 acres. L6/75 SR7348
Location: MNH adjoining The Chesapeake Bay.
Persons mentioned: John Covill, Gent. (assignor of land rights). William Durand (neighbor).

Waterman/Waters, Nicholas

Lockwood's Guift 8/4/1685 – 500 acres. LNS2/100
SR7371
Location: WRH in Herring Creek Swamp.
Persons mentioned: **James White** (neighbor*). Note: The tract
cannot be drawn and the actual acreage cannot be
determined due to incomplete boundary course information
in the patent document.*

Water Town 11/20/1662 – 120/120 acres. L5/621 SR7347
Location: WRH at the head of the West River.
Persons mentioned: **Thomas Ford & James Scott** (original
owners)

Watkins, John

Unnamed Patent 8/9/1658 – 300 acres. LQ/111 SR7345
Location: WRH next adjoining the land of **Roger Gross**.
Persons mentioned: **Thomas Miles** (assignor of land rights
and transporter of his wife **Elizabeth** to this Province here to
inhabit). *Note: The tract cannot be drawn and the actual
acreage cannot be determined due to incomplete boundary
course information in the patent document.*

Watkin's Hope 8/5/1664 – 300/281 acres. L7/301 SR7349
Location: WRH on the north side of the West River next
adjoining a tract called Essex.
Persons mentioned: **Elizabeth Rawden & Samuel Beinger**
(persons transported by Watkins into this Province here to
inhabit). **Edward Lloyd, Esq.** (assignor of land rights).

Watkins His Purchase Res. 9/1/1681 – 554/529 acres.
LCB2i/219 SR7367
Location: WRH at the mouth of the Rode River.
Persons mentioned: **Roger Gross** (original owner).

Watkin's Inheritance Res. 10/1/1682 –300/296 acres.
LCB2i/218 SR7366

Location: WRH adjoining the West River
Persons mentioned: Roger Gross, Richard Ewen, & Benjamin Lawrence (neighbors).

Wayman, Leonard

Owen Wood Thickett 2/18/1688 – 200/174 acres. LNSBi/280 SR73770
Location: SRH in the forke near the northmost branch of the Patuxent River.
Persons mentioned: John Duvall (assignor of land rights).

Tangerine 10/10/1695 – 10/10 acres. L23/317 SR7365
Location: SRH on the South Runn of the South River near the mouth of Walker's Branch.
Persons mentioned: Daniel Ellet (assignor of land rights). Richard Snowden (neighbor). George Nettlefold (former owner of Snowden's adjoining tract).

Wayman's Marsh 6/10/1706 – 55/45 acres. LCDi/298 SR7376
Location: SRH on the North Branch of the Patuxent River next adjoining a tract called Poll Cat Hill.
Persons mentioned: James Carroll (assignor of land rights). *Note: This patent is included because the Certification and/or Survey date is within the targeted period.*

Welch/Welsh, John & Sylvestre

Arnold Gray Res. 10/20/1703 – 605/605 acres. LCDi/61 SR7376
Location: MNH on the north side of the South River.
Persons mentioned: Richard Arnold & John Gray (original owners). Rachel Gray (wife of John). Coll Henry Darnall (Surveyor General). *Note: This tract was initially granted as a 300-acre tract to Richard Arnold and John Gray in 1668. Gray and his wife Rachel died by 1671, and their portion was regranted to Arnold who then sold it to John Welsh. Welsh's Last Will & Testament devised the tract in equal*

*portions to his sons John & Sylvestre. A resurvey determined that the tract contained a total of 605 acres rather than the 300 acres certified. After paying rent for the increased acreage, the tract was regranted to the brothers in roughly equal portions. Note: Sylvestre sold his portion to John in 1708. John (or his estate) sold the entire tract to **Gerald Hopkins** in 1789.*

Welch/Welsh, John

Preston's Enlargement 8/8/1670 – 65/40 acres. L13/29 SR7355

Location: Three-holes area in the woods adjoining Beaver Dam Runn.

Persons mentioned: **George Yate** (assignor of land rights). *Note: The 3-hole area is not a hundred. This designation identifies a small number of tracts adjoining a cliff with three holes that served as a landmark. Other than being in Ann Arundell Manor, there is nothing in the patent documents to indicate where this cliff or these tracts were located.*

The Enlargement 5/25/1704 - 97 acres. LDD5i/440 SR7378

Location: SRH near the head of the South River next adjoining tracts called Arnold Gray & Maddox's Adventure.

Persons mentioned: **Joseph King** (assignor of land rights). *Note: The tract cannot be drawn and the actual acreage cannot be determined due to incomplete boundary course information in the patent document.*

Welding, Henry *(Planter)*

Henry's Park 11/12/1686 – 184/184 acres. L22/287 SR7363

Location: B&TNH on the south side of the Patapsco River adjoining Deep Creek.

Persons mentioned: **John Granger** (neighbor). *Note: The patent/survey document places this tract in Baltimore County. MSA Land Index #55 places it in Anne Arundel*

County. I have included it here based on its location.

Wells, Benjamin

Benjamin's Addition - 6/10/1671 - 40/41 acres. L14/287
SR 7356
Location: HCH adjoining a tract called Holland's Hills.
Person's mentioned: Richard Wells (brother and assignor of
land rights). Richard Deaver (neighbor).

Wells, James

Mascall's Haven 7/1/1671 – 100/89 acres. L16/216
SR7357
Location: B&TNH on the south side of the Patapsco River at
the mouth of a small creek.
Persons mentioned: John Mascall (assignor of land rights).
John Inchport & William Davis (persons transported by
Mascall to this Province to inhabit).

Wells, Richard (Churgeon)

Wells 2/29/1659 – 600 acres. L4/534 SR7346
Location: HCH on the west side of Herring Creek Bay and
on the south side of Carter's Branch.
Persons mentioned: None. *Note 1: A marginal note states
that "This patent is surrendered and a new warrt is granted
for the same quantity of land this 13th day of July, 1663."
The new warrant was probably used to obtain a later tract
of the same acreage located close to this one. See "Wells"
below. Note 2: The tract cannot be drawn and the actual
acreage cannot be determined due to incomplete boundary
course information in the patent document.*

Benjamin's Choyce 9/9/1663 - 280/278 acres. L5/296
SR7347
Location: HCH to the west of Herring Creek Bay in the
woods.
Persons mentioned: **Benjamin Wells** (son), **Mary Herrings,
George Symonds, William Thompson, Timothy Owens,
Charles Ryder** (persons transported by **Richard Wells** into

this Province here to inhabit).

Little Wells 9/9/1663 – 100/96 acres. L5/497 SR7347
Location: HCH
Persons mentioned: Anthony Salloway (neighbor).

Wells 9/10/1663 - 600/600 acres. L5/508 SR7347
Location: HCH in Herring Creek Bay at the mouth of
Carter's Cove.
Persons mentioned: Francis Holland (neighbor), Coll.
Edward Carter (former owner of Holland's tract).

Well's Hills 7/20/1664 – 420 acres. L7/204 SR7349
Location: HCH in the branches of Ship Creek.
Persons mentioned: Anthony Salloway (neighbor). *Note:
MSA Land Index #54 states that this tract was certified at
450 acres. However, the patent document shows the
certified acreage to be 420 acres. The actual acreage could
not be determined because of incomplete boundary course
information in the patent document.*

West Wells 7/29/1664 350/462 acres. L7/206 SR7349
Location: HCH between the branches of Herring Creek and
Fishing Creek.
Persons mentioned: James Ogden, William Jackson, John
Weaver, John Webster, Samuel Hill, William Linkhorn, &
Ann Price (persons transported by Richard Wells into this
Province here to inhabit in 1660).

Brendsley Hall 9/9/1699 – 800/815 acres. LQ/278 SR7345
Location: WRH next adjoining a tract called Hooker's
Purchase.
Persons mentioned: John Cathin, Ann Brookland, Roger
Guthridge, Thomas Williams, Mathias Stevenson,
Katherine Griffin Bonnor, a negro, John Taylor, Thomas
Horby, Edward Harris, John Waters, Jane Hodges,
Charles Lewen, John Martin, and Ann Chaplain (persons

transported by **Richard Wells** into this Province here to inhabit).

Wells, Robert
> **Bednall Green** - 9/1/1670 - 180/175 acres. L14/79 SR7356
> <u>Location:</u> HCH on Herring Creek next adjoining a tract called Benjamin's Choyce.
> <u>Persons mentioned:</u> **Richard Wells, Benjamin Wells, M. Holland, & William Hunt** (neighbors).

Westhill, George
> **Scornton** 5/2/1659 – 800/715 acres. L4/39 SR7346
> <u>Location:</u> SRH on the south side of South River at the head of Brown's Creek.
> <u>Persons mentioned:</u> **George Hisson** (assignor of land rights). **Thomas Besson** (neighbor).

Wheeler, John
> **Wheeler's Lott** 8/10/1683 – 200 acres. LSDA/98 SR7369
> <u>Location:</u> B&TNH on Cattaile Creek between the Magothy and Ann Arrundall *(Severn)* Rivers next adjoining tracts called Randall's Range, Lewis'Addition, and Hopkins Fancy.
> <u>Persons mentioned:</u> **George Yate** (assignor of land rights). **Charles Randall** (neighbor). *Note: The tract cannot be drawn and actual acreage cannot be determined due to incomplete boundary course information.*

Wheelock, Edward
> **Wheelock's Chance** 9/8/1670 – 50 acres. L14/65 SR7356
> <u>Location:</u> B&TNH
> <u>Persons mentioned:</u> **Thomas Knighton** (assignor of land rights). **John Ray & Richard Moss** (neighbors). *Note: The tract cannot be drawn and the actual acreage cannot be determined due to incomplete boundary course information in the patent document.*

Wheelock's Lott 7/20/1673 – 100/102 acres. L15/34
SR7347
Location: B&TNH on the north side of the Patapsco River on Bodkin Creek.
Persons mentioned: **Robert Wilson** (assignor of land rights).
Note: The patent document states that the tract is located in Baltimore County but that it is held in the manor of Ann Arundell. Based on the limited information available either assertion could be correct so I have included here.

Strong's Leavings 7/12/1675 – 125/130 acres. L19/457
SR7360
Location: B&TNH on the east side of Severn River on Ferry Creek by Strong's Branch.
Persons mentioned: **George Yate** (Deputy Surveyor). **Baker Brook** (Surveyor Generall). **Thomas Meares, John Homewood, William Slade & Emmanuel Drew** (neighbors).

White, James

The Addition 9/16/1666 – 50/50 acres. L10/131 SR7352
Location: WRH in Herring Creek Swamp next adjoining land he now liveth upon.
Persons mentioned: **George Yate & John Taylor** (assignors of land rights).

White's Folly 9/20/1666 – 30/28 acres. L10/151 SR7352
Location: WRH near Herring Creek Swamp
Persons mentioned: **George Yate, Gent.** (assignor of land rights). **John Cumber** (neighbor).

White, Jerome. Esq.

White's Hall 5/12/1665 – 1,800/1,800 acres. L7/587
SR7349
Location: SRH on the South Runn near the head of the South River.
Persons mentioned: **John Freeman** (neighbor).

The Iron Mine 4/10/1668 – 500/502 acres. L11/332
SR7353
Location: SRH on the west side of the South Runn of South
River next adjoining a tract called White's Hall.
Persons mentioned: George Nettlefold (neighbor).

St. Jerome's 4/10/1668 – 300/300 acres. L11/334 SR7353
Location: HCH next adjoining tracts called Quick Sale and
Portland Mannor.
Persons mentioned: John Burridge (neighbor).

White's Plaines 8/8/1669 – 2,000/2,002 acres. L12/401
SR7354
Location: SRH on the north side of Stockett's Runn next
adjoining The Patuxent River.
Persons mentioned: None.

Portland Landing 9/2//1672 – 206/206 acres. L17/202
SR7358
Location: HCH next adjoining the Patuxent River.
Persons mentioned: None.

Portland Manor 12/8/1662 – 2,000/5,127 acres. L5/428
SR7347
Location: HCH next adjoining tracts called Portland Landing
and Ann Arundell Manor.
Persons mentioned: Richard White (father), John Burrage
& Abraham Birkhead (neighbors).

Whiteacre/Whittiar, John
> **Whiteacre's Chance** 3/29/1696 – 150/152 acres. LC3i//358
> SR7377
> Location: B&TNH in Elk Ridge near a branch of the
> Patuxent River next adjoining a tract called Talbott's
> Resolution.
> Persons mentioned: None. *Note: This tract lies in present day*
> *Howard County.*

Whittiar's Purchase 4/10/1696 – 79/75 acres. LWD/125 SR7372-2

Location: B&TNH in Elk Ridge next adjoining a tract called Whittiar's Chance.

Persons mentioned: John Doderidge (assignor of land rights). John Dorsey (neighbor). *Note: This tract lies in present day Howard County.*

Williams, Benjamin

Williams His Addition 6/12/1687 – 26/24 acres. LNS2i/732 SR7371

Location: SRH on the south side of the South River next adjoining Huggings' Cove and the riverside.

Persons mentioned: Charles Gorsuch (assignor of land rights).

Williams His Angle 6/1/1688 – 15/15 acres. LNS2i/597 SR7371

Location: SRH on the south side of the South River next adjoining a tract called Covell's Folly.

Persons mentioned: John Dorsey (assignor of land rights). Coll. William Burges, Richard Cheney, & Ann Covell (neighbors).

Addition 10/23/1697 – 166/169 acres. LDD5i/205 SR7378

Location: B&TNH on the North Branch of the Patuxent River next adjoining a tract called William's Contrivance,

Persons mentioned: None. *Note: This tract was located in Baltimore County at the time of the patent/survey. I have included it because the land had been, and would again be, designated as Anne Arundel County before being absorbed into present day Howard County.*

William's Contrivance 6/1/1700 – 327/346 acres. LDD5l 355 SR7378

Location: B&TNH on the north side of the Patuxent River next adjoining his own tract called Addition.

Persons mentioned: None. *Note: This tract was located in Baltimore County at the time of the patent/survey. I have included it because the land had been, and would again be, designated as Anne Arundel County before being absorbed into present day Howard County.*

Bare Neck -11/1/1701 - **151/155 acres.** LDD5i/210 SR7376
Location: HCH on a Branch of the Patuxent River about 12 miles from the head of the South River.
Persons mentioned: Clement Hill (Surveyor Generall.). Neale Clarke (neighbor).

Wilson, John

Bersheba -7/29/1664 - **100/100 acres.** L7/212 SR7349
Location: HCH on the east side of the Patuxent River and on the west side of the main branch of Lyons Creek.
Persons mentioned: John Burrage (assignor of land rights). Christopher Burkitt (neighbor). *Note: The patent document states that this tract is in Calvert County. However, it is located on the east side of Lyon's Creek and it is also shown in the Rent Rolls as an Anne Arundel County tract in the Herring Creek Hundred.*

Wilson, Robert

Utopia 1/10/1670 – **320 acres.** L14/137 SR7356
Location: B&TNH on the west side of the Patapsco River adjoining Rumbly Marsh.
Persons mentioned: Thomas Knighton & Thomas Taylor (assignors of land rights). Hugh Kinsey, Paul Kinsey, Jr., (orphan of Paul Kinsey), & John Brown (neighbors). *Note: The tract cannot be drawn and the actual acreage cannot be determined due to incomplete boundary course information in the patent document.*

The Plaine 7/10/1671 – **300/294 acres.** L16/135 SR7357

Location: SRH on the west side of a branch of the Patuxent River by a great marsh.

Persons mentioned: John Pawson (assignor of land rights). John Howerton (neighbor). *Note: This tract is located in present day Prince George's County.*

Wilson's Inlargement 5/1/1672 – 60 acres. L16/577 SR7357

Location: B&TNH on the south side of the Patapsco River and on the north side of Curtis Creek.

Persons mentioned: The Orphans Kinsey & Richard Mascall (neighbors). *Note: The actual acreage could not be determined due to incomplete boundary course information in the patent document.*

Little Town 5/11/672 – 80 acres. L16/570 SR7357

Location: B&TNH on the south side of the Patapsco River next adjoining a tract called Harborrow.

Persons mentioned: Paul Kinsey (neighbor). *Note: The actual acreage could not be determined due to incomplete boundary course information in the patent document.*

Wilson's Grove 7/5/1672 –200/188 acres. L16/385 SR7357

Location: SRH between the heads of the South & Severn Rivers next adjoining tracts called White's Hall & Abingdon.

Persons mentioned: Robert Proctor, John Gaither, & Jerome White, Esq. (neighbors). *Note: From MSA Land Index #73: The tract was sold to John & James Powell and by the Powells to William Hunt who devised it to his daughter and son-in-law Elizabeth & John Duvall (1689-IH# i/66).*

Herford 5/1/1675 – 260/228 acres. L16/384 SR7357

Location: MNH between the heads of the South and Severn Rivers.

Persons mentioned: George Yate (assignor of land rights).
John Gater & Cornelius Howard (neighbors).

Withers, Samuel

Wither's Durand 5/20/1663 – 250 acres. L5/266 SR7347
Location: MNH on the south side of the Severn River at
Howell's Creek.
Persons mentioned: Thomas Tolley (neighbor). *Note: The
tract cannot be drawn and the actual acreage cannot be
determined due to incomplete boundary course information
in the patent document.*

Wither's Outlett 8/5/1664 – 100/91 acres. L7/283 SR7349
Location: MNH on the south side of the Severn River at
Saughier's Creek.
Persons mentioned: None. *Note: From MSA Tract Index
#73: Devised to son Samuel Withers, Jr., and sold by him
to Richard Hill in 1685.*

Wood, John

Woodstock 4/27/1710 – 200/191 acres. LDD5i/443
SR7378
Location: B&TNH between the main branch of the Magothy
River and Mill Branch near the Lower Rocks.
Persons mentioned: John Carroll (surveyor). Robert
Proctor & John Howard, Jr. (neighbors). *Note: This patent
is included because the certification and/or survey date is
within the targeted period.*

Wood, Thomas

Woodcock's Nest 8/10/1683 – 30/25 acres. LSDA/184
SR7369
Location: B&TNH on a branch of the Maggity River next
adjoining Cypress Swamp.
Persons mentioned: Henry Hanslap & Coll. Thomas Taillor
(assignors of land rights). Edward Bates & Adam Bowsey
(neighbors).

Woolchurch, Henry *(Planter)*

Leonard's Neck 9/24/1663 – 300/300 acres. L5/582
SR7347
Location: B&TNH on the south side of the Maggity River
and on the west side of Maggity Creek at the mouth.
Persons mentioned: **Leonard Strong & John Genier**
(assignors of land rights). *Note: one hundred acres of the
rights certified for this tract were due Woolchurch for
marrying the "relict" of **Leonard Gunnis** who earned these
rights by transporting daughter **Janie** into this Province to
inhabit.*

Woolchurch's Rest 9/24/1663 – 110/84 acres. L5/581
SR7347
Location: B&TNH on the north side of the Severn River at
Woolchurch Point.
Persons mentioned: **John Ellis, Joseph Seeres, & William
Cole** (persons from whom **Woolchurch** purchased three
smaller tracts and merged them into this tract).

Woolman, Richard *(Planter)*

Harwood 9/6/1659 – 100 acres. L4/106 SR7346
Location: WRH on the west side of the Three Island Bay on a
branch of the Road River.
Persons mentioned: **Robert Harwood** (owner of the original
survey of this tract). *Note 1: A later patent (9/16/1664) has
been found in L7/447. Note 2: See footnote for the following
patent. Note 3: The tract cannot be drawn and the actual
acreage cannot be determined due to incomplete boundary
course information in the patent document.*

Harwood 9/16/1664 – 150 acres. L7/447 SR7349
Location: WRH on the north side of the Rode River next
adjoining a tract called Hasslin.
Persons mentioned: **Robert Harwood** (owner of former
survey). **Jerome Hasslin** (neighbor). *Note: The language of*

this patent is almost identical to the language of the above (9/6/1659) version except that the later patent mentions an adjoining tract called Hasslin that did not exist at the time of the earlier patent. Note 2: The tract cannot be drawn and the actual acreage cannot be determined due to incomplete boundary course information in both patent documents. Note 3: No explanation found as to why Wollman re-patented this tract ten years after the first patent or why/how the tract grew by 50% in acreage during the period between patents.

Worthington, John, Jr.

Meare's Expectation & Howardston 7/27/1702 – 316/335 acres. LDD5i/470 SR7378

Location: B&TNH by the Severn River next adjoining tracts named Brownton & Lusby.

Persons mentioned: **John Brice** *(probably Brisco)* & **John Worthington**, (the elder) deceased. *Note: Brice obtained a special warrant, on behalf of John Worthington, Jr., son and heir of John Worthington, to resurvey & merge these two Worthington-owned tracts into one.*

Wyatt, Nicholas

Wyatt 11/22/1651 – 90 acres. LAB&H/264 SR7344

Location: MNH on the north side of the South River on Howard's Creek.

Persons mentioned: **Matthew Howard & Samuel Underwood** (neighbors).

Beare Ridge 8/11/1664 - 175/209 acres. L7/355 SR7349

Location: MNH on the south side of the Severn River at the head of a swamp.

Persons mentioned: None. *Note: **Thomas Griffith** of Virginia claimed 350 acres of land in February 1664, for transporting **Nicholas Wyatt** and others to this Province to inhabit (L7/507 SR7349).*

Wayfield 7/14/1664 – 100/80 acres. L7/353 SR7349
Location: South side of Severn River by an Indian Path adjoining a tract called Hope.
Persons mentioned: **Henry Sewell** (neighbor). *Note 1: The Indian Path referred to in the patent document is present day Maryland Route 178 (General's Highway). Note 2: Wyatt sold the tract to **Richard Warfield** & **Edward Gardner** for 3,000 pounds of tobacco in 1688 (JH2/181).*

Wyatt's Hills 8/8/1664 – 60/54 acres. L7/345 SR7349
Location: MNH on the south side of the Severn River adjoining the land he now liveth upon.
Persons mentioned: None.

Wyatt's Ridge 8/4/1664 – 450/504 acres. L7/237 SR7349
Location: MNH between the branches of the South River and the main Branch of Broad Creek.
Persons mentioned: **Thomas Turner** & **Richard Preston** (assignors of land rights).

Wyatt's Harbor 5/2/1668 – 100 acres. L11/361 SR7357
Location: MNH on the south side of the Severn River at Wyatt's Point.
Persons mentioned: **George Yate** & **Daniel Jennifer** (assignors of land rights*). Note: The tract cannot be drawn and the actual acreage cannot be determined due to incomplete boundary course information in the patent document.*

Wyneat, Thomas
> **Wyneat's Range 9/8/1674 – 40/40 acres.** L18/215 SR7359
> Location: SRH on the main branch of the Road River.
> Persons mentioned: **George Yate** (assignor of land rights).
> **John Bufford** (neighbor).

Yate, George

The Chance 9/1/1666 – 25/42 acres. L10/123 SR7353
Location: B&TNH on the east side of the Severn River.
Persons mentioned: Henry Woolchurch (neighbor).

The Happy Choice 5/10/1671 – 300/384 acres. L16/239
SR7357
Location: SRH on the east side of the Patuxent River among
the branches.
Persons mentioned: Thomas Knighton (assignor of land
rights).

Yate's Inheritance 9/4/1668 – 170/210 acres. L12/134
SR7354
Location: B&TNH on the south side of the Maggity River at
the mouth.
Persons mentioned: Capt. James Connaway (assignor of
land rights).

Locust Thickett 5/1/1672 – 200/196 acres. L14/583
SR7356
Location: B&TNH on the south side of the Patapsco River
near Swan Creek next adjoining a tract called Mascall's
Haven.
Persons mentioned: Robert Wilson- & Robert Davidge
(assignors of land rights).

The Plaine 9/26/1677 – 120/117 acres. L20/40 SR7361
Location: SRH on the south side of the South River by
Walker's Branch.
Persons mentioned: George Holland (assignor of land
rights). George Walker (neighbor).

Radnidge 7/10/1677 – 160/164 acres. L11/183 SR7353
Location: B&TNH on the south side of the Patapsco River
opposite the Rockes.
Persons mentioned: Richard Moss (assignor of land rights).

Mascall's Rest 6/24/1678 – 230/232 acres. L20/397
SR7361
Location: B&TNH on the west side of the Patapsco River.
Persons mentioned: **Richard Mascall** (deceased former
owner). The **Orphans Kinsey** (neighbors). *Note: This tract
was patented by Richard Mascall in 1671. By judgement of
the Provincial Court on 6/1/1679, the tract became
escheated unto the Lord Proprietor for non-payment of the
rent due. George Yate obtained the tract by paying 2,000
lbs. of tobacco.*

Denchworth 7/18/1679 – 250/239 acres. L20/250 SR7361
Location: B&TNH on the south side of the Patapsco River on
a branch of Curtis Creek.
Persons mentioned: **Quinton Parker** (former neighbor).
William Slade (neighbor). *Note: The patent/survey document
places this tract in Baltimore County. MSA Land Index #55
places it in Anne Arundel County. I have included it here
based on its location.*

Come by Chance 8/10/1684 – 214/219 acres. LSDA/438
SR7369
Location: MNH on the north side of the South River near
Smith's Creek next adjoining a tract called Wither's Outlett.
Persons mentioned: **Henry Hanslap** (assignor of land rights).
Walter & Zephaniah Smith (neighbors).

Yieldhall, William
Yieldhall's Island 7/6/1679 – 100 acres. L20/311SR7361
Location: MNH on the south side of the Severn River and on
the south side of Sunken Ground Creek by a marsh adjoining
The Round Bay.
Persons mentioned: **George Holland** (assignor of land
rights*). Note: The tract cannot be drawn and the actual
acreage cannot be determined due to incomplete boundary
course information in the patent document.*

Narrow Neck 10/5/1683 – 41/39 acres. LSDA/441 SR7360
Location: MNH on the south side of Severn by The Round
Bay at the head of Sunken Ground Creek.
Persons mentioned: Henry Hanslap (assignor of land rights).

Young, John

> **Young's Range 3/15/1704 – 300/300 acres.** LDD5i/212
> SR7378
> Location: MNH on the east side of the main runn of the
> Severn River 6 miles above a bridge called Severn Bridge.
> Persons mentioned: None. *Note: The reference to a Severn
> Bridge could have been to Severn Ridge.*
>
> **Young's Locust Plaine 4/10/1704 – 150/152 acres.**
> LDD5i/137 SR7378
> Location: B&TNH on the south side of the Patapsco River on
> Mill Branch.
> Persons mentioned: None. *Note: The patent/survey document
> places this tract in Baltimore County. MSA Land Index #55
> places it in Anne Arundel County. I have included it here
> based on its location.*

Young, Richard, Jr.

> **Young Richard 12/4/1663 – 500/234 acres.** L6/77 SR7345
> Location: B&TNH on the north side of the Severn River near
> Burle's Creek at Pascall's Cove.
> Persons mentioned: Himself, **Dorothy** his wife, **George,
> Richard,** & **William** his sons (persons transported by
> Richard Young, deceased, into this Province here to inhabit).
> **Edward Lloyd, Ralph Hawkins,** & **William Blay**
> (neighbors). *Note: The grant consists of three unadjoined
> tracts. The largest of the three (260 acres) could not be
> drawn and the actual acreage could not be measured, due to
> incomplete boundary course information in the patent
> document. This accounts for the large overall acreage
> discrepancy.*

Young, Samuel

Brushy Neck 10/28/1699 – 200/213 acres. LCC4i/161 SR7375

Location: MNH on the south side of the Severn River at Shipping Creek and at the head of a cove by Collier's Branch.

Persons mentioned: None. *Note: The grant conveyed two adjoining tracts with the combined acreage shown above.*

The Addition 10/29/1704 – 80/80 acres. LSDF/540 SR7360

Location: MNH on the north side of the South River.

Persons mentioned: **Robert Clarkson** (neighbor)

Young, Theodore & Phillips, Robert,

Truswell 8/10/1684 30/32 acres. LSDA/438 SR7369

Location: HCH in Herring Creek Swamp on the South Branch of Deep Creek.

Persons mentioned: **Henry Hanslap** (assignor of land rights).

Young, Theodorus

Dorrus His Chance 8/1/1673 – 116/114 acres. L17/157 SR7358

Location: WRH in a swamp near to Cattaile Slash and next adjoining a tract called Baldwin's Addition.

Persons mentioned: **George Yate & Capt William Burges** (assignors of land rights), **John Baldwin** (neighbor).

Beetenson, John 11
Beetenson, Lydia 5
Beinger, Samuel 230
Bell, Elizabeth 11
Bell, George 158
Bell, Thomas 11(2), 48
Bellot, Michael 83
Belt, Humphrey 168
Bennet, John 11
Bennett, Ann 35
Bennett/Bennet, Richard, Esq.
  35(2), 111, 147, 166, 224
Bennett, Tristram 217
Benson, Daniel 12
Benson, Elizabeth 12
Benson, Steven 12
Besson, Ann (dau) 12
Besson, Ann (wife) 12
Besson, Thomas, Capt. 7, 12, 13,
  21, 28, 82, 212, 235
Besson, Thomas, Jr. 12, 13
Bevin, Charles 169
Bewsey, William 13
Biggs, Seth 13
Billingsly, Francis 13, 129
Billingsly, John, Maj. 30
Birkhead 15
Birkhead, Abraham 11, 14, 17, 27,
  237
Birkhead, Christopher 15(2)
Birmingham, Jacob 16
Birmingham, Michael 16
Bishop, Roger 17
Blackwell, Mary 109
Blackwell, Thomas 17, 93
Bladen, William 17, 101
Blaies, William 1
Bland, Thomas 18, 64(2)
Blay, Edward 18,108; 202
Blay, William 18(2), 78, 247
Blea, William 202
Blomfield, John 56
Blomfield, M. 194

Blunt, James 74
Boarman, Edward 18
Bodware, Richard 19
Body/Boddy, John 19, 191
Boetler, Charles 56, 84, 110
Bond, Benjamin 19
Bond, Peter 19, 207
Bond, Thomas 20
Bonner, James 20, 80(2), 103,
  108(2), 168
Bonner, John 213
Bonnor, Katherine Griffin 234
Bonwart, Richard 15
Boon, Humphrey 20
Booth, John 170
Boring, John 148(2)
Bosley, Thomas 72
Boswell, Ralph 51, 116
Bowles, Christopher 213
Bowsey, Adam 241
Bowsley, Edward 144
Boyde, James 176
Boyde, John 21
Bozill, Rize 201
Bradley, Thomas 55, 92, 152, 222,
  223
Breadwart, Richard 15
Brewer, John 21, 44, 139, 183, 220
Brewer, John, Jr. 21
Brewer, Joseph 22
Brewer, Mrs. 175
Brewer, William 89
Brice, John 22, 243
Brooke, Baker, Esq. 89, 106, 114,
  187(2), 236
Brookland, Ann 234
Brooksby, John 22
Brosn, David 85
Brown, Elizabeth Sisson 82
Brown, Ellis 21(2), 22, 26, 44
Brown, Francis 158
Brown, James 23, 70
Brown, John 23, 47, 239

Gassaway, Nicholas 32, 82, 87, 94, 141, 195, 218, 220
Gates, Ann 83(2)
Gates. Jane 83(2)
Gates, Joseph 83(2)
Gates, Thomas, Ensign 83
Gearfe, Thomas 9
Genier, John 242
George 223
Gibbs, Edward 83
Gibbs, Mary 227
Gibbs, William 10, 84
Gill, Stephen 198
Gillium, John 56
Gleve, Thomas 125
Glover, Ann 19
Goddfrey, Elias 201
Goldsbury/Gouldsbury, Robert 84, 109
Good, Joseph 109
Goodrick, Henry 68, 84, 148
Gordon, Alexander 75, 84, 104
Gorsuch, Charles 90, 238
Gosnell/Goswell, William 85, 204
Gossum, Elizabeth 220
Gossum, Ester 19
Gossum, Patrick 26, 84, 183, 220
Gott, Richard 52, 85
Gover, Robert 85
Grammar/Grammer/Gramer, John 14(2), 86, 99, 183
Grammar, Robert 35
Grange, John 87, 177
Granger, John 232
Gray, John 2, 4, 7, 10, 18, 40, 54, 72, 73, 78, 87(2), 108, 141, 143(2), 155, 165, 169, 192, 199, 203, 215, 231
Gray, Rachel 231
Gray, Zacariah 159
Green, John 3, 4, 89
Green, Joseph 144
Green, Nicholas 172

Green(e), George 56, 89
Greenbury, Nicholas 90, 120, 172, 184, 219
Greenwood, Armigill 81, 84, 90, 109, 168
Greenwood, Christian 90
Gremmell, Ann 122
Greniston, James 90, 165
Gresham, John 91
Griffin, Catherine Baldwin 5
Griffin, Charles 5
Griffith, Thomas 243
Griffith, William 91, 161
Grimes, Ann 92
Grimes, William 26, 91(2), 92, 199
Grinnell, William 158
Gross, Nicholas 92
Gross, Thomas 93
Gross/Grosse, Roger 92, 157(2), 230(2), 231
Gudgeon, Lawrence 93
Gudgeon, Robert 93(2)
Guisse, John 93
Gullock, Thomas 94
Gunnis, Janie 242
Gunnis, Leonard 242
Guthridge, Roger 234
Hadwell, William 71
Hage, John 161
Hale, Henry 47
Hale, Henry, Jr. 47
Halifield, Joseph 185
Hall, Christopher 94, 175
Hall, Edward 27
Hall, Faith Wilson 212
Hall, Henry 41, 94
Hall, John 31(2), 95, 147, 196
Hall, Josias 95, 112, 134
Hall, Richard 69, 212, 221
Hall, Thomas 161, 218(2)
Hallitt, Jacob 95
Hammond, John, Maj./Coll. 26, 41, 77, 96, 120, 124, 208

Hammond, Thomas 59, 96(2), 162
Hanslap, Henry 1, 10, 13, 15, 19,
    24, 29(2), 43(2), 48, 49, 57, 89,
    91, 97(2), 106, 119, 120, 124,
    125, 131, 142, 143, 144, 151,
    152(2), 153, 162, 171, 174, 178,
    190, 191, 193, 199, 211, 223,
    229(2), 241, 246, 247, 248
Harbitt, Elinor 97, 151
Harding, Matthew 97
Harness, Elinor 98
Harness, Isaac 98(2)
Harness, Jacob 98(2)
Harness, Susan 98
Harness, William, Jr. 98
Harness, William 98
Harney, William 226
Harper, Stephen 74
Harrington, John 160
Harris, Edward 234
Harris, Elizabeth 99
Harris, John 99, 126
Harris, Richard 73
Harris, Thomas 63
Harris, William 15, 99
Harrison/Harrisson, Richard 99,
    110
Harrisson, John 176
Harsbottle, John 100
Harwood, John 3
Harwood, Robert 100, 242(2)
Harwood, Thomas 44, 111, 141,
    142, 222, 226
Hasslin, Jeremy/Jerome 100, 242
Hat, William 170
Hatt, Ann 75
Hawes, John 109
Hawkins, John 100,108
Hawkins, Ralph 17, 63, 101, 156,
    218, 247
Hawkins, William 101
Haxling, Jeremy 196
Hay, Andrew 35

Haywood, John 102, 108
Heath, James 102, 103
Heathcoat/Heathcoate/Heathcote,
    Nathaniel 103, 158, 213
Hedge, Thomas 93, 103, 128
Hendrickson, John 118
Herman, John 200
Herring, Bartholemew 104, 158
Herring, John 104
Herrings, Mary 233
Highman, Lawrence 222
Hill, Abel 104, 213
Hill, Clement 104, 194(2), 212, 239
Hill, Clement, Jr. 105(3)
Hill, Elizabeth 4
Hill, Joseph 98
Hill, Richard, Capt. 6(2), 16, 60,
    105, 106, 146, 241
Hill, Samuel 234
Hill, William 72
Hilliard, Dariell 171
Hilliard, Thomas 28
Hills, Elizabeth 161
Hills, William 89, 107
Hipsley, Thomas 182
Hisson, George 235
Hodges, Jane 234
Holeman, Abraham 107
Holland, Anthony 28, 81, 108, 142,
    165, 178
Holland, Cecilia xvii
Holland, Francis, 69(2), 85, 86,
    109, 111, 155, 234
Holland, Francis, Jr. 109
Holland, George 24(2), 42, 43, 45,
    48, 69(2), 75, 86, 95, 96, 110,
    136, 137, 149, 180, 183, 198,
    203, 207, 245, 246
Holland, M. 235
Holland, Mary 109
Holloway, John 83
Holloway, Oliver 111
Holt, Elizabeth 85

Homewood, James 111, 113
Homewood, John 3, 112, 113, 115, 218, 236
Homewood, Robert 85
Homewood, Thomas 89, 112, 113(2)
Hooker, Thomas 6(2), 52, 56, 80(2), 108, 115
Hope, Edward 41, 116
Hope, George 2, 116, 129, 130, 157, 191
Hopkins, Charles 70
Hopkins, Gerald 232Hopkins, William 23(2), 24(2), 35, 56, 117(2), 118(2), 125, 159, 184, 191, 223(2)
Horby, Thomas 234
Horne, William 44
Horner, James 120
Horner, Richard 45
Horner, William 226
Horring, Ann Burroughs Barnett 31
Horring, John 31
Horsley, Joseph 137
Howard, Cornelius 35, 59, 60, 61, 102, 120, 121, 122, 127(2), 225, 241
Howard, Cornelius, Jr. 124
Howard, Elinor 122
Howard, John 50(2), 55, 61(2), 70, 82, 121(2), 122(3), 123, 127, 188, 200, 207
Howard, John, Jr. 123, 126, 228, 241
Howard, Mary 124Howard, Matthew 10, 21, 27, 35, 102(2), 121, 122, 124, 125, 127, 152, 153, 174, 208, 214, 223, 227, 243
Howard, Phillip 23, 123, 124, 126, 145, 180, 229
Howard, Robert 146
Howard, Ruth, Mrs. 66

Howard, Samuel 59, 60, 61, 121, 122, 127
Howell, Elizabeth 127
Howell, Thomas 69, 127, 170
Howerton, John 86, 127, 240
Hubbard, Robert 19
Hudson, John 128
Huggings, Richard 128(2), 177, 182(2)
Humphrey, Robert 166
Hunt, Edward 130
Hunt, Elizabeth 131, 240
Hunt, William 36, 69, 109(2), 110, 128, 155(2), 235, 240
Hunt, Wolfran 129
Hutton, John 128
Hyde, William 214
Illingsworth, Richard 129
Inchport, John 233
Jackson, Arnold 217
Jackson, Isaac 129
Jackson, James 11, 129
Jackson, William 234
James, Ann 130
James, Charles 210
James, Dalton 204
James, James 130
James, John 130(2)
James, Robert 15, 94
James, William 130
Jeffe, Thomas 96, 131
Jeffe, William 131
Jennifer, Daniel 42, 244
Johnson, Davy 113, 131
Johnson, Edward 214
Jones, Ann 132
Jones, Annis 132
Jones, Edward 100, 131
Jones, Elizabeth 15, 48
Jones, John 103, 131
Jones, John, Jr. 132
Jones, Joshua 100
Jones, Richard 144

Phillips, Robert 248
Pickson, Ann 213
Pierpoint, Amos 3, 82, 174, 184, 207
Pierpoint, Arnis 174
Pierpoint, Elizabeth 174
Pierpoint, Elizabeth (the elder) 174
Pierpoint, Hannah 174
Pierpoint, Henry 174(2), 175, 209, 223
Pierpoint, Jabez/Jabes 124, 163, 175, 208
Piersen, Thomas 67
Pine, John 125
Piny, Henry 35
Pinkstone/Pinkston/Pinxton, Peter 175
Poole, David 36, 39, 67, 75, 87, 195
Porter, Frances 177
Porter, Peter 23, 118, 120, 176, 177, 229
Porter, Peter, Jr. 177
Potter, Ann 77
Powell, James 177, 240
Powell, John 177, 240
Pratt, Thomas 6(2), 116, 177(2)
Preston, Richard, Gent. 10, 115, 137, 178, 202, 221, 224, 244
Preston, Thomas 2
Price, Ann 234
Price, Edward/Edwin 43, 97, 179(2)
Price, Elizabeth 179
Price, Mordecai 154
Priest, Robert 107
Prior, Thomas 177
Pritchard, Abraham 15
Proctor, Elizabeth Freeman 76
Proctor, Robert 4, 40, 41, 43, 76, 78, 79(2), 89, 106, 126, 180, 229, 240, 241
Prosser, John 15
Puddington, Comfort 182

Puddington, George 10, 19, 28, 44, 66, 128, 154, 182(3), 197, 203, 226
Puddington, Jane 182
Puddington, Mary 182
Purnell, Richard 182
Pyther, Ann 26
Pyther, William/Will 26, 112, 183
Pyther, William, Jr. 26
Raffey, John 43
Randall, Charles 235
Randall, Christopher 78, 88, 183
Rawden, Elizabeth 230
Rawlings, Richard 184
Ray, John 8, 119, 184, 235
Read, Elizabeth 185
Read, William 185(2)
Reade, Thomas 185
Reynolds, Thomas 40
Rice, Roger 135
Richardson, Daniel 41
Richardson, Francis 56
Richardson, John 186
Richardson, Lawrence/Larrance 93, 186
Richardson, Lawrence/Larrance, Jr. 186
Richardson, Sarah 186(2)
Richardson, Sarah (the younger) 186
Richardson, Thomas 3(2), 10(2), 19, 27, 52, 63, 89, 96, 126, 131, 139, 143, 145(2), 174, 186, 187, 208(2), 212, 214, 215
Richardson, William 8, 103, 115, 138, 187
Ridgely 130
Ridgely, Elizabeth 225
Ridgely, Henry 41(2), 77, 91, 99, 126, 187, 188, 198, 226
Ridgely, Henry, Jr. 187, 188, 189
Ridgely, Robert 1, 55, 202, 203, 222

Smith, Edward 202
Smith, Franklin 48
Smith, James 51, 72, 203
Smith, John 13, 45, 144
Smith, Manuell 204
Smith, Margaret, Burrage 204
Smith, Mary 12
Smith, Nathan 15, 38, 48, 155, 164, 169, 203, 204
Smith, P. 102
Smith, Philemon 85, 204
Smith, Richard 197
Smith, Walter 53, 97, 204, 246
Smith, Zephaniah 48, 49, 97, 163, 204, 246
Smithrick, Thomas 218
Smitz, Nathan 109
Snowden, Richard 138, 165, 205, 231
Snowden, Richard, Jr. 69, 154, 205, 220
Sollers, John 36
Solling, Harman 206
Sophir, George 224
South, Thomas 102
Southard, James 107
Sparrow, Elizabeth 206
Sparrow, Elizabeth (The Elder) 206, 214
Sparrow, Soloman 62, 167, 168, 202, 206
Sparrow, Thomas 13, 42, 166, 214, 218
Sparrow, Thomas (III) 206
Sparrow, Thomas, Jr. 206
Spencer, John 206
Spencer, William 166
Sporne, Nicholas 34
Spriggs, Thomas 133, 207
Sprye, Oliver 201, 224
Standish, Alexander ix
Stear, Richard 207
Stedloe, Thomas 125

Stephens/Stevens, Charles 48, 72, 92, 122(3), 147, 207(2), 208
Stephenson, William 132
Stevens, William 208
Stevenson, Mathias 234
Steward, David 175
Stimson/Stinson, John 40, 79, 153, 184, 208
Stimson, Rachel Beard Clarke 40
Stimson, William 74
Stinchcomb, Nathaniel 209
Stockett, Francis 209(2), 210
Stockett, Henry 209(2), 210
Stockett, Thomas 209(2), 210
Stockeley, Anthony 109
Stone, Edward 21
Stone,Thomas vii, 207
Strahan, Samuel James 109
Streith, Susan 158
Stringer, John 44
Strong 209
Strong, Elizabeth 183, 210, 211(2)
Strong, Leonard 149, 150, 210(3), 211, 242
Struther, John 201
Sturton, George 96, 181, 211
Suggs, William 72
Sumers, John 211
Summerland, John 99, 211
Sutton, John 22, 211
Sutton, Thomas 10, 84, 212
Symmons/Symonds, George 212, 234
Talbott, Edward 38, 155, 173, 212, 213
Talbott, George, Esq. 106, 145, 162, 219
Talbott, John 212
Talbott, Richard 7, 8(2), 52, 71, 81, 103, 142, 187(2), 201, 212, 213(2)
Talbott, Susan 213
Tashberg, John ix

INDEX OF TRACTS

Tract Name	Owner's Name	Year	Page
Angle (The)	Hill, Richard, Capt. Captain	1684	107
Ann Arundell Manor, Part Of	Franklin, Robert	1674	75
Anthony's Purchase	Smith, Anthony	1699	202
Arnold Gray	Arnold, Richard & Gray, John	1668	2
Arnold Gray Resurveyed	Welch, John & Sylvester	1703	231
Ashman's Hope	Ashman, George	1695	2
Asketon, John	Askew, John	1659	2
Ayne	Hanslap, Henry	1683	97
Baily's Content	Bayly, Richard	1687	9
Baker's Addition	Baker, Morris	1688	3
Baker's Chance	Baker, Morris	1687	3
Baker's Folly	Bayley, Richard	1671	8
Baker's Increase	Baker, Morris	1668	4
Baldwin's Addicion	Baldwin, John	1664	4
Baldwin's Addicon	Baldwin, John	1664	4
Baldwin's Chance	Baldwin, John	1695	5
Baldwin's Neck	Baldwin, John	1651	4
Ball's Enlargement	Ball, William	1674	6
Bare Neck	Williams, Benjamin	1701	239
Bare Neck	Beard, Richard	1687	10
Bare Neck	Ball, William	1671	5
Bare Neck	Proctor, Robert	1684	181
Barren Neck	Devoir, Richard	1664	57
Barren Neck (The)	Ewen, Richard	1663	70
Barren Point	Pascall, George	1665	169
Barwell's Choice	Barnwell, John	1665	6
Barwell's Enlargement	Barwell, John	1682	7
Barwell's Purchase	Barwell, John	1671	6
Batchellor's Choice	Hall, Henry	1699	95
Batchellor's Hall	Medcalfe, John	1695	151
Batchellor's Hope	Saunders, James	1670	195
Batchellor's Hope	Vennell, John	1669	224
Batchellor's Hope (The)	Phelps & Green	1666	172
Bate's Chance	Bates, Edward	1672	7
Batia Purchase	Hill, Clement, Jr.	1698	105
Batten's Due	Batten, Fernando	1677	8
Beard's Dock	Beard, Richard	1663	9
Beard's Habitation	Beard, Richard	1663	9

Tract Name	Owner's Name	Year	Page
Beare Neck	Meade, Francis	1681	149
Beare Ridge	Wyatt, Nicholas	1664	243
Beasley's Neck	Hill, Richard	1673	106
Beaver Dam Neck	McConnough, Dennis	1662	149
Beaver Dam Neck	Gray, John	1671	87
Beazlely's Neck Resurveyed	Hill, Richard	1675	106
Beckley	Thomas, Phillip	1650	217
Bednall Green	Wells, Robert	1670	235
Bedworth His Addition	Bedworth, Richard	1672	11
Beetenson's Adventure	Beetenson, Edward	1678	11
Bell's Haven Resurveyed	Burnett Richard & Elizabeth	1684	29
Bell's Haven	Bell, Thomas	1665	11
Ben's Discovery	Warfield, Benjamin	1704	227
Benjamin's Addition	Wells, Benjamin	1671	233
Benjamin's Choyce	Wells, Richard	1663	233
Benjamin's Fortune	Lawrence, Benjamin	1679	138
Bennett's Chance	Bennett, John	1684	11
Bennett's Island	Carter, Edward, Capt.	1658	35
Bennett's Park	Bennett, John	1688	12
Benson Park	Warfield, John & Alexander	1701	227
Benson's Park	Benson, Daniel	1696	12
Bersheba	Wilson, John	1664	239
Besson's Den	Besson, Thomas	1650	12
Bessonton	Besson, Thomas, Captain	1650	13
Betty's Poynt	Bayly, Richard	1685	8
Bigg's Purchase	Biggs, Seth	1707	13
Bipartite	Parsons, Thomas & Shaw, John	1659	168
Birkhead's Adventure	Birkhead, Abraham	1679	14
Birkhead's Chance	Birkhead, Abraham	1666	14
Birkhead's Choice	Birkhead, Abraham	1667	14
Birkhead's Lott	Birkhead, Christopher	1665	15
Birkhead's Meadow	Birkhead, Christopher	1664	15
Birkhead's Mill	Birkhead, Abraham	1683	14
Birkhead's Parcel	Birkhead, Christopher	1663	15

Tract Name	Owner's Name	Year	Page
Birkhead's Right	Birkhead, Abraham	1685	15
Blackwell's Search	Blackwell, Thomas	1694	17
Bland's Quarter	Bland, Thomas	1681	18
Blay's Neck	Blay, Edward, Jr.	1678	18
Body's Adventure	Body, John	1676	19
Bold Venture	Ketlin, Richard	1700	134
Bolealmanack	Hawkins, John	1668	100
Bond's Forrest	Bond, Peter	1678	19
Bonnerston	Bonner, James	1659	20
Boyde's Chance	Boyde, John	1684	21
Brampton	Beard, Richard	1659	9
Brandy	Warfield, Richard	1683	229
Brendon	Kinsey, Paul	1663	135
Brendsley Hall	Wells, Richard	1669	234
Brewer's Chance	Brewer, John	1687	21
Brewerston	Brewer, John	1659	21
Brewerston Resurveyed	Brewer, Joseph	1710	22
Bridge Hill	Stockett, Henry	1671	209
Bright Seate	Price, Edward	1673	179
Broad Creek	Fuller, William	1659	78
Brooksby's Point	Brooksby, John	1680	22
Broome	Beard, Richard	1659	9
Broome Resurveyed	Ridgely, Henry	1670	188
Brown & Clark	Brown, John & Clark, John	1666	23
Brown's Adventure	Boon, Humphrey	1672	20
Brown's Chance & Dorsey's Friendship	Brown, Thomas	1702	25
Brown's Encrease	Hopkins, William	1670	120
Brown's Fancy	Brown, William	1695	26
Brown's Folly	Browne, Thomas	1679	24
Brown's Forrest	Brown, Thomas	1695	25
Brown's Peace	Brown, Thomas	1676	24
Brown's Quarter	Brown, James	1677	23
Browne's Chance	Browne, Thomas	1687	24
Brownly	Browne, Thomas	1659	24
Brownstone	Browne, Thomas	1659	24
Brownton	Brown, John & Clark, John	1650	23
Browton Ashley Resurveyed	Holland, Francis	1670	110

Tract Name	Owner's Name	Year	Page
Browton Ashley	Holland, Francis	1664	109
Bruerton	Bruer, John	1659	26
Brushy Neck	Baldwin, John	1665	5
Brushy Neck	Filer, Robert	1663	71
Brushy Neck Resurveyed	Francis, Thomas	1683	74
Brushy Neck	Bates, Edward	1665	7
Brushy Neck	Dawson, Abraham	1665	55
Brushy Neck	Tyler, Robert	1665	223
Brushy Neck	Young, Samuel	1699	248
Brushy Neck Bottom	Hopkins, William	1664	118
Bruton	Bruton, John	1664	27
Bruton Grimes	Bruton, John & Grimes, William	1664	26
Bruton's Hope	Bruton, John	1671	27
Buck Stands	Cumber, John, Jr.	1664	52
Burges	Burges, William	1651	28
Burges His Right	Burges, Edward	1688	27
Burges' Choice	Burges, William	1666	28
Burgh (The)	Burges, William	1650	28
Burle Bank	Burle, Robert	1650	28
Burle's Hill	Burle, Robert	1658	29
Burle's Park	Burle, Steven	1684	29
Burle's Town Land	Burle, Robert	1663	29
Burntwood	Gudgeon, Robert	1676	93
Burntwood Common	Gudgeon, Robert & Lawrence	1684	93
Burradge	Burradge, John	1659	29
Burrage	Burrage, John	1663	30
Burrage Blossom	Burrage, John	1663	30
Burrage's End	Burrage, John	1665	31
Bush Bay	Pawley, Lionel	1670	169
Carr's Forrest	Carr, Nicholas	1661	32
Champe's Adventure	Champe, John	1670	36
Chance	Taylor, Robert	1685	214
Chance	Frizzell, William	1664	77
Chance	Carroll, Charles	1705	33
Chance (The)	Roper, Thomas	1665	192
Chance (The)	Howard, Cornelius	1664	121
Chance (The)	Yate, George	1666	244

Tract Name	Owner's Name	Year	Page
Chandler's Grove	Chandler, Thomas	1664	36
Charles His Forrest	Baker, Morris	1688	3
Charles His Gift	Ladd, Richard	1676	136
Charles' Hill	Stephens, Charles & Howard, John	1662	207
Charles' Hills	Stephens, Charles	1679	207
Chathley's Well	Chathley, Thomas	1704	36
Chelsy	Draper, Lawrence	1695	62
Cheney Hill	Cheney, Richard	1659	37
Cheney Neck	Cheney, Richard	1663	37
Cheney's Hazard	Cheney, Richard	1663	37
Cheney's Purchase	Cheney, Richard	1663	37
Cheney's Resolution	Cheney, Richard	1663	37
Cheney's Rest	Cheney, Richard	1663	37
Chew's Resolution Mannour	Chew, Samuel	1694	38
Chew's Right	Chew, Sammuell	1665	38
Chew's Vinyard	Chew, Samuel	1695	38
Chilcott's Increase	Chilcott, James	1672	39
Child's Reserve	Child, Abraham	1683	39
Chilton	Child, Abraham	1681	39
Chinkapinn Forrest	Lorbitt, John	1694	144
Choice (The)	Dearing, John	1666	55
Clark of the Councill	Clark, Richard	1701	41
Clarke's Enlargement	Clarke, Neale	1687	41
Clarke's Inheritance	Clarke, Neale	1670	40
Clarke's Luck	Clarke, Neale	1685	41
Clarke's Purchase	Clark, William	1688	40
Clarke's Walk	Clarke, Richard	1702	42
Clarkenwell	Clark, John	1665	39
Clarkston	Clark, Matthew	1659	39
Clarye's Hope	Parrish, Edward	1664	166
Clink	Galloway, William	1651	80
Clink	Galloway, William	1659	80
Coape's Hill	Coape, George	1683	43
Cockey's Addition	Cockey, William	1683	43
Cockley's Addition	Cockley, William	1684	42
Cole Cliffs	Cole, Thomas	1651	43
Cole's Point	Cole, Thomas	1665	44
Collierby	Brewer, John, Jr.	1678	21
Collierby	Collier, John	1654	44
Come By Chance	Yate, George	1684	246

Tract Name	Owner's Name	Year	Page
Come By Chance	Hanslap, Henry	1682	97
Complement (The)	Homewood, Thomas	1672	114
Conant's Chance	Conant, Robert	1680	44
Conclusion (The)	Foster, Richard	1666	73
Content	Saughier, George	1683	195
Contest (The)	Hopkins, William	1681	119
Coombe (The)	Butler, Tobias	1659	32
Cordwell	Merriott, John	1682	153
Cornfield Creek Plain	Turner, Thomas	1670	222
Corrant (The)	Hooker, Thomas	1683	115
Cossill	Collier, John	1659	44
Covell's Cove	Lambert, Ann	1661	137
Covell's Folly	Lambert. Ann	1663	137
Covill	Covill, John	1651	46
Coxby	Cox, Edward	1650	46
Coxes Enlargement	Cox, Christopher	1689	46
Coxes Forrest	Cox, Christopher	1684	46
Coxes Range	Cox, Christopher	1686	47
Cromwell's Adventure	Cromwell, John & William	1671	47
Cromwell's Addition	Cromwell, Richard	1687	47
Crosses Forrest	Cross, John	1695	49
Crouches Calf Pasture	Crouch, William	1666	50
Crouches Mill Dam	Crouch, William	1666	50
Crouches Triangle Addition	Crouch, William	1665	50
Crouches Tryangle	Crouch, William	1662	50
Crouchfield	Crouch, William	1665	49
Crouchley's Choice	Crouchley, Thomas	1676	51
Cuckold's Pointe	Cockley, William	1695	43
Cumber's Ridge	Cumber, John	1662	51
Cumberston	Cumber, John	1679	51
Cumberston Grainge	Cumber, John, Jr.	1662	52
Cumberton	Cumber, John	1659	51
Curtis Neck	Kinsey, Paul	1663	134
Daborne's Hope	Daborne, Thomas	1666	52
Daborne's Inheritance	Daborne, Thomas	1668	52
Dann	Paca, Robert	1663	164
Davidge's Meadows	Davidge, John	1701	53
Davis His Rest	Davis, Evan	1672	54

Tract Name	Owner's Name	Year	Page
Davis' Pasture	Davis, Isaac	1700	54
Davistone	Davis, Thomas	1701	54
Dearing's Encrease	Dearing, John	1688	56
Dearing's Gullier	Dearing, John	1668	56
Dearing's Increase	Dearing, John	1666	55
Deaver's Purchase	Devoir, Richard	1662	57
Deep Creek Point	Dawson, Abraham	1663	55
Deep Creek Neck	Tyler, Robert	1664	222
Deep Creek Point	Turner, Thomas	1665	222
Deep Point	Hopkins, William	1671	117
Denchworth	Yate, George	1679	246
Desert (The)	Blackwell, Thomas	1696	17
Devise	Davies, Thomas	1659	54
Devore's Range	Devore, Richard	1675	58
Diamond (The)	Browne, Thomas	1681	24
Diligent Search (The)	Richardson, William	1678	187
Dinah Ford Beaver Dam	Ford, Thomas	1663	72
Dividing Point (The)	Johnson, Davy	1665	131
Dodderidge's Forrest	Dodderidge, John	1696	58
Dodon	Stockett, Francis	1671	209
Dorrell's Inheritance	Dorrell, Paul	1668	58
Dorrell's Luck	Dorrell, Paul	1687	59
Dorrus His Chance	Young, Theodorus	1673	248
Dorsey	Dorsey, Edward	1668	59
Dorsey's Addition	Dorsey, Joshua	1680	62
Dorsey's Adventure	Dorsey, John	1688	61
Dorsey's Search	Dorsey, John	1696	61
Dort	Duhaddaway, Jacob	1659	63
Doughoregan	Carroll, Charles	1700	32
Doughoregan (& The Addition)	Carroll, Charles	1709	34
Dryer's Inheritance	Dryer, Samuel	1695	63
Duke's Cove	Ewen, Richard, Maj.	1659	70
Duke's Cove Resurveyed	Kinsey, Paul, Jr.	1671	136
Dunkin's Chance	Dunken, Patrick	1708	64
Dunkin's Luck	Dunken, Patrick	1684	64
Durand's Place	Durand, Alice	1664	64
Duvall's Addition	Duvall, Marin	1670	67
Duvall's Dellight	Duvall, John	1695	65
Duvall's Pasture	Duvall, Lewis	1705	66

Tract Name	Owner's Name	Year	Page
Duvall's Range	Duvall, Marin	1672	67
Duvall's Range Resurveyed	Lynthicum, Hezikiah	1703	145
Duvall's Range Resurveyed	Duvall, John	1695	65
Eagle's Nest	Gross, Nicholas	1681	92
Eagleston's Range	Eagleston, Bernard	1680	67
Edge's Addition	Edge, Daniel	1683	68
Edward's Neck	Edwards, John	1668	68
Efford's Chance	Efford, John & Goodrick, H	1677	68
Efford's Delight	Efford, William	1704	69
Elinor's Neck	Price, Edward & Elizabeth	1700	179
Elizabeth's Fancy	Clarke, Richard	1702	41
Elizabetha	Strong, Elizabeth	1670	210
Elk Thickett	Davis, Robert	1700	54
Elk Thickett Resurveyed	Phelps, Walter	1701	173
Elke Thickett	Arbuckle, Archibald	1659	1
Emmerton's Addition	Emmerton, Humphrey	1680	69
Emmerton's Range	Emmerton, Humphrey	1680	69
Encrease (The)	Hopkins, William	1671	119
Encrease (The)	Howard, Cornelius	1700	121
Encrease (The)	Minter, John	1668	154
Enlargement (The)	Welch, John	1704	232
Equality (The)	Saunders, James	1687	195
Escheat land called Barron Neck	Brice, John	1704	22
Essex	Batten, Fernando	1664	7
Eversail	Duvall, Lewis	1707	66
Ewen Upon Ewenton	Ewen, Richard	1668	71
Ewen's Addition	Ewen, Richard	1664	7
Expectation (The)	Meares, Thomas	1665	150
Favor (The)	Bond, Benjamin	1682	19
Favor (The)	Galloway, Samuel	1678	80
Ferfatt	Bayly, Richard	1672	8
Fingual	Carroll, James	1704	34
First Pattent for Prevention	Richardson, William	1700	187
Fish Pond (The)	Tench, Thomas	1704	216
Floyd's Adventure	Floyd, James	1695	72

Tract Name	Owner's Name	Year	Page
Fuller's Luck	Fuller, Mary	1701	77
Gadd's Hill	Hall, John	1688	95
Gadsby's Adventure	Gadsby, John	1694	78
Galloway	Galloway, Richard	1662	80
Gardner's Chance	Gardner, Christopher	1672	81
Gardner's Folly	Gardner, Christopher	1665	81
Gardner's Warfield	Gardner, Edward & Warfield, Richard	1669	81
Garret's Town	Cussack, Michael	1685	52
Gatenby	Gates, Thomas, Ensign	1658	83
Gater's Range	Gaither, John	1679	79
George's Fancy	Ashman, George	1687	2
Georgeston	Saughier, George	1659	194
Gibbs His Folly	Gibbs, William	1685	84
Gift (The)	Collier, William	1676	44
Gift (The)	Galloway, Richard, Jr.	1676	80
Girles Porcon (The)	Kirkland, Robert	1702	136
Godwell Resurveyed	Parker, George	1679	165
Goldsbury's Choice	Goldsbury, Robert	1672	84
Good Mother's Endeavor (The)	Howard, Elinor	1698	122
Gordon	Gordon, Alexander	1659	84
Gosnell's Adventure	Gosnell, William	1684	85
Gover's Ferin	Gover, Robert	1677	85
Gover's Hills	Gover, Robert	1680	86
Gover's Venture	Gover, Robert	1679	86
Gowery Banks	Ford, Thomas	1663	72
Gozwell's Choice	Gozwell, William	1695	85
Grammar's Chance	Grammar, John	1666	86
Grammar's Chance Resurveyed	Harrisson, Richard	1699	99
Grammar's Parrott	Grammar, John	1667	86
Graves End	Norman, George	1670	159
Gray Lands	Turner, Thomas	1665	222
Gray's Adventure	Baker, Ralph	1687	4
Gray's Chance	Gray, John	1684	88
Gray's Increase	Gray, John	1681	88
Gray's Land	Gray, John	1688	89
Gray's Land	Gray, John	1684	88
Gray's Lott	Gray, John	1687	88

Tract Name	Owner's Name	Year	Page
Gray's Range	Gray, John	1676	88
Great Bonnerston Resurveyed	Holland, Anthony	1671	108
Great Bonnerston	Bonner, James	1659	20
Great Piney Neck	Hopkins, William	1666	118
Green Spring	Proctor, Robert	1684	181
Green's Beginning	Green, John	1683	89
Greenbury	Green, John	1664	89
Greenbury's Forrest	Greenbury, Nicholas	1680	90
Greene's Town	Greene, George	1673	89
Greeniston Resurveyed	Painter, Richard	1683	165
Greenspring	Proctor, Robert	1673	180
Greenwood	Greenwood, Armigill	1663	90
Greniston	Greniston, James	1683	90
Griffith's Lott	Griffith, William	1695	91
Grime's Enlargement	Grimes, William	1695	92
Grimes Addition	Grimes, William	1672	92
Grimeston	Grimes, William	1665	91
Grosses Increase	Gross, Thomas	1685	93
Gullock's Folly	Gullock, Thomas	1679	94
Guy's Rest	Meeke, Guy	1670	151
Guy's Will	Meeke, Guy	1672	152
Hall's Inheritance	Hall, Christopher	1670	94
Hall's Palace	Hall, Henry	1695	94
Hall's Parcel	Hall, Josias	1683	95
Hallit's Lott	Hallit, Jacob	1680	95
Hamilton	Skidmore, Edward	1664	201
Hamm (The)	Bedworth, Richard & Thornbury, Samuel	1669	11
Hammond's Forrest	Hammond, John, Major	1696	96
Hammond's Pasture	Hammond, John	1682	96
Hampton's Enlargement	Taylord, William	1702	216
Hanslap's Range	Hanslap, Henry	1681	97
Happy Choice (The)	Yate, George	1671	245
Happy Choice (The)	Gray, John	1688	89
Harbitt's Clear	Harbitt, Elinor	1686	97
Harborow	Kinsey, Paul	1664	135
Hare Hill	Porter, Peter	1674	177
Harness	Harness, William	1652	98

Tract Name	Owner's Name	Year	Page
Harness' Range	Harness, Isaac	1670	98
Harnesses Gift	Harness, Jacob	1684	98
Harris His Mount	Harris, William	1677	99
Harrises Beginning	Harris, John	1695	99
Harrisson's Lott	Harrisson, Richard	1688	99
Harrissons' Enlargement to Grammar's Chance	Harrisson, Richard	1699	99
Harwood	Woolman, Richard	1659	242
Harwood	Woolman, Richard	1664	242
Haslenut Ridge	Gray, John	1665	87
Hasslin	Hasslin, Jeremy	1658	100
Hawkins	Hawkins, Ralph	1652	101
Hawkins Habitation Resurveyed	Bladen, William	1703	17
Hawkins Habitation	Hawkins, Ralph	1665	101
Hawkins His Range	Hawkins, William	1679	101
Hawkins His Addition	Hawkins, William	1695	102
Hawkins His Choice	Hawkins, William	1684	102
Hawkins Neck	Hawkins, Ralph	1665	101
Hazlenut Ridge Resurveyed	Tideings, Richard	1690	218
Health (The)	Lytfoot, Thomas	1684	145
Heart (The)	Bewsey, William	1681	13
Heath's Landing	Heath, James	1704	103
Heath's Meadow	Heath, James	1702	102
Heath's Purchase	Heath, James	1702	102
Hedge Park	Hedge, Thomas	1675	103
Heir's Purchase (The)	Marsh, Sarah	1664	147
Henry's Addition	Sewell, Henry	1673	197
Henry's Encrease	Sewell, Henry	1679	197
Henry's Park	Welding, Henry	1686	232
Herford	Wilson, Robert	1675	240
Herring	Herring, Bartholemew	1654	104
Herring Creek Road	Burrage, John	1685	31
Herring's Purchase	Herring, John	1684	104
Hester's Habitation	Beard, Hester	1679	9
Hickory Hills	Franklin, Robert	1667	74
Hickory Ridge	Stevens, Charles	1695	207
Hill's Chance	Hill, Clement, Jr.	1698	105
Hillington	Hill, Abel	1683	104
Hockley	Ebden, William	1670	68

Tract Name	Owner's Name	Year	Page
Huckleberry Forrest	Beard, Richard	1687	10
Huggings' Advantage	Huggings' Richard	1664	128
Hunt's Chance	Hunt, William	1663	128
Hunt's Range	Hunt, Wolfran	1684	129
Hunting Ridge	Clarke, Richard	1702	42
Huntington Quarter	Ridgley, Henry Jr. & Henry Sr.	1696	187
Idle Combe (The)	Pascall, George	1665	169
Indian Range (The)	Franklin, Robert & Beard, Richard	1665	74
Intacke (The)	Norwood, John	1659	161
Iron Mine (The)	White, Jerome	1668	237
Ironstone Hill	Gibbs, Edward	1685	83
Jackson's Chance	Jackson, James	1687	130
Jackson's Venture	Jackson, Isaac	1686	129
Jacob's Point	Smith, James	1676	203
James His Fancy	James. John	1685	130
James' Hill	James, John	1664	130
Jane's Inheritance	Sisson, Jane	1668	200
Jeff's Increase	Jeffe, Thomas	1682	131
Jeff's Search	Jeff, William	1688	131
Jerrico	Crosley, William	1663	48
John's Cabbin Ridge	Beard, Richard	1666	10
Jones His Lott	Jones, William	1673	132
Jordan's Adventure	Jordan, Thomas	1664	133
Kendall's Enlargement	Kendall, Daniel	1702	133
Kendall's Delight	Kendall, Daniel	1701	133
Kendall's Purchase	Kendall, John	1696	134
Kent	Batten, Fernando	1673	8
Kequeston Choice	Benson, Steven	1663	12
Kickalan's Choice	Symmons, George & Hall, Richard	1704	212
King's Venture	King, Joseph	1704	134
Knavery Discovered	Frissell, John	1699	76
Knavery Prevented	Selby, John	1702	196
Knighton's Fancy	Knighton, Thomas	1672	136
Knighton's Purchase	Knighton, Thomas	1688	136
Knocker's Hale	Saundry, Francis	1672	195
Lancaster Plaine	Hudson, John	1676	128

Tract Name	Owner's Name	Year	Page
Landing (The)	Proctor, Robert	1668	180
Landing (The)	Underwood, Thomas	1664	224
Landing Place (The)	Clark, Neale	1663	40
Landisell	Lloyd, Edward	1659	141
Landisell	Owens, Richard	1652	163
Lappston	DeLapp, Adam	1659	56
Lappston II	Delapp, Adam	1664	57
Lark's Hill	Larkin, John	1663	138
Larkin's Choice	Larkin, John	1670	138
Larkinton	Brewer, John	1663	21
Lavall	Duvall, Marin	1658	67
Lawe's Chance	Lawe, William	1675	138
Leonard's Neck	Woolchurch, Henry	1663	242
Levell (The)	Cross, John	1683	49
Lewis His Addition	Lewis, Henry	1680	139
Linham's Search	Linham, John	1688	139
Linnescomb's Lott	Linnescomb, Thomas	1677	140
Linnescomb's Stopp	Linnescomb, Thomas	1677	139
Linneston	Dorrell, Paul	1668	58
Linthicum Walks	Linthicum, Thomas	1701	140
Little Beginning	MacClannin, James	1709	149
Little Brushy Neck	Hopkins, William	1672	119
Little Brushy Neck Resurveyed	Hopkins, William	1682	119
Little Buxton	Lockwood, Robert	1687	143
Little Hawkins	Hawkins, Ralph	1652	101
Little Netlam	Askew, John	1665	3
Little Piney Neck	Hopkins, William	1664	118
Little Town	Wilson, Robert	1672	240
Little Town	Sumers, John	1704	240
Little Wells	Wells, Richard	1663	234
Littleworth	Hill, Richard, Captain	1686	105
Littleworth	Guisse, John	1706	93
Lloyd's Chance	Lloyd, John	1686	141
Lockwood's Adventure	Lockwood, Robert	1679	142
Lockwood's Addition	Lockwood, Robert	1673	141
Lockwood's Great Park	Lockwood, Thomas	1688	143
Lockwood's Guift	Waterman, Nicholas	1685	230
Lockwood's Lott	Lockwood, Robert	1674	142

Tract Name	Owner's Name	Year	Page
Lockwood's Luck	Lockwood, Robert	1698	143
Lockwood's Park	Lockwood, Robert	1683	143
Lockwood's Range	Lockwood, Robert	1676	142
Lockwood's Security	Lockwood, Robert	1683	142
Locust Neck	Parrish, Edward	1671	167
Locust Neck	Horner, James	1651	120
Locust Thickett	Owings, Richard	1688	163
Locust Thickett	Yate, George	1672	245
Locust Thickett	Burle, Steven	1684	29
Locust Thickett (The)	Harding, Matthew	1688	98
Long Lane	Hill, Clement	1698	104
Long Neck	Dorrell, Elizabeth	1665	58
Long Reach	Dorsey, Edward, Major	1694	59
Long Venture	Stimson, John	1673	208
Lord's Bounty	Smith, Nathan	1685	204
Lott (The)	Towgood, Josias	1704	219
Love's Neck	Love, Robert	1664	144
Lower Fuller Resurveyed	Reade, Thomas	1659	186
Luck	Gardner, Mary	1689	82
Lucke	Murphy, Patrick	1695	157
Lucky Hole	Bond, Thomas	1702	20
Luffman's Due	Luffman, William	1685	144
Lugg Ox	Duvall, John	1702	65
Lunn's Addition	Lunn, Edward	1683	144
Lusby	Lusby, Robert	1664	144
Lydia's Rest Resurveyed	Baldwin, John	1681	5
Maddox Adventure	Maddox, Thomas	1683	146
Maid Stone	Hunt, William	1663	129
Maiden (The)	Howard, Mary	1683	124
Maidenstone	Strong, Elizabeth	1659	210
Major's Choice	Dorsey, Edward, Major	1688	60
Major's Fancy	Dorsey, Edward, Major	1695	60
Manors of Ann Arrundell & Portland Res.	Baltimore, Lord, Lord Proprietor	1698	6

Tract Name	Owner's Name	Year	Page
March (The)	Gardner, Edward	1673	81
Margaret's Fields Resurveyed	Saughier, George	1670	194
Marlborough Plaine	Pinxton, Peter	1707	176
Marshe's Forrest	Marsh, John	1696	146
Marshe's Seat	Hall, John	1661	95
Martin's Nest	Faulkner, Martin	1680	71
Mary's Mount	Myles, Thomas	1664	158
Maryes Delight	Calvert, William	1669	32
Mascall's Haven	Wells, James	1671	233
Mascall's Hope	Mascall, Richard	1699	148
Mascall's Rest	Mascall, Richard	1670	148
Mascall's Rest	Yate, George	1678	245
Mascalls Adventure	Mascall, Richard	1671	148
Mavorne Hill	Tuckesbury, William	1679	221
Mayden Croft	Draper, Lawrence	1688	62
Mear's Expectation & Howardston	Worthington, John, Jr.	1702	243
Meares	Meares, Thomas	1659	149
Medcalfe's Chance	Medcalfe, John	1681	150
Medcalfe's Mount	Medcalfe John	1681	151
Meeke's Rest	Meeke, Guy	1680	152
Merriken	Merriken, Christine	1666	152
Merriton's Fancy	Merriton, John	1687	153
Middle Burrow	Greenbury, Nicholas	1688	90
Middle Land (The)	Cattline, Henry	1666	35
Middle Neck	Underwood, Thomas	1665	224
Middle Neck (The)	Goodrick, Henry	1668	84
Middle Plantation	Duvall, Marin	1664	67
Middle Plantation Resurveyed	Duvall, Lewis	1708	66
Milford	Proctor, Robert	1685	181
Mill Haven	Larkin, John	1682	138
Mill Land	Proctor, Robert	1683	180
Mill Meadow	Hill, Richard, Captain	1682	106
Mitchell's Addicion	Mitchell, William	1704	154
Mitchell's Chance	Mitchell, William	1686	154
Mitley's Purchase	Mitley, Christopher & Elizabeth	1698	154
Moore's Morning Choice	Moore, Mordecai, Dr.	1695	155

Tract Name	Owner's Name	Year	Page
Morley	Morley, Joseph	1663	155
Morley's Choyce	Morley, Joseph	1671	155
Morley's Grove	Morley, Joseph	1670	156
Morley's Lott	Morley, Joseph	1667	155
Morley's Lott	Morley, Joseph	1670	155
Moss His Purchase	Moss, Richard	1687	156
Mosses Discovery	Moss, Ralph	1702	156
Mosses Purchase	Moss, Richard	1666	156
Mountain Neck	Hammond, Thomas	1665	96
Mt. Gilboa	Dorsey, John	1702	62
Murphy's Choice	Murphy, Patrick	1684	157
Mutual Consent (The)	Underwood, Samuel & Cockley, William	1685	223
Narrow (The)	Leafe, Francis	1679	139
Narrow Neck	Yieldhall, William	1682	246
Neale's Purchase	Neale, Johnathan	1695	158
Nealson	Clarke, Neale	1659	40
Neglect (The)	Dunkin, Patrick	1665	64
Neglect (The)	Chaffinch, John	1709	36
Netlam	Askew, John	1664	3
Nettleland	Nettlefold, George	1662	159
New Worster	Tolly, Thomas	1679	219
New Year's Guift	Carroll, Charles	1706	34
Nicholson's Adventure	Nicholson, John	1685	159
Nicholson's Addition	Nicholson, John	1695	159
Norman's Dams	Norman, John	1668	159
Norman's Fancy	Norman, George	1670	159
North Crouchfield	Crouch, William	1659	50
Norwood	Norwood, John	1651	160
Norwood	Norwood, John	1658	160
Norwood's Angles	Norwood, Andrew	1683	160
Norwood's Fancy	Norwood, John	1659	161
Norwood's Recovery	Norwood, Andrew	1686	160
Oatley	Oatley, Christopher	1651	161
Obligation	Stockett, Thomas	1670	210
Oblong (The)	Holland, George	1683	110
Orphan's Addition	Guggeon, Robert & Lawrence	1685	93
Orphant's Inheritance (The)	Sisson, Elizabeth	1666	200

Tract Name	Owner's Name	Year	Page
Orrourck	Orrourck, James	1666	162
Orwick's Fancy	Orwick, James	1684	162
Owen Wood's Thickett	Wayman, Leonard	1688	231
Owen's Range	Owen, Richard	1696	163
Paca His Chance	Paca, Robert	1679	164
Padgett	Padgett, William	1659	164
Papa Ridge	Parrish, Edward	1674	167
Parker's Encrease	Croker, Thomas & Merrica, Hugh	1696	47
Parker's Encrease	Parker, Quinton	1669	165
Parrishes Choice	Parrish, Edward	1670	167
Parrishes Delay	Parrish, Edward	1671	167
Parrishes Park	Parrish, Edward	1664	166
Parrishes Purchase	Parrish, John	1700	167
Parry's Purchase	Parry, John	1700	168
Parson's Hill	Parsons, Thomas	1666	168
Pascall's Chance	Pascall, George	1664	168
Pascall's Purchase	Selby, Edward	1667	196
Pascall's Purchase Surplus	Heath, James	1705	103
Paul's Neck	Kinsey, Paul	1663	135
Pawson's Plaine	Pawson, John	1670	169
Peake	Heathcote, Nathaniel	1678	103
Peasley's Inheritance	Peasley, John	1680	170
Peasley's Lott	Peasley, John	1685	170
Peasley's Neck	Peasley, Francis	1666	170
Pendenny	Lloyd, Edward, Esq.	1659	140
Pennington's Search	Pennington, William	1695	171
Petticoate's Rest	Petticoate, William	1679	172
Pettybone's Rest	Pettybone, Richard	1673	172
Phantascoe	Boarman, Edward	1705	18
Phelp's Increase	Phelps, Walter	1681	173
Phelps His Luck	Phelps, Walter	1687	173
Phelps His Choice	Phelps, Walter	1685	173
Phelps His Luck	Phelps, Walter	1695	173
Philke's Rest	Philke, Edward	1680	174
Phillip's Fancy	Cromwell, William	1684	48
Phillip's Pillaged Lott	Dowell, Phillip	1700	62
Pierpoint's Branch	Pierpoint, Henry	1673	175
Pierpoint's Chance	Pierepoint, Amos	1688	174

Tract Name	Owner's Name	Year	Page
Pierpoint's Lott	Pierpoint, Henry	1666	174
Pierpoint's Range	Pierpoint, Jabes	1695	175
Pierpoint's Rocks	Pierpoint, Henry	1672	175
Piney Point	Phelps, Thomas	1668	172
Pinkston's Folly	Pinkston, Peter	1700	176
Pinkstone's Delight	Pinkstone, Peter	1696	175
Pinxton's Randan	Pinxton, Peter	1707	176
Piny Plaine	Bayly, Richard	1685	8
Plaine (The)	Yate, George	1677	245
Plaine (The)	Tyler, Robert & Dawson, Abraham	1664	222
Plaine (The)	Wilson, Robert	1671	239
Plaine (The)	Pawson, John	1671	170
Plaine (The)	Hope, George	1673	116
Planter's Pleasure	Penn, Edward	1699	171
Pleasant Hills (The)	Lytfoot, Thomas	1686	146
Plumpton	Walker, George	1663	225
Point Lookout	Merriken, Hugh	1695	153
Poll Cat Hill	Gaither, John	1687	79
Poplar Hill	Selby, Thomas & Edward	1655	197
Poplar Knowle	Talbott, Richard	1659	213
Poplar Neck	Marsh, Thomas	1652	147
Poplar Neck	Beard, Richard	1663	10
Poplar Plaine	Howard, Matthew	1685	126
Poplar Ridge	Proctor, Robert	1684	181
Poplar Ridge	Gassaway, Nicholas	1654	82
Port of Annapolis	Carroll, Charles	1701	33
Porter's Hill	Porter, Peter, Jr.	1659	177
Portland Landing	White, Jerome	1672	237
Portland Manor	White, Jerome, Esq.	1662	237
Portland Manor Part Of	Lazenby, Charles Calvert	1701	139
Portland Manor Part Of	Darnall, Henry, Coll	1696	53
Pound (The)	Beard, Richard	1687	10
Powell's Inheritance	Powell, John & James	1685	177
Pratt's Choice	Pratt, Thomas	1671	178
Pratt's Choice Resurveyed	Pratt, Thomas	1673	178
Pratt's Neck	Pratt, Thomas	1672	178

Tract Name	Owner's Name	Year	Page
Pratt's Security	Pratt, Thomas	1683	178
Preston's Cliffs	Preston, Richard	1658	178
Preston's Enlargement	Welch, John	1670	232
Proctor's Chance	Proctor, Robert	1679	180
Proctor's Forrest	Proctor, Robert	1673	180
Proctor's Park	Proctor, Robert	1683	181
Prop's Gift	Heathcote, Nathaniel	1680	103
Providence	Garrett, Amos	1700	82
Puddington	Puddington, George	1650	182
Puddington's Enlargement	Puddington, George	1661	182
Puddington's Harbor	Puddington, George	1663	182
Purnell's Angle	Purnell, Richard	1683	183
Push Pinn	Jones, John	1700	131
Pytherston	Pyther, William	1659	183
Quicksale	Burrage, John	1664	29
Rachell's Hope	Maddox, Thomas	1683	146
Rainge (The)	Burges, George	1684	27
Rams Gott Swamp	Gott, Richard	1659	85
Randall's Fancy	Randall, Christopher	1680	183
Randall's Purchase	Randall, Christopher	1680	184
Randall's Range	Randall, Christopher	1681	184
Range	Medcalfe, John	1703	151
Range (The)	Baker, Morris	1671	3
Range (The)	Constable, Henry	1687	46
Range (The)	Lytfoot, Thomas	1684	145
Range (The)	Goodrick, Henry	1668	84
Range Resurveyed	Medcalfe, John	1703	151
Rantor's Ridge	Browne, Thomas	1705	25
Rattlesnake Neck	Devoir, Richard	1684	57
Rattlesnake Point	Illingsworth, Richard	1667	129
Rawling's Purchase	Rawlings, Richard	1682	184
Rawlings	Rawlings, Richard	1680	184
Ray's Chance	Ray, John	1667	185
Read's Lott	Read, William	1665	185
Read's Lott	Read, William	1665	185
Rich Neck	Duvall, Marin & Young, William	1665	66
Rich Neck	Hammond, John Coll	1684	96
Rich Neck (The)	Rockhold, John	1666	190
Richardson's Joy	Richardson,	1666	186

Tract Name	Owner's Name	Year	Page
Ridge (The)	Lawrence Conaway, James & Turner, Thomas	1669	45
Ridgely's Beginning	Ridgely, William	1679	189
Ridgely's Beginning	Ridgely, Henry	1695	188
Ridgely's Chance	Ridgely, William	1694	189
Ridgely's Forrest	Ridgely, Henry	1686	188
Ridgely's Lott	Ridgely, Henry, Jr.	1695	188
Rigby	Rigby, James	1659	189
Robert's Luck	Franklin, Robert, Jr.	1671	75
Robin Hood's Forrest	Snowden, Richard	1686	205
Robinston	Robinson, Henry	1659	190
Rockhold's Purchase	Rockhold, John	1696	190
Rockhold's Range	Rockhold, John	1684	190
Rockhold's Search	Rockhold, John	1696	191
Rockwould	Rockhold, Robert & John	1659	191
Rocky Point	Lambert, Ann	1679	137
Roedown Security	Taylor, Thomas, Esq.	1675	215
Rooker's Range	Rooker, Thomas	1702	191
Roole's His Chance	Rooles, Christopher	1681	191
Roper Gray	Roper, William & Gray, John	1683	192
Roper's Neck Resurveyed	Roper, Thomas	1673	192
Roper's Range	Roper, William	1670	193
Roper's Yard (The)	Roper, Thomas	1664	192
Rosse	Meeke, Guy	1679	152
Roundabout Hill	Gaither, John	1685	79
Rowdown	Taylor, Thomas	1670	215
Rudnidge	Yate, George	1677	245
Ruly's Search	Ruly, Anthony	1696	193
Rutland's Purchase Inlarged	Rutland, Thomas	1700	193
Salmon's Hill	Salmon, Ralph	1663	194
Samuel's Purchase	Thomas, Samuel	1699	217
Sanetley	Chew, Samuell	1664	38
School House (The)	Grammer, John	1659	86
Scornton	Westhill, George	1659	235
Scotland	Essen, John	1659	69
Scott's Folly	Scott, Edward	1695	195

Tract Name	Owner's Name	Year	Page
Security (The)	Brewer, John	1663	21
Selby Clifts	Billingsly, Francis	1650	13
Selby's Enlargement	Selby, Matthew	1670	197
Selby's Marsh	Selby, Edward	1658	196
Selby's Stopp	Selby, Edward, Jr.	1688	196
Sewall's Fancy	Sewall, Henry	1704	198
Sewell's Increase	Sewell, Henry	1680	198
Sharp Pointe	Roberts, Andrew	1666	189
Shaw's Folly	Shaw, John	1666	198
Shaw's Folly Resurveyed	Shaw, John	1672	198
Shepheard's Choice	Shepheard, Nicholas	1686	199
Shepheard's Forrest	Sheppard, Nicholas	1702	199
Shepheard's Grove	Shepheard, Nicholas	1683	199
Shepheard's Right	Shepheard, Nicholas	1673	199
Shipley's Choice	Shipley, Adam	1681	200
Silverston	Salaway, Anthony	1659	194
Skidmore	Skidmore, Edward	1663	201
Slade's Addition	Slade, William	1671	202
Slade's Addition	Slade, William	1695	202
Slade's Hope	Slaid, William	1664	201
Slatbourne	Proctor, Robert	1676	180
Smith	Smith, Zephaniah	1650	204
Smith's Delight	Smith, Nathan	1665	203
Smith's Desire	Smith, Edward	1686	202
Smith's Forrest	Smith, Philemon	1695	204
Smith's Neck Resurveyed	Owen, Ann	1684	162
Smith's Neck	Owen, Richard	1650	163
Smith's Range	Hopkins, William	1679	119
Smith's Range	Solling, Harmann	1666	206
Smith's Rest	Smith, Walter	1662	204
Smithfield	Smith, Nathan	1664	203
Soldier's Delight	Pawley, Lionel	1671	169
Soldier's Fortune	Miller, Christopher	1704	154
Soloman's Desire	Hills, William	1666	107
Soloman's Purchase	Sparrow, Soloman	1695	206
South Canton Resurveyed	Clarkson, Robert, Jr.	1680	42
South Canton	Taylor, Thomas & Elizabeth	1659	214
Sparrow's Addition	Sparrow, Thomas	1675	206

Tract Name	Owner's Name	Year	Page
Sparrow's Rest	Sparrow, Thomas	1659	206
Spencer's Search	Spencer, John	1683	206
Spring Point	Kinsey, Paul	1663	135
St. Edmund's	Parker, William	1661	166
St. Jeromes	White, Jerome	1668	237
St. Jeromes & Portland Landing	Darnall, Henry Coll	1700	53
St. Thomas' Neck	Parsons, Thomas	1664	168
Stear's Park	Stear, Richard	1695	207
Stephen's Forrest	Stephens, Charles	1709	208
Stinchcombe's Addition	Stinchcombe, Nathaniel	1672	209
Stinson's Choice	Stinson, John	1684	209
Stones (The)	Rowles, Thomas	1705	193
Stony Hills	Everet, Richard	1695	70
Strawberry Plaine	Hopkins, William	1664	117
Strong's Leavings	Wheelock, Edward	1675	236
Sturton's Rest	Sturton, George	1671	211
Suffolk	Batten, Fernando	1683	8
Summerland's Lott	Summerland, John	1683	211
Surplus Land in Cheney Neck	Burroughs, William & Ann	1696	31
Sutton's Addition	Sutton, Thomas	1688	212
Sutton's Choice	Sutton, Thomas	1681	212
Swan Cove	Drue, Emmanuel	1665	63
Swan Neck Resurveyed	Smith, James	1674	203
Swan Neck	Lloyd, Edward, Esq.	1659	140
Talbott's Angles	Talbott, Edward	1686	213
Talbott's Hope	Richardson, William	1677	187
Talbott's Land	Bishop, Roger	1687	17
Talbott's Ridge	Talbott, Richard	1664	213
Talbott's Ridge Resurveyed	Talbott, Edward & John	1676	212
Talbott's Search	Bishop, Roger	1687	17
Talbott's Timber Neck	Talbott, Richard	1664	213
Tangerine	Wayman, Leonard	1695	231
Tanyard (The)	Thurston, Thomas	1665	217
Taylor's Addition	Taylor, Thomas	1672	215
Taylor's Chance & Hale	Taylor, Thomas	1663	214
Taylor's Search	Taylor, Thomas	1688	215

Tract Name	Owner's Name	Year	Page
Taylord's Enlargement	Taylord, William	1702	216
Tearecoate Thickett	Lockwood, Robert	1687	143
Thomas Towne	Reade, Thomas	1659	185
Thornbury's Addition	Bodware, Richard	1684	19
Timber Neck	Huggings, John & Wheeler, John	1665	128
Timber Neck	McCubbin, John	1665	149
Timber Neck	Budd, William	1695	27
Timber Neck	Proctor, Robert	1684	181
Timber Neck	Stephens, Charles	1695	208
Todd	Todd, Thomas	1651	218
Todd's Harbor	Todd, Thomas	1671	218
Todd's Pasture	Todd, Thomas	1674	219
Todd's Range	Todd, Thomas	1664	218
Tolley's Point Resurveyed	Hill, Richard, Captain	1684	106
Tolley's Point	Tolley, Thomas	1683	219
Towhhill Choice	Gossum, Patrick	1652	85
Town Neck	Utie, Nathaniel	1650	224
Town Neck on the Severn	Smith, Zephaniah	1650	204
Townhill	Townhill, Edmond	1659	220
Tredhaven Point	Richardson, Thomas	1671	187
Trent	Morley, Joseph & Gray, John	1666	155
Treover	James, John	1701	130
Triangle (The)	Lockwood, Robert	1670	141
Triangle (The) Resurveyed	Roberts, Andrew	1681	189
Triangle Neck	Lloyd, Robert	1666	141
Troster's Purchase	Troster, John	1661	221
Troy	Dorsey, John	1695	61
Truroe	Turner, Thomas	1664	221
Truswell	Young, Theodorus & Phillips, Robert	1684	248
Tryall (The)	Harsbottle, John	1698	100
Tryall (The) (Certification)	Jones, Edward	1685	131
Tryangle (The)	Taylor, Thomas	1672	215
Turkey Hill	Pratt, Thomas	1664	177
Turkey Island	Clarke, Neale	1696	41
Turkey Island	Hill, Abel	1677	104

Tract Name	Owner's Name	Year	Page
Turkey Neck	Snowden, Richard	1698	205
Turkey Quarter	Clark, Neale	1663	40
Tyler's Lott 1	Tyler, Robert	1680	223
Tyler's Lott II	Tyler, Robert	1666	223
United Friendship (The)	Grange, John	1671	87
Unnamed Cert	Blay, William	1652	18
Unnamed Cert	Harwood, Robert	1651	100
Unnamed Cert	Pyther, William	1650	183
Unnamed Cert	Lloyd, Edward	1650	140
Unnamed Cert	Strong, Leonard	1651	211
Unnamed Cert	Ewen, Richard	1652	70
Unnamed Cert	Marsh, Thomas	1651	147
Unnamed Cert	Marsh, Thomas	1651	147
Unnamed Cert	Myles, Thomas	1652	157
Unnamed Cert	Porter, Peter	1651	176
Unnamed Cert	Smith, Zephaniah	1651	205
Unnamed Cert	Herring, Bartholemew	1652	104
Unnamed Cert	Marsh, Thomas	1651	147
Unnamed Cert	Warring & Davis	1651	229
Unnamed Cert	Burrage, John	1665	31
Unnamed Cert (2 tracts)	Meares, Thomas	1651	150
Unnamed Cert	Drew, Hugh & Emmanuel	1652	63
Unnamed Cert	Brown, Ellis	1652	22
Unnamed Cert	Fuller, William	1651	77
Unnamed Cert	Parker, William	1651	165
Unnamed Cert	Burrage, John	1665	31
Unnamed Cert	Tolley, Thomas	1651	219
Unnamed Patent	Jones, Robert	1658	132
Unnamed Patent	Pell, William	1658	171
Unnamed Patent	Groose, Roger	1658	92
Unnamed Patent	James, John	1658	130
Unnamed Patent	Howard, Matthew	1650	124
Unnamed Patent	Howell, Thomas	1658	127
Unnamed Patent	Townhill, Edmond	1658	220
Unnamed Patent	Emmerson, Thomas	1658	69
Unnamed Patent	Fuller, William	1658	77
Unnamed Patent	Chew, Ann Ayres	1658	37
Unnamed Patent	Norwood, John	1658	161
Unnamed Patent	Watkin, John	1658	230
Unnamed Patent	Parker, William	1666	166

Tract Name	Owner's Name	Year	Page
Unnamed Patent (2 tracts)	Carter, Edward	1651	35
Unnamed Patent (3 tracts)	Crouch, William	1650	49
Unnamed Patent	Darnall, Henry, Coll	1687	53
Unnamed Patent	Homewood, Thomas	1663	113
Unnamed Patent	Jones, John	1658	132
Unnamed Patent	MacDowell, William	1651	146
Unnamed Patent	Homewood, John	1663	112
Upper Toynton	Richardson, Larrance	1662	186
Upton	Truman, Thomas	1664	221
Utopia	Wilson, Robert	1670	239
Vale Of Pleasure (The)	Gullock, Thomas	1685	94
Valley of Owen (The)	Owen, Richard	1705	164
Velmeade	Dearing, John	1667	56
Vennell's Inheritance	Vennall, John	1658	225
Vines His Fancy	Vines, William	1697	225
Vinson Parke	Warfield, John & Alexander	1702	228
Wade's Encrease	Wade, Robert	1679	225
Wadlington	Homewood, John	1664	112
Walters' Adventure	Walters, John	1677	226
Wardner's Neck	Wardner, James	1658	226
Wardner's Neck Resurveyed	Wardner, James	1668	227
Wardridge	Wardner & Ridgely	1664	226
Wardrop	Wardner, James	1663	227
Wardrop Ridge	Dunken, Patrick	1663	64
Warfield's Forrest	Warfield, Richard	1673	228
Warfield's Plaines	Warfield, Richard	1681	228
Warfield's Range	Warfield, John & Richard	1696	228
Warfield's Right	Warfield, Richard	1674	228
Warringston	Warring, Sampson	1663	229
Water Town	Waterman, Nicholas	1662	230
Water's His Lott	Snowden, Richard, Jr.	1704	205
Waterford	Jones, William	1676	132
Watkins	Myles, Thomas	1652	157
Watkins His Purchase Resurveyed	Watkins, John	1681	230
Watkins Inheritance Resurveyed	Watkins, John	1681	230

Tract Name	Owner's Name	Year	Page
Woodstock	Wood, John	1710	241
Woodyard (The)	Howard, John & Stephens, Charles	1663	122
Woodyard (The)	Haywood, John	1671	102
Woolchurch Rest	Woolchurch, Henry	1663	242
Wrighten	Terratt, Nicholas, Jr.	1697	217
Wrighton	Taylor, William	1650	216
Wyatt	Wyatt, Nicholas	1651	243
Wyatt's Harbor	Wyatt Nicholas	1668	244
Wyatt's Hills	Wyatt, Nicholas	1664	244
Wyatt's Ridge	Wyatt, Nicholas	1664	244
Wyneat's Range	Wyneat, Thomas	1674	244
Yate's Inheritance	Yate, George	1668	245
Yieldhall's Island	Yieldhall, William	1679	246
Young Richard	Young, Richard, Jr.	1663	247
Young's Locust Plaine	Young, John	1704	247
Young's Range	Young, John	1704	247
Younger Besson	Besson, Thomas, Jr.	1659	13

Appendices

A - Anne Arundel County Hundreds

B - Broad & Town Neck Hundred

C – Middle Neck Hundred

D – South River Hundred

E – West River Hundred

F – Herring Cr. Hundred

Anne Arundell County Hundreds

Broad and Town Neck

Middle Neck

South River

West River

Herring Creek

Broad & Town Neck
Hundred

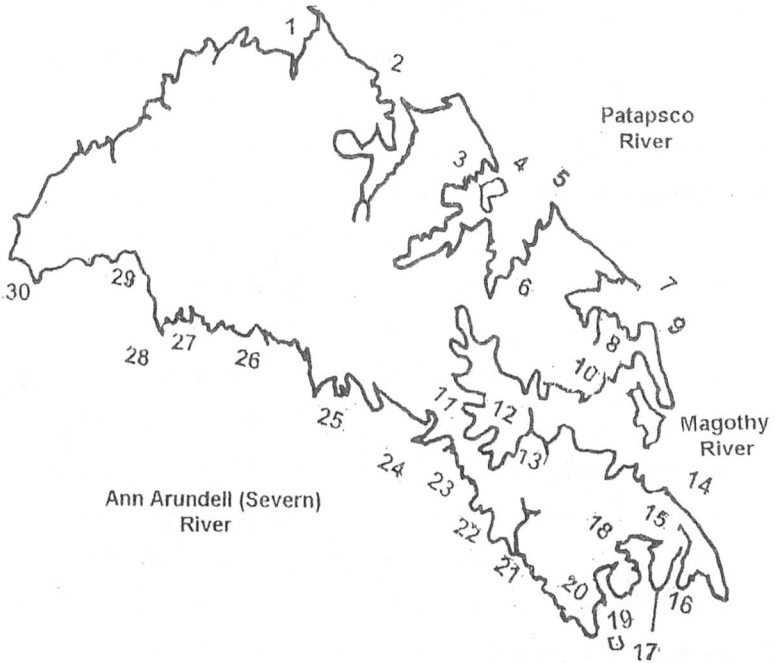

Patapsco
River

Magothy
River

Ann Arundell (Severn)
River

1. Curtis Cr.	12. Piney Neck Br.	23. Catlyn Br.
2. Nabb's Cr.	13. Forked Cr.	24. Hopkins' Cove
3. Cox Cr.	14. Deep Cr.	25. Timber Neck Cr.
4. Stoney Cr.	15. Harness Cr.	26. Crouche's Cr.
5. Rock Cr.	16. Ferry Cr.	27. Round Bay
6. White's Cove	17. Providence	28. Swan Poynt
7. Back Cr.	18. Town Cr.	29. Foster's Nest Pt.
8. Bodkin Cr.	19. Sear's Cr.	30. Williams' Cove
9. Old Man Cr.	20. Cooper's Br.	31. Cedar Point
10. Broad Cr.	21. Poplar Tavern Br.	
11. Bate's Br.	22. Brown's Cove	

Middle Neck Hundred

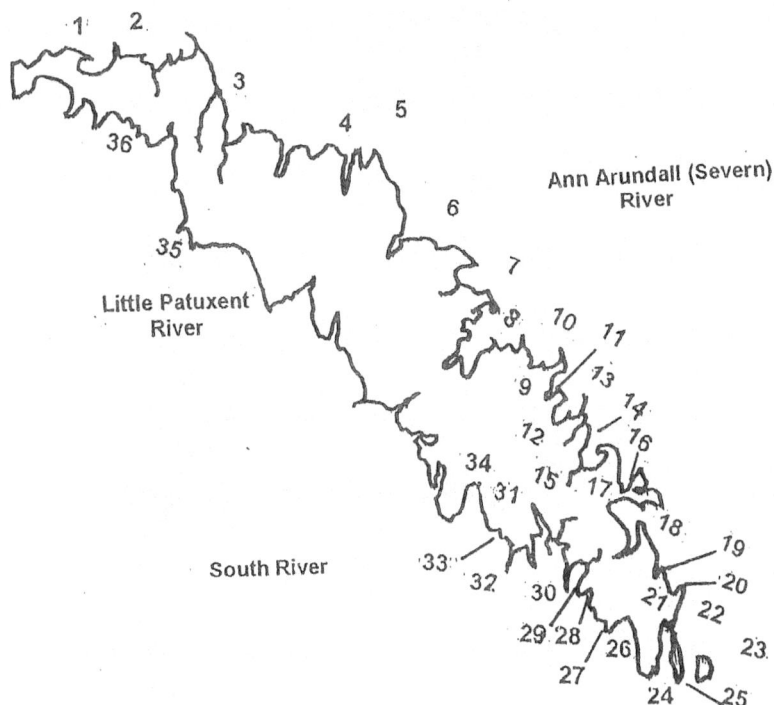

Ann Arundall (Severn) River

Little Patuxent River

South River

1. Indian Cr.
2. Spring Br.
3. Cypress Cr.
4. Plum Cr.
5. Plum Pt.
6. Fox Cr.
7. Long Pt.
8. Round Bay
9. Rockhold's or Jones's Cr.
10. Wyatt's Cr.
11. Marshes or Hockley Cr.
12. Underwood's Cr.
13. Hammond's Cr.
14. Bustion's Cove
15. Warner's or Norwood's Cr.
16. Freeman's Cove
17. Deep or Dorsey's Cr.
18. Todd, Acton, Shipping or Clarkson's Cr.
19. Beasley's Cr.
20. Howell's Cr.
21. Durand's Cr.
22. Saughier's Cr.
23. Tolley Point
24. Fishing Cr.
25. Thomas Pt.
26. Cherrystone Cr.
27. Oatley Cr.
28. Harness Cr.
29. Smith's Cr.
30. Enlargement or Roper's Cr.
31. Green Ginger Cr.
32. Hamilton Cr.
33. Cubbin's Cove
34. Broad Cr.
35. Towser's Br.
36. Rogues Harbor Br.

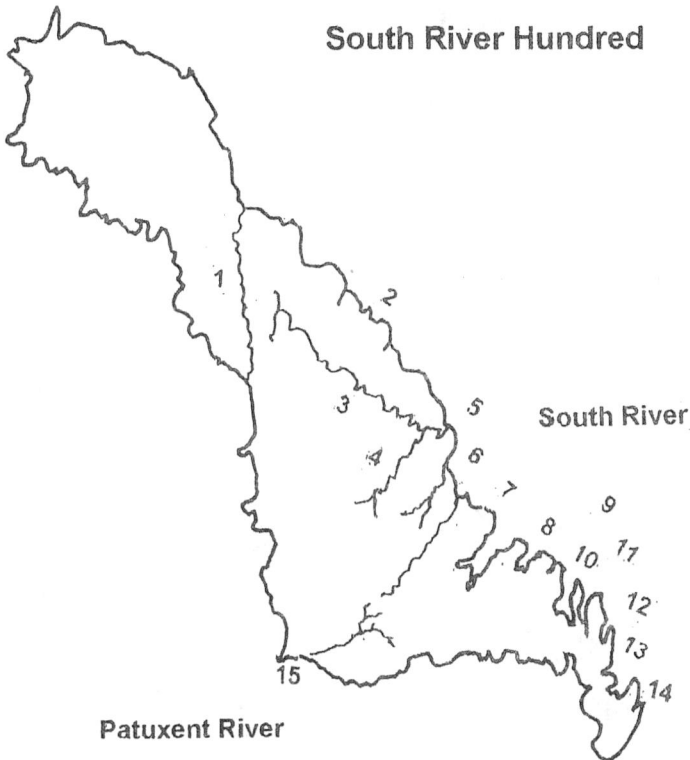

South River Hundred

South River

Patuxent River

1. Little Patuxent River	7. Jacob's or	11. Pyther's Cr.
2. North Runn	Beard's Cr.	12. Gossum Cr.
3. South Runn	8. Puddington Cr.	13. Selby Bay
4. Western Br.	9. Mott's Cr.	14. Pennington's
5. Nettlefold's Cr.	10. Glebe or	Ponds
6. The Flat Creek	Burges' Cr.	15. Stockett's Cr.

West River Hundred

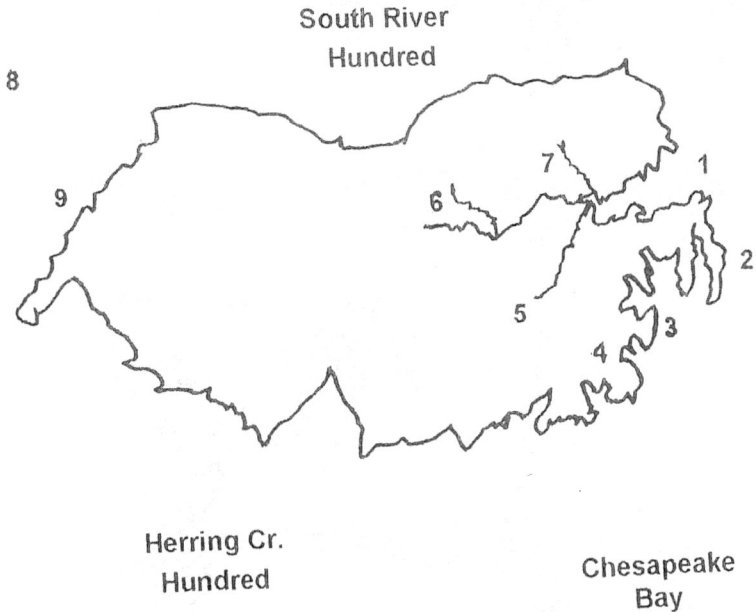

South River
Hundred

8

9

6

7

1

2

5

3

4

Herring Cr.
Hundred

Chesapeake
Bay

1. Road (Rhode) River
2. Long Point
3. West River
4. Smith Cr.

5. South Fork of
   Muddy Cr.
6. Muddy Cr.
7. Mill Br.

8. Prince George's
   County
9. Patuxent
   River

Herring Creek Hundred

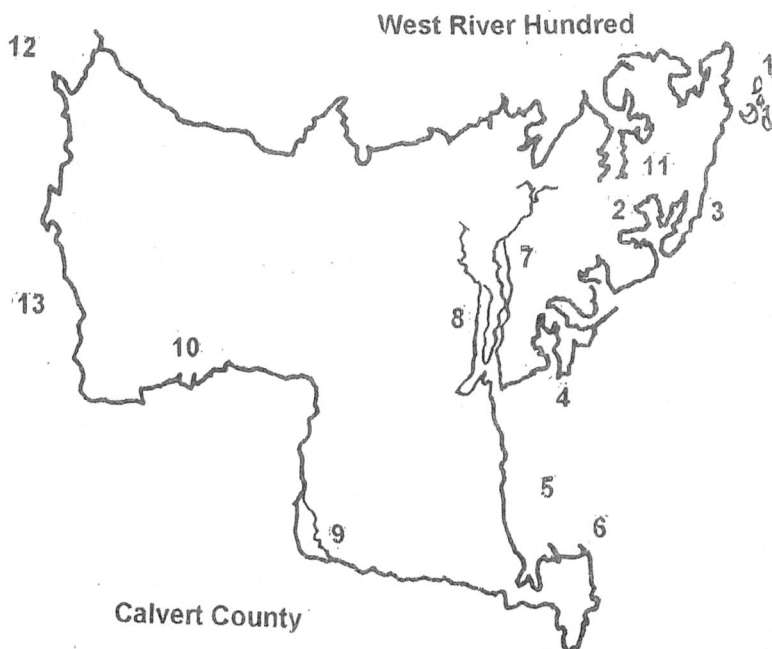

West River Hundred

Calvert County

1. Three Sisters
2. Deep Creek
3. Franklin's Pt.
4. Parker's Cr.
5. Herring Bay
6. Holland Pt.
7. Gott's Cr.
8. Herring Cr.
9. Hall's Cr.
10. Lyon's Cr.
11. South Cr.
12. Prince George's Co.
13. Patuxent River